WAVERLY®

decorating projects you can make

Meredith® Books
Des Moines, Iowa

Meredith® Press
An imprint of Meredith® Books

WAVERLY® Decorating Projects You Can Make
Editor: Amy Tincher-Durik
Art Directors: Marisa Dirks, Gayle Schadendorf
Copy Chief: Terri Fredrickson
Copy and Production Editor: Victoria Forlini
Editorial Operations Manager: Karen Schirm
Managers, Book Production: Pam Kvitne, Marjorie J. Schenkelberg
Contributing Copy Editor: M. Peg Smith
Contributing Proofreaders: Becky Danley, Maria Duryee, Kathy Roth Eastman
Indexer: Kathleen Poole
Electronic Production Coordinator: Paula Forest
Editorial and Design Assistants: Kaye Chabot, Mary Lee Gavin, Karen McFadden

Meredith® Books
Publisher and Editor in Chief: James D. Blume
Design Director: Matt Strelecki
Managing Editor: Gregory H. Kayko
Executive Editor, Home Decorating and Design: Denise L. Caringer

Director, Operations: George A. Susral
Director, Production: Douglas M. Johnston
Executive Director, Sales: Ken Zagor

Vice President and General Manager: Douglas J. Guendel

Meredith Publishing Group
President, Publishing Group: Stephen M. Lacy
Vice President-Publishing Director: Bob Mate

Meredith Corporation
Chairman and Chief Executive Officer: William T. Kerr

Chairman of the Executive Committee: E. T. Meredith III

WAVERLY®
President, Waverly Lifestyle Group: Dale Williams
Vice President, Marketing and Licensing: Carolyn A. D'Angelo
Director, Design, Licensed Product: Susan Bennie
Design Director, Licensing: Kristin Osterberg

Waverly® is a registered trademark of F. Schumacher & Co.

Making your own soft furnishings (window treatments, pillows, chair slipcovers and cushions, and bedding) gives you the opportunity to choose exactly the right fabrics, colors, and patterns for the individual rooms of your home. When you allow yourself creative freedom to mix and match fabrics and incorporate interesting—and sometimes unexpected—trims and other embellishments to your projects, you create a living space that is uniquely yours.

Skill Levels

The projects in this book have been assigned skill levels and time requirements based on the following definitions:

Beginner: One who is familiar with basic sewing terms, such as seam line, seam allowance, grain line of fabric, and selvage edge. Experience with a sewing machine includes making seams, hemming, gathering, and installing zippers and welting. The beginner can work precisely from illustrations.

Intermediate: One who is comfortable with basic sewing terms and uses sewing techniques such as understitching and topstitching; can make custom paper patterns following written and illustrated instructions; has constructed a simple garment; and can make facings, install zippers, and make buttonholes.

Advanced: One who completely understands sewing terms and measurements; feels confident with the complexity of incorporating multiple elements in project construction; and easily makes paper patterns from illustrations. Sewing experience includes details, such as ruching.

Before You Begin

Please keep the following in mind when choosing projects to create:

The time required for each project is a general guide; actual time required will depend on individual skill levels and circumstances.

Use the yardage indicated in each project materials list as a guideline; you may require additional yardage to match design repeats or one-way designs. Take measurements and make patterns before purchasing fabric to eliminate frustration and save time and money.

Read all instructions carefully before beginning a project. If you encounter unfamiliar sewing terms in the instructions, please check the Glossary (page 217) for help. See the Credits (page 220) for a complete listing of the fabrics shown in the photos of each project.

Some projects, such as cornice boxes, require that you work with lumber. If you do not own wood-cutting equipment or do not feel confident cutting it yourself, many lumber companies will make simple cuts free of charge. Note, however, that you may still require a jigsaw or table saw to cut shaped pieces.

Consult the numerous sidebars located throughout the book for additional information, inspiration, and instructions. See the Table of Contents (pages 5 to 7) for a complete listing; the sidebars are listed in green type.

Many materials lists request that you use a vanishing fabric marker. The most common type is air-soluble, which makes a bright colored mark on your fabric that vanishes within 24 to 48 hours. Others, such as the water-soluble variety, need to be washed out and may react to the dyes or finishing agents used in the manufacture of your fabric, causing permanent marks. Regardless of which you choose, always test your marking tool on a scrap of fabric to ensure satisfactory results. Note that heat can make any temporary mark permanent, so do not press fabric after it is marked (you may, however, press it after the ink has disappeared). Finally, if neither air- nor water-soluble markers will work for your needs, try tailor's chalk, which can easily be removed with a small stiff-bristle brush.

When instructed to finish a project's raw edges, use whatever stitch appeals to you, including zigzag or narrow hem. If you own a serger, you may serge the edges.

About Waverly

For more than 75 years, Waverly has maintained a reputation for design excellence and quality home furnishings. As a premier home furnishings brand, Waverly provides all of the decorating elements you need to make your home the perfect embodiment of your individual style, including the fabrics featured throughout this book. If you are looking for additional inspiration, consult these books: *Waverly Inspirations: Your Guide to Personal Style* and *Waverly At Home with Color*.

table of contents

table of contents

living
rooms

At the heart of every home is a living room. Large or small, this room is all about bringing people together, making it the perfect showcase for handsome draperies and customized pillows.

See page 48 for pillow instructions.

Use a vibrant color scheme
to satisfy your modern and country design
sensibilities. A sleek striped Roman shade lifts into
neat folds to let in light and easily lowers at night to
provide privacy. The striped scarf reinforces the easy,
breezy decorating style. Repeat the fabric on a pillow
for a unified effect.

bright and bold

Although Roman shades traditionally mount inside the window frame, the example at left is installed outside the window opening for complete window coverage. The mounting board rests on 2-inch-long inside corner braces installed above the window.

Soften the Roman shade by pairing it with a gently pleated scarf. The classic no-sew topper extends only two-thirds of the way down the window to avoid interfering with seated guests. (You could also team the scarf with blinds and shades or curtain panels.)

Use the vibrantly striped scarf fabric for a classy pillow. To make a pattern for matching stripes in the pillow, use tracing paper, which allows you to see the exact pattern placement on the fabric. With accurate cutting, the pieces will fit together beautifully—and if there is a slight mismatch at the center, simply hide it (and accent the pillow) with a tassel or decorative medallion.

For a complete custom look, use fabric scraps to embellish lampshades and photo mats. The fruit motifs on the lampshade were affixed with spray adhesive. To create the photo mats, cut mat board to fit a standard 8x10" frame, leaving a 4x6" opening for the photo. Wrap the fabric around the mat and adhere it to the back with spray adhesive.

See page 48 for basic pillow instructions.

materials

54"-wide decorator fabric*
Strips cut from
    contrasting fabric*
Small O-rings*
Roman shade cord*
2 (2") inside corner braces
1×2 pine board*
$1/2$"-diameter dowel*
Cleat with fasteners
4 (1") No. 8 wood screws
4 (2") No. 8 wood screws
4 screw eyes

tools

Handsaw
Electric drill and drill bits
Screwdriver
Staple gun and $1/4$" staples

sewing tools

Sewing machine
Iron and ironing board
Scissors
Tape measure
Pins
Vanishing fabric marker

skill level: intermediate
time required: 1 day
*Purchase materials after
taking measurements.

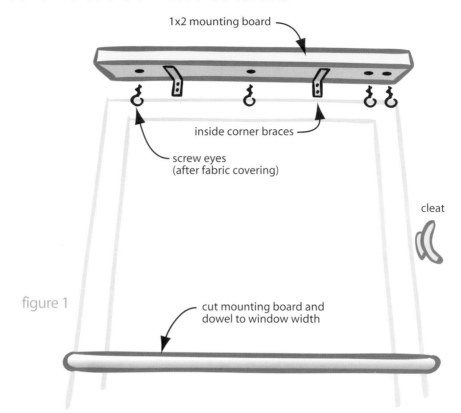

1x2 mounting board

inside corner braces

screw eyes
(after fabric covering)

cleat

cut mounting board and
dowel to window width

figure 1

1 Measure the window width and cut the 1×2 board and dowel to this measurement. Install the inside corner braces with 2" wood screws. Set the dowel aside (use it to weight the lower edge of the finished shade). Center the board on the corner braces with one narrow edge of the board against the wall (Figure 1). Mark the pilot holes to attach the board to the braces. Mark additional points for screw eyes 2" from each end and at the center. Mark a pilot hole for a fourth screw eye 1" from the right end of the board. Drill the pilot holes, then set the board aside.

2 Place the cleat on the right side of the window frame, about midway between the top and bottom to hold the cords taut (Figure 1). If you have small children in your home, place the cleat close to the top of the frame to eliminate the risk of possible entanglement. Drill pilot holes in the frame or wall and mount the cleat.

3 Measure the window height from the top of the board. Divide the length by 6, dropping any remainder for the number of pleats in the finished shade. For the additional length needed to make a tuck at each pleat, multiply the number of pleats in the finished shade by 4.

4 Cut a length of fabric the measured window height plus 7" for the mounting and casing and the number calculated for the pleats. Measure the window width. Add 3" to the measured width for the cut width of fabric. To determine the number of O-rings needed, multiply the number of pleats in the finished blind by 3. You will need cord 6 times the measured height plus 2 times the measured width.

5 Cut a strip from contrasting fabric to be used as an accent on the Roman shade, adding a $3/8$" allowance on each long edge of the strip to turn under. (A striped fabric was used on page 10. The striped section is $2^1/4$" wide and was cut 3" wide to allow the small blue stripe on the outer edges to show.) Measure the length needed against the length of the shade. Turn under $1/4$" on each long edge of the strip. Press. Place the strip $3^1/2$" from each long edge. Topstitch the strip to the shade, stitching each edge in the same direction, from the lower edge of the shade to the top edge.

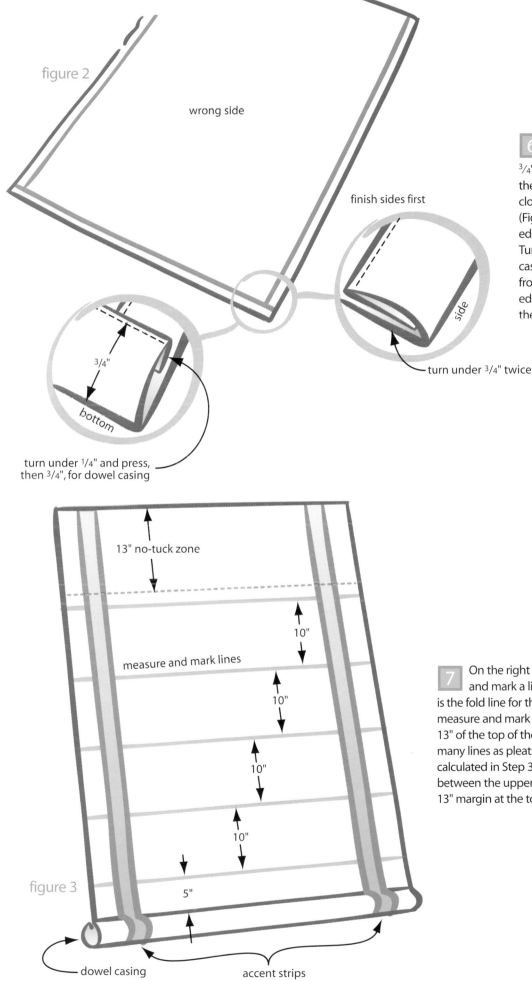

figure 2

wrong side

finish sides first

side

turn under ³/₄" twice

3/4"

bottom

turn under ¹/₄" and press,
then ³/₄", for dowel casing

6 On the shade, turn under each side edge ³/₄" twice. Press. Working on the wrong side, edgestitch close to the folded edge (Figure 2). On the bottom edge, turn under ¹/₄". Press. Turn under ³/₄" for the dowel casing and press. Working from the wrong side, edgestitch the casing close to the folded edge.

13" no-tuck zone

10"

measure and mark lines

10"

10"

10"

5"

figure 3

dowel casing

accent strips

7 On the right side of the shade, measure and mark a line 5" from the casing; this is the fold line for the first tuck. From this line, measure and mark lines every 10" to within 13" of the top of the shade (Figure 3). Mark as many lines as pleats in the finished shade calculated in Step 3. There may be a gap between the uppermost line and the 13" margin at the top of the blind.

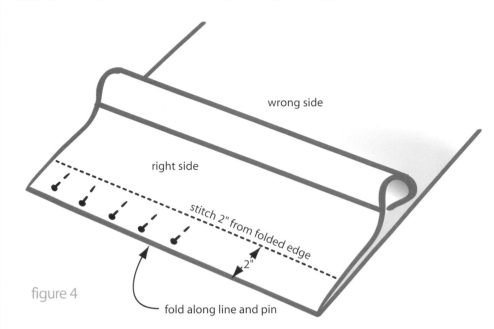

wrong side

right side

stitch 2" from folded edge

2"

figure 4

fold along line and pin

8 Fold the shade along the first line. Pin the layers together. Stitch 2" from the folded edge, forming a tuck (Figure 4). Be sure the stitching line is no more than 2" from the fold: If the tucks are stitched too deeply, the shade will be too short. Fold each line in turn and stitch the tucks. Remove the marks from the fabric. Press each tuck flat, creasing the fold. Lay each tuck toward the bottom of the shade. Press the shade on the front and back.

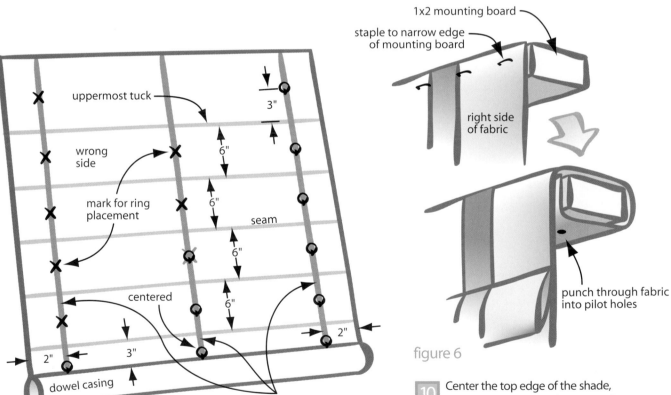

uppermost tuck

wrong side

mark for ring placement

seam

centered

2"

3"

dowel casing

draw lines from rings

3"

6"

6"

6"

6"

2"

figure 5

1x2 mounting board

staple to narrow edge of mounting board

right side of fabric

punch through fabric into pilot holes

figure 6

9 On the wrong side of the shade, use a needle and thread to stitch one O-ring to the dowel casing 2" from each side edge and at the center of the shade. Draw lines straight up the shade from each ring. Mark placements for additional rings halfway between each tuck along each line. Place the final ring 3" above the uppermost tuck (Figure 5). Stitch the rings to the shade at each mark.

10 Center the top edge of the shade, wrong side down, on the narrow front edge of the mounting board. Staple the fabric to the board. Wrap the fabric smoothly around the board, overlapping the first edge (Figure 6). Punch a small hole through the fabric into each pilot hole. Set the board on the corner braces; install with 1" wood screws. Install screw eyes in the pilot holes. Insert the dowel into the bottom casing.

11 For the left-hand cord, cut a length of cord equal to the window width plus 2 times the window length. Tie one end of the cord to the lowest ring on the left side of the shade, opposite the cleat. For the center cord, cut a length $1/2$ the width plus 2 times the length. Tie one end of this cord to the lowest ring in the center of the shade. Tie one end of the remaining cord to the lowest ring on the right side of the shade. Thread each cord through the column of rings to the screw eye at the top of the column. Thread the cords to the right toward the cleat. Thread all cords through the extreme right screw eye. Pull the cords to take up the slack and trim the cord ends even. To raise the shade, gently pull the cords together.

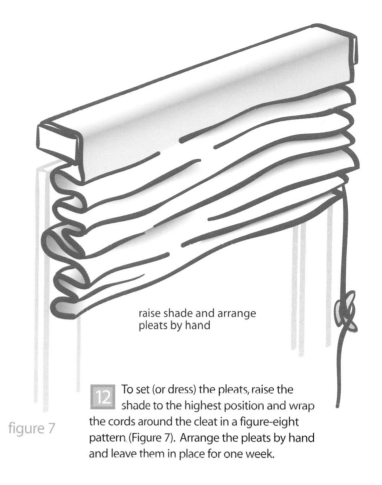

raise shade and arrange pleats by hand

figure 7

12 To set (or dress) the pleats, raise the shade to the highest position and wrap the cords around the cleat in a figure-eight pattern (Figure 7). Arrange the pleats by hand and leave them in place for one week.

HARDWARE MADE EASY

the inside corner brace

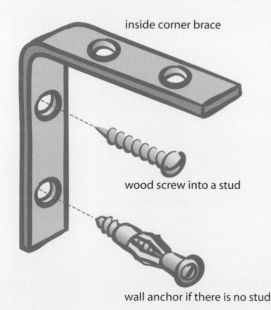

inside corner brace

wood screw into a stud

wall anchor if there is no stud

Mounting a board on L-shape inside corner braces is quite easy.

■ Metal inside corner braces, in sizes from 1" to 4", are often mistakenly called "L-brackets." Ask for inside corner braces at hardware and home improvement stores.

■ Choose the brace size based on the weight you expect it to hold. In most applications, a 2" brace will do the job. Attach the brace to the wall with wood screws into a stud, using wall anchors where there is no wall stud. Set the board on top of the braces and attach it with wood screws.

■ To mount a board outside the window frame, measure from the top of the board to the windowsill or floor, depending on the curtain style. Use the length of the mounting board as the window width measurement.

window scarf

materials

54"-wide decorator fabric*
⅞"-wide fusible adhesive tape*
2 wooden pegs or
  curtain tiebacks
Hardware to mount pegs

tools

Electric drill and drill bits
Screwdriver

sewing tools

Tape measure
Iron and ironing board
Scissors

skill level: beginner
time required: ¹/₂ day
*Purchase materials after
taking measurements.

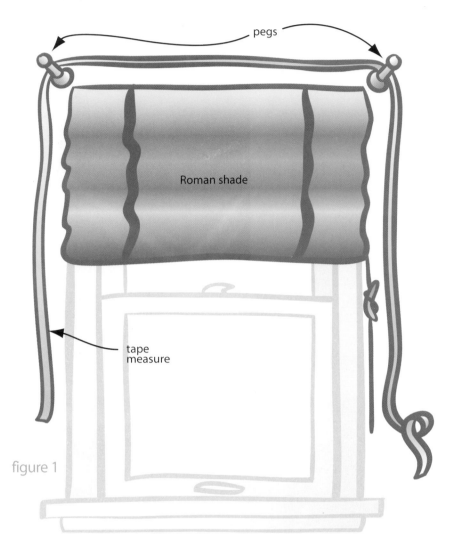

pegs

Roman shade

tape
measure

figure 1

wrong side

fusible adhesive

figure 2

1 Install the wooden pegs or tiebacks slightly above and outside the top of the Roman shade. Drape a tape measure over the pegs to determine the scarf length (Figure 1). In general, a symmetrically placed window scarf should extend two-thirds of the way down the window.

2 From a single width of decorator fabric, cut a piece the measured length plus 2". Trim the selvages. On one long edge, measure 12" in from each corner. Cut diagonally from this point to the adjacent corner on each long edge.

3 On the wrong side, following the manufacturer's instructions, apply fusible tape to each raw edge; remove the paper backing. Turn under each edge by the width of the fusible surface. Trim the fabric corners for a neat application (Figure 2). Fuse the hems in place.

4 Fold the scarf accordion-style to make casual pleats and drape the scarf over the pegs. Pull down the center to form a drape. Arrange the pleats at the sides.

draping a window scarf

Change the style of your window dressing by rearranging the scarf.

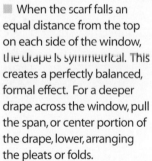

■ When the scarf hangs lower on one side than the other, the drape is asymmetrical and creates a feeling of energy and movement in a window treatment. If you drape a pair of tall, narrow windows, pull each scarf lower on the outside of the pair.

■ When the scarf falls an equal distance from the top on each side of the window, the drape is symmetrical. This creates a perfectly balanced, formal effect. For a deeper drape across the window, pull the span, or center portion of the drape, lower, arranging the pleats or folds.

■ For a casual, off-the-shoulder look, cut a long scarf to drape and swirl over a wooden pole. Fold, scrunch, and knot the fabric to create a soft, pleasing presentation.

window scarf how to

materials

18"-square pillow form
1 yard 54"-wide striped
    decorator fabric
14" invisible zipper
Tracing paper

sewing tools

Sewing machine
Iron and ironing board
Vanishing fabric marker
Pins
Needle and thread
Scissors
Tape measure
Liquid ravel preventer
Zipper foot

skill level: intermediate
time required: 4½ hours

mitered stripe pillow

1 Cut an 18" square from tracing paper. Diagonally fold the square from corner to corner. Crease. Open the square and fold on the opposite diagonal. Crease. Open the square and cut along the creases to make four identical triangle patterns.

2 Place one pattern on the fabric to determine the placement of the fabric design on the pillow. For the pillow shown on page 19, the green stripe bordered on either side by a red stripe is the center stripe in the pillow piece. When the four pieces are combined, the stripe intersects at the pillow center, and the remaining stripes make chevrons along the seams.

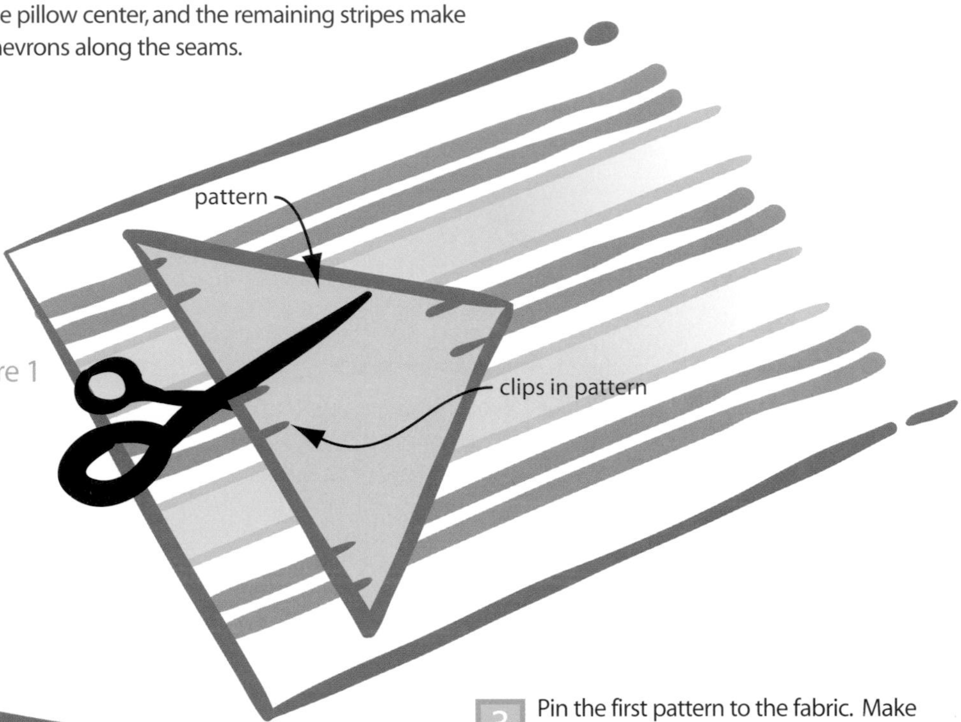

pattern

clips in pattern

figure 1

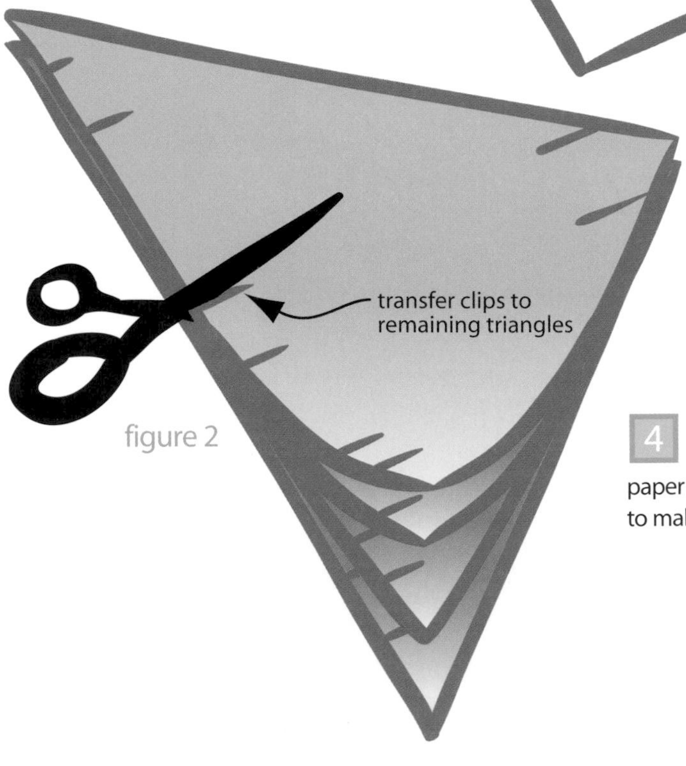

transfer clips to
remaining triangles

figure 2

3 Pin the first pattern to the fabric. Make small clips within the seam allowance in the pattern to mark the placement of the stripes (Figure 1).

4 Remove the pattern from the fabric. Stack the first pattern on the remaining paper triangles. Transfer the clips to the triangles to make identical patterns (Figure 2).

5 Pin each pattern on a single layer of fabric, matching the stripes to the clips in the pattern edges. Inspect the pattern placement to ensure each fabric piece will be identical. Mark a $1/2$" seam allowance around all edges of each pattern piece. Cut out the triangles on the marked lines.

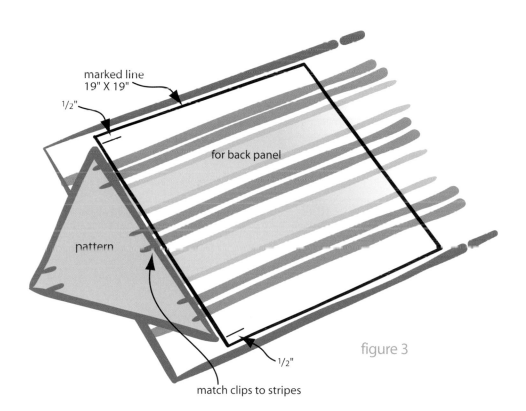

marked line
19" X 19"

$1/2$"

for back panel

pattern

figure 3

$1/2$"

match clips to stripes

6 For the back panel, place one pattern section on the fabric, matching the clips to the stripes in the fabric (Figure 3). Mark a line on the fabric $1/2$" beyond each long end of the pattern. Using the marked lines as a guide, cut a 19" square. Set the back panel aside.

7 With right sides together and raw edges aligned, pin two pairs of triangles together along one diagonal edge, matching the stripes. Using a $1/2$" seam allowance, stitch the pieces together on the pinned edge. Stitch the remaining pair of triangles together on one edge in the same manner. Check the seams for the alignment of the stripes. Press the seams open.

8 With right sides together and raw edges aligned, pin the long edges of the resulting triangles together, matching the stripes and center seam. Using a $1/2$" seam allowance, stitch the pieces together. Check the seam for the alignment of the stripes. Press the seam open. If the seams don't quite match at the center, add a tassel or button over the intersection after the pillow front is sewn to the pillow back.

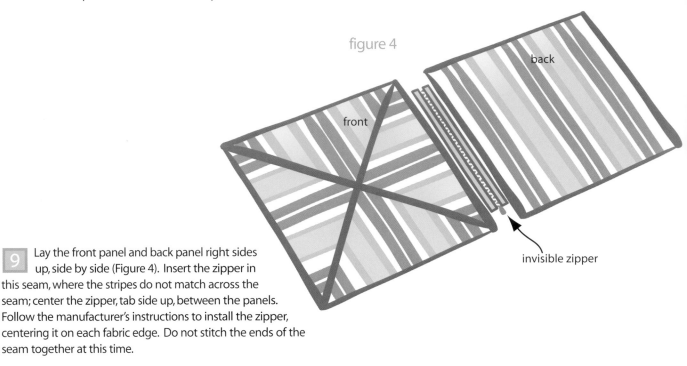

figure 4

front

back

invisible zipper

9 Lay the front panel and back panel right sides up, side by side (Figure 4). Insert the zipper in this seam, where the stripes do not match across the seam; center the zipper, tab side up, between the panels. Follow the manufacturer's instructions to install the zipper, centering it on each fabric edge. Do not stitch the ends of the seam together at this time.

10 With right sides together and raw edges aligned, pin the side edges of the front panel to the back panel, matching the stripes. Using a $1/2$" seam allowance, stitch the pinned edges together. Check the alignment of the stripes. Press the seams open, then turn to the right side and press.

11 Turn to the wrong side. With right sides together and raw edges aligned, pin the seams at each end of the zipper. Using a $1/2$" seam allowance and the zipper foot, stitch the ends of the seam. Press the seam open. Open the zipper. With right sides together and raw edges aligned, pin the remaining open edge of the panels together (the edge opposite the zipper). Using a $1/2$" seam allowance, stitch the front panel to the back panel along the pinned edge. Press the seams open.

12 Clip the corners, then turn to the right side through the zipper. Press the seams. Using a needle and thread, hand-stitch the tassel to the center front of the cover. Insert the pillow form into the cover and close the zipper.

designing with mitered seams

Change the placement of the pattern pieces to yield a variety of effects.

Concentric Squares: Change the layout of the pattern pieces to create a pillow front of concentric squares (Figure 1). By placing the long side of the paper triangles along the stripe, you create boxes of graduated size on the pillow front.

Hourglass Imagery: Use the triangular pattern pieces to cut two pieces from two contrasting fabrics. Position the fabrics across the center from each other to create an hourglass image on the pillow front (Figure 2). With solid fabrics or small prints, it will be easier to match the center of the panel. To accentuate the hourglass image, do not sew a button or tassel to the center of the panel.

Faux Wrap: Cut two pairs of triangles from two contrasting fabrics. Arrange the fabric pairs on opposite sides of the square to make an hourglass shape. From the remaining fabric, cut two 12× 3" lozenge-shape pieces. With right sides together and raw edges aligned, stitch the pieces together using a 1/4" seam allowance, pivoting the stitching at the points and leaving an opening in one side for turning. Press the seam and clip the corners and curves, then turn to the right side and place the seam on edge. Turn the raw edges at the opening to the inside and press. Hand-stitch the opening closed. Make a knot at the center of the piece and stitch the knot to the center of the pillow front (Figure 3).

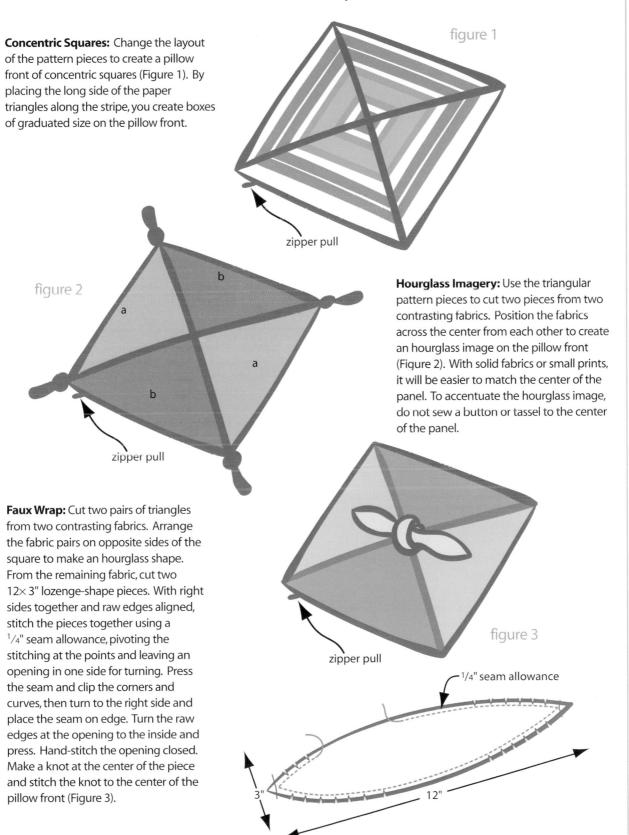

figure 1

zipper pull

figure 2

b

a

a

b

zipper pull

figure 3

zipper pull

1/4" seam allowance

3"

12"

Tie the pattern palette in your room together

by using remnants from draperies in distinctive pillows and other accents throughout the room. Bay windows add light, character, and a sense of spaciousness to a room; highlight them with a trimmed valance and simple gathered drapery panels.

custom companions

Framing each window with its own pair of draperies creates intimacy and softens a room by day. A shirred valance on a continuous valance shelf unifies the treatment and accents the architecture. Tassel fringe and cord emphasize the details of the valance, which conceals the traverse rods.

Choose a companion fabric to line the valance. Here, the flirty curved edge reveals a bit of the valance lining at each pleat. For lining or backing the long panels, use traditional white or ivory lining—from the outside, it will tend to disappear, adding to your home's curb appeal.

Repeating fabric elements within a room unifies the design. In this room, for example, the fabric in the window treatment appears on the upholstered seat of the side chair and on the sofa pillows. The pillows don't display the fabric in full; rather, they accent a portion of the striped floral.

The width of the appliqué pieces for each pillow is determined by the width of the floral stripe featured at the center of the pillow. If you work with an all-over design, plan for the three appliqué strips to be equal widths, or arrange them symmetrically if they are unequal widths. The complete design should cover approximately one-half to two-thirds of the total width of the pillow front.

See page 108 for drop-in seat instructions.

materials

54"-wide decorator fabric*
54"-wide contrasting fabric*
54"-wide lining fabric*
Tassel fringe*
Cord*
1×4 pine boards*
6 (4") inside corner braces
12 (2") No. 8 wood screws
12 (3/4") No. 8 wood screws
Finishing nails (dark color)
3 two-way traverse rods
Curtain pins*

tools

Electric drill and drill bits
Handsaw
Push pins
Staple gun and 1/4" staples

sewing tools

Sewing machine
Iron and ironing board
Pins
Tape measure
Vanishing fabric marker
Needle and thread

skill level: advanced
time required: 2 1/2 days
*Purchase materials after
taking measurements.

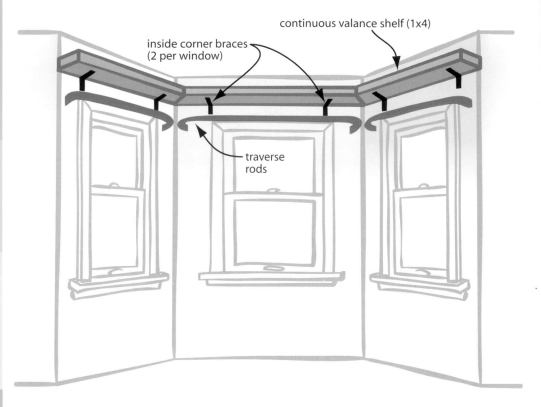

figure 1

1 Plan for the 1×4 boards to span the windows and the wall sections between the windows as a continuous valance shelf; the boards will meet in the corners of the bay. Install two inside corner braces above each window with 2" screws. Place the 1×4 boards on the corner braces; the ends of the boards should just meet (Figure 1). Mark and cut the ends, if necessary. Drill pilot holes through the corner braces into the boards and attach them with 3/4" screws. For the traverse rods, measure the width of each window, including the wall sections that are part of the bay. Mount the traverse rods outside the window frames. Position the rods end-to-end so the panels in the corners of the bay will appear as one.

2 Measure the width of the bay by measuring the front edge of the valance shelf, including the return. If working with solid or miniprint fabrics, multiply the measurement by 2 for the required width of the valance panel. Measure from the top of the valance shelf to the floor. Divide the measurement by 4 to determine the finished length of the valance; the valance must be at least 8" long. Trim the selvages from the fabric and contrasting fabric. Cut enough fabric lengths to make the required fullness, ensuring that each piece starts at the same point in the fabric repeat. Using a 1/2" seam allowance, stitch the lengths together, matching the pattern repeat. To create a special effect with the placement of a motif or stripe in the fabric, as in the valance shown on page 22, purchase enough fabric to cut one or two additional lengths to add to the valance width, if needed.

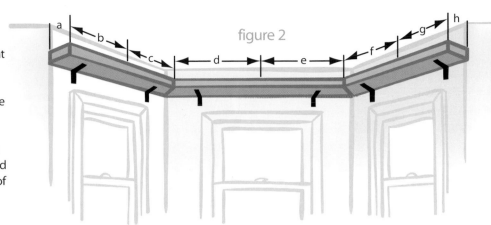

figure 2

3 The valance has one pleat at the center of each window and at each inside corner and outside corner of the bay. Divide the valance shelf into 8 sections (Figure 2). Sections A and H are the return sections. Sections B, C, D, E, F, and G begin and end at the center of a pleat. Measure the length of each section.

mark center of each pleat

valance

match pattern motif to center of pleat

lining

measure 2 times the length of each section

2a 2b 2c 2d 2e 2f 2g 2h

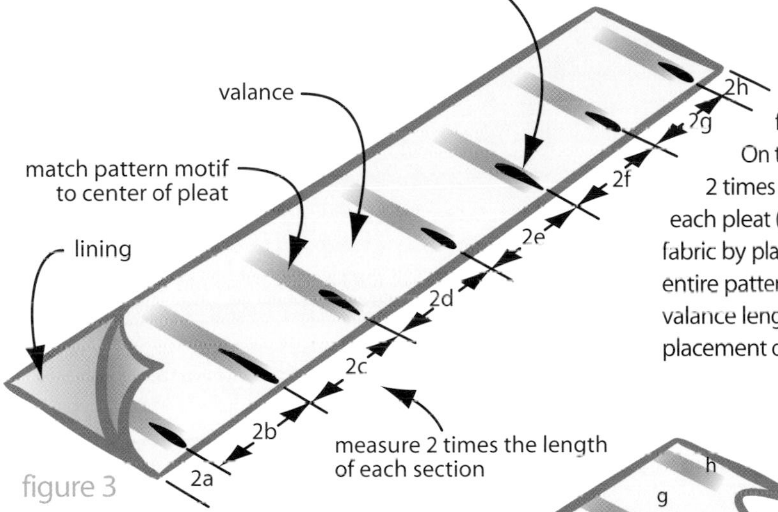

figure 3

4 Stack the lining and valance front, right sides together, with the valance front on top. Note the upper edge of the valance. On the wrong side of the valance front, measure 2 times the length of each section. Mark the center of each pleat (Figure 3). To emphasize a motif or stripe in the fabric by placing the motif at the center of the pleat, shift the entire pattern. It may be necessary to cut and seam additional valance lengths to each end in order to achieve the desired placement of motifs.

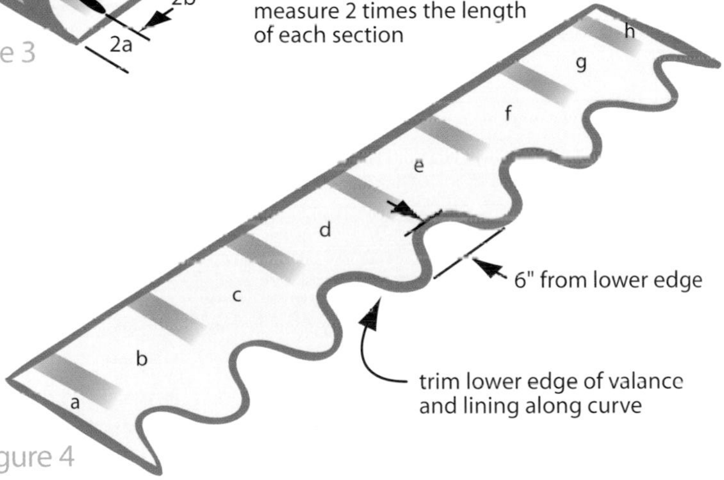

a b c d e f g h

6" from lower edge

trim lower edge of valance and lining along curve

figure 4

5 Draw a line from the marks for the centers of the pleats to the lower edge of the valance. At each mark, measure 6" into the valance from the lower edge. Draw a uniform curve from the raw edge to the 6" mark and back to the raw edge (Figure 4) to create scallops in the lower edge at each pleat. Trim the lower edge of the valance and lining along the marked curves.

6 With right sides together and using a ½" seam allowance, stitch the lower edges of the valance and lining together. Clip the curves. Stitch the upper edges together and press the seams open. Turn the valance to the right side, through the side openings. Place the seams on edge. Press flat. On each end, turn under the valance and lining ½". Press. Edgestitch through all layers.

7 Measure the tassel fringe to the lower edge of the valance and add 2". Apply ravel preventer to the braid portion of the fringe. Let dry. Cut the fringe through the ravel preventer and apply more ravel preventer to the cut ends. Turn under 1" at each end. Stitching both edges of the braid in the same direction, topstitch the fringe to the lower edge of the valance.

8 On the sewing machine, loosen the upper thread tension and set a long stitch length. On a scrap of fabric and lining stacked together, test gathering stitches and pull the bobbin thread to gather. Measure 1" from the top edge of the valance. Beginning and ending at the marked center of the pleats, stitch a line of gathering stitches, leaving long tails of thread when starting and stopping. Stitch a second line of gathering stitches ⅜" from the top edge, parallel to the first line. Pull the bobbin threads together in both lines of stitching to draw up the fabric.

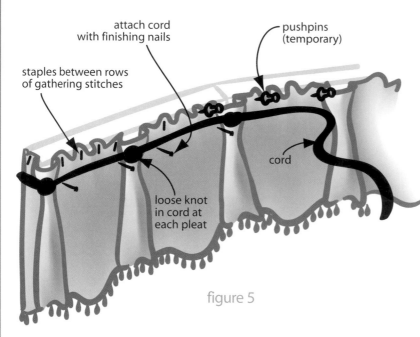

attach cord
with finishing nails

pushpins
(temporary)

staples between rows
of gathering stitches

cord

loose knot
in cord at
each pleat

figure 5

9 Adjust the gathers and shape the inverted pleats by hand. Fit the valance to the shelf. Temporarily hold the valance in place with pushpins on the front edge of the shelf as you work. Staple the valance to the shelf between rows of gathering stitches. Apply ravel preventer to the cord ends. Let dry. Use finishing nails to tack the cord to the valance over the gathers and staples. Make loose knots in the cord at each pleat (Figure 5).

10 For the draperies, measure the window height from the top of the rod to the floor. Add 10" to the measured height for the cut length of the front panels. Measure the width of each window to the traverse rod, including the return at each end of the rod. Cut two front panels for each window from fabric the measured length and as wide as the measured width plus 3". Be sure each piece starts at the same point in the fabric repeat. Cut two panels from lining for each window the measured height plus 4" and the measured width. If necessary, seam together fabric and lining lengths for the required width.

11 Lay each front panel right side up. Place the top edge of the lining 3" below the top edge of the panel. Smooth the lining down the length of the panel. Trim the lining 1" narrower than the front panel on both sides. Slide the lining to one side edge. Measure and mark 8" from the top edge and 12" from the bottom edge. Using a ½" seam allowance, stitch the front and lining together between the marks. Slide the lining to the opposite edge of the drapery front. Stitch the front and lining together in the same manner. Press the seams open.

12 Turn the drapery to the right side. Lay the lining side up. Center the lining over the drapery front with 1" of drapery fabric turned to the lining side. Press the folds and seams.

13 Turn the top edge of the lining back away from each drapery front. Turn the drapery fronts under 4", mitering the corners. Press. Turn under the side edges of the lining ½". Turn under the top edges of the lining 1¼". Press. Using a needle and thread, stitch the lining to the drapery fronts along all folded edges (Figure 6). Also stitch the angle folds of the drapery fronts.

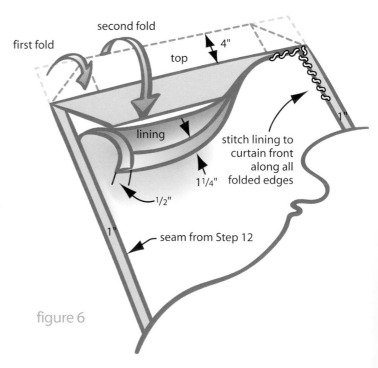

second fold

first fold

4"

top

lining

stitch lining to
curtain front
along all
folded edges

1¼"

½"

1"

1"

seam from Step 12

figure 6

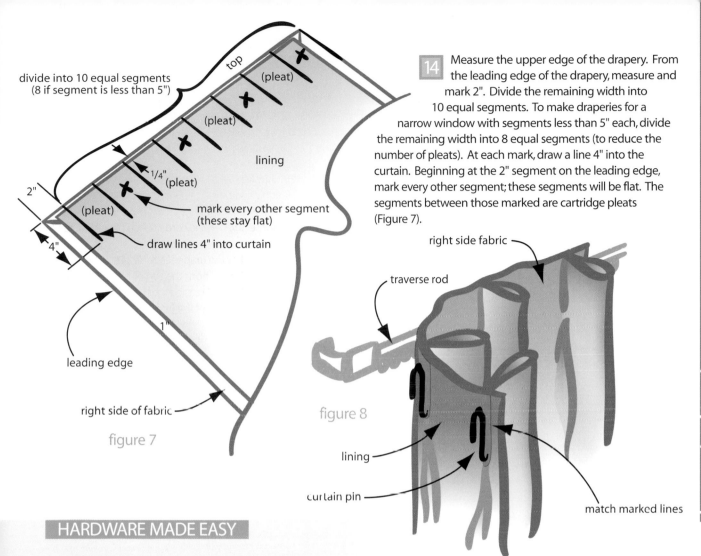

divide into 10 equal segments (8 if segment is less than 5")

top

(pleat)

(pleat)

(pleat)

lining

1/4" (pleat)

2"

(pleat)

mark every other segment (these stay flat)

draw lines 4" into curtain

4"

1"

leading edge

right side of fabric

figure 7

right side fabric

traverse rod

figure 8

lining

curtain pin

match marked lines

14   Measure the upper edge of the drapery. From the leading edge of the drapery, measure and mark 2". Divide the remaining width into 10 equal segments. To make draperies for a narrow window with segments less than 5" each, divide the remaining width into 8 equal segments (to reduce the number of pleats). At each mark, draw a line 4" into the curtain. Beginning at the 2" segment on the leading edge, mark every other segment; these segments will be flat. The segments between those marked are cartridge pleats (Figure 7).

15   Fold each pleat, matching the marked lines. Topstitch through all layers at the lines (Figure 8). Insert curtain pins into the back of each pleat and at the top corners of each panel. Adjust the pins to allow the top edge of the curtain to conceal the traverse rod. Hang the hook portion of the pins through the carriers on the rod.

16   Turn under the drapery front hem so the edge meets the floor. Pin. Remove the draperies from the rod. Keeping the lining edge free, press the fold, then open it. Measure 6" from the fold and trim the excess. Turn under the raw edge of the drapery front to meet the crease for the hem. Press. Refold the hem, mitering the corners at the ends. Hemstitch the folded edge.

17   Turn under the lining 1" shorter than the drapery front. Press. Measure 2" from the fold and trim the excess. Turn under the raw edge to meet the crease. Turn under the side edges ½". Press. Working from the wrong side, edgestitch the hem close to the folded edge. Using a needle and thread, stitch the lining and drapery together below the side seams. Hang the draperies on the rod.

18   Follow the manufacturer's instructions to set up the cords on the traverse rods. To open and close the draperies, pull the cords.

HARDWARE MADE EASY

decorative traverse rod

pull mechanism hidden behind decorative front

traverse rods move curtains by a pull mechanism across the window. Two-way draw traverse rods split a pair of curtains at the window center to move to each side. One-way draw rods pull a single panel to one side of the window. Follow the instructions provided by the manufacturer for easy installation of these rods.

Originally, traverse rods looked utilitarian, like adjustable rods, but decorative traverse rods are now on the market. Some look like brass cafe rods with rings, while others resemble wood poles and rings. The pull mechanisms are hidden on the backside of a decorative front.

materials

16"-square pillow form
$3/4$ yard 54"-wide decorator fabric
$3/4$ yard 54"-wide accent fabric
$3/4$ yard 54"-wide accent fabric
$1^1/2$ yards gimp
$2^1/4$ yards tassel fringe
Invisible thread
14" zipper

sewing tools

Sewing machine
Iron and ironing board
Vanishing fabric marker
Pins
Needle and thread
Scissors
Tape measure
Liquid ravel preventer
Pressing cloth

skill level: intermediate
time required: $3^1/2$ hours

creative custom pillows

1 Cut two 17" squares from the main pillow fabric for the front and back panels. Cut one 2×17" strip for the zipper flap. If working with a fabric design that has an obvious top and bottom, cut the zipper flap to match the lower edge of the back panel. Cut out one strip from accent fabric (such as the floral stripe in the sample pillow) to the desired width, adding a $1/4$" allowance on each long edge. To make it easier to design the pillow front, allow excess length on the strip to allow you to position the motifs in the stripe. Cut two 17"-long strips from a second accent fabric (a check in the sample pillow) the width of the first accent strip plus 1".

2 On the front panel, center and arrange the accent fabrics. Measure from the side edge of the pillow front to the edge of the check fabric and add $1/2$" for the placement line of the check accent. Remove the accent fabrics from the front panel.

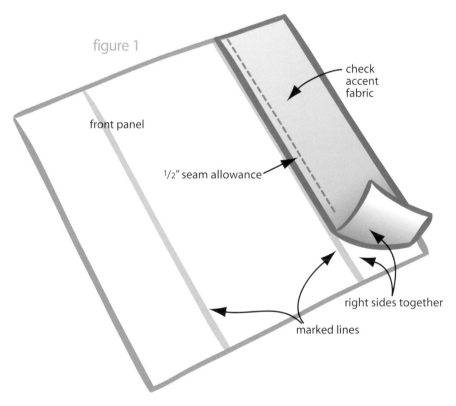

figure 1

check accent fabric

front panel

$1/2$" seam allowance

right sides together

marked lines

3 Measure from each side edge of the front panel and mark lines for the placement of the check accents. With right sides together, align one raw edge of one check accent strip with each marked line, allowing the accent strips to extend beyond the side edges of the front panel. Using a $1/2$" seam allowance on the check, stitch the check accent strips to the panel along the marked lines (Figure 1). Press the seam. Turn the check accent strips toward the center of the front panel. Press.

4 Center the floral stripe piece on the front panel, covering the raw edges of the check accents. Zigzag over each long raw edge of the floral stripe piece, stitching through the check fabric and the front panel. Trim the ends of the floral strip even with the front panel.

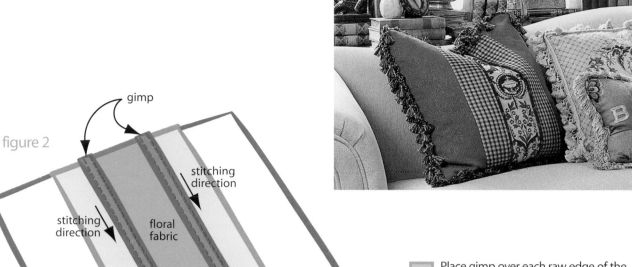

figure 2

gimp

stitching
direction

stitching
direction

floral
fabric

checked fabric

figure 3

right side of fabric

stitch zipper tape
to zipper flap

back panel

zipper facedown

right side of fabric

zipper flap

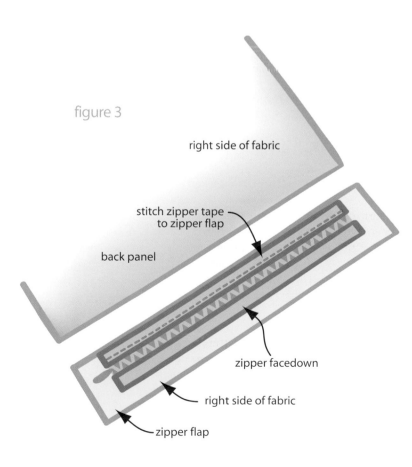

5 Place gimp over each raw edge of the center strip. Thread the top of the machine with invisible thread and load conventional thread on the bobbin. Using a long stitch length and stitching both edges in the same direction, topstitch the gimp to the front panel along each long edge of the floral piece (Figure 2). Turn the panel to the wrong side. Press the stitches.

6 On the right side of the front panel, align the braid of the tassel fringe with the raw edges of the panel, with the fringe toward the center of the panel. Pin in place. Clip the braid at the corners. Where the braid ends meet, overlap the ends ¹/₂". Apply liquid ravel preventer to the cut ends. Let dry. Using a long stitch length, baste the trim to the panel along the inner edge of the braid. Press the panel on the wrong side. Set the front panel aside.

7 Lay the back panel and the zipper flap right side up. Center the zipper facedown on the left long edge of the zipper flap (Figure 3), aligning the zipper tape with the raw edge of the flap. Using the zipper foot, stitch the zipper tape to the zipper flap. Turn the zipper faceup and press the seam.

8 On the bottom edge of the back panel, turn under 1¼" and press. Open the fold. Center the zipper on the lower raw edge, aligning the raw edge of the fabric with the zipper tape (Figure 4). Using the zipper foot, stitch the zipper tape to the edge. Press.

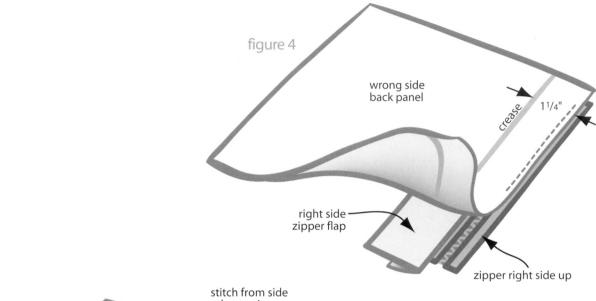

figure 4

wrong side
back panel

crease

1¼"

right side
zipper flap

zipper right side up

figure 5

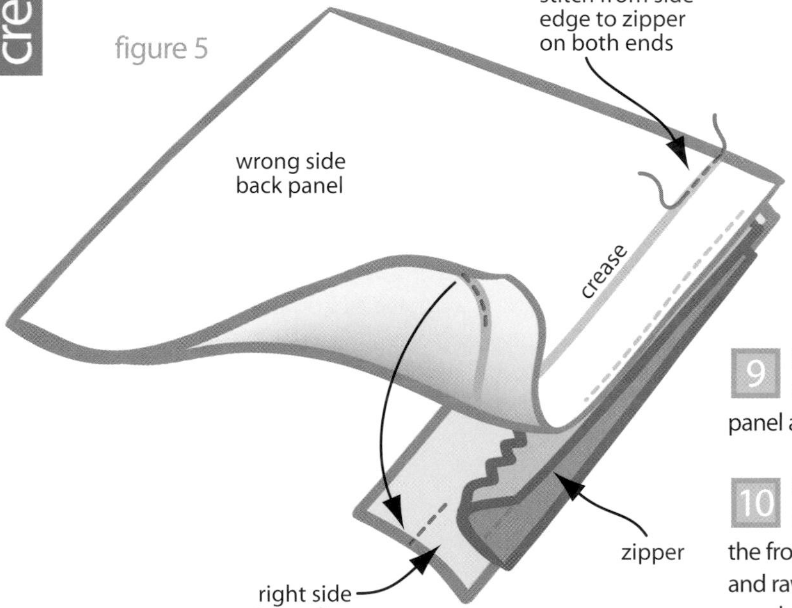

stitch from side
edge to zipper
on both ends

wrong side
back panel

crease

right side
zipper flap

zipper

9 Stitch along the crease at both ends of the zipper (Figure 5), beginning stitching at the side edges of the panel and stopping at the zipper. Refold the crease and press.

10 Compare the zippered back panel to the front panel. If necessary, trim the zippered back panel to match the front panel. Open the zipper. With right sides together and raw edges aligned, stitch the back panel to the front panel along the previous basting line on the front panel. Pivot the stitching at the corners. Clip the corners. Apply liquid ravel preventer to the cut edges of the braid. Let dry. Press the seam.

11 Turn to the right side through the zipper. Reach inside the cover to push out the corners. Cover the seam and fringe with a pressing cloth. Press the seam from the right side. Insert the pillow form into the cover.

MORE GOOD IDEAS

one-of-a-kind pillows Combine techniques and materials to make your own designer pillows.

figure 1

gimp

pleated fabric

tassel fringe

Pleat fabric strips to create texture in custom fabrics (Figure 1). Cut a strip about 3 times as long as the finished length of the pillow front to allow plenty of fabric play as you make the pleats. If you work with scraps or short lengths left over from another sewing project, stitch the short strips together and hide the seams in the creases of the pleats. To hold the pleats in place, baste the pleated fabric to a strip of nonwoven interfacing. Cover the pleats with a pressing cloth soaked in a solution of 1 cup water and $1/4$ cup distilled white vinegar (the vinegar press makes the pleats permanent). Press firmly.

Appliqué a motif from one fabric onto another to combine two designs. Apply paper-backed fusible web to the wrong side of the appliqué fabric, following the manufacturer's instructions. Cut out the motif or design. Remove the paper backing and fuse the motif to the front panel of the pillow. Use a satin stitch to cover all the cut edges of the appliqué (Figure 2). To add dimension to the motif, accent portions of the design with satin stitching.

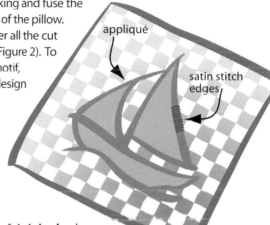

appliqué

satin stitch edges

figure 2

fringe

welting

fabric panel

stitch in the ditch

figure 3

Create a **fabric badge** by framing a small fabric panel with a combination of trims, such as loop fringe with a sculpted or scalloped edge and welting made from a complementary fabric. Place the badge (the fabric-and-trim unit) at the center of the front panel. Stitch in the ditch between the fabric and the welting to secure the badge to the front panel (Figure 3).

TECHNIQUES MADE EASY

directional stitching

Why does it matter which direction you stitch when applying braid or trim to a pillow? The feed dog on the sewing machine pulls the fabric under the needle as you stitch. If you stitch down one side of a trim, then turn the fabric around to stitch up the other, the feed dog will rumple the fabric on the underside of the trim. The result is a trim that twists or pulls out of shape and fabric that lumps.

To avoid this, stitch along each side of the trim in the same direction. Identify one end of the trim as the starting point and place it under the machine first. When you reach the end, cut the threads and return to the starting point to stitch the remaining side. This way, the trim will lie flat on the fabric.

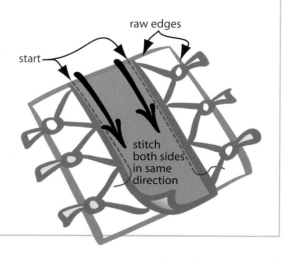

raw edges

start

stitch both sides in same direction

Slipcovers transform chairs
and sofas—why not pillows? Layering fabric,
such as coordinating solids or prints, over a pillow
cover adds richness and shifts the color emphasis in
the room. The red check on the pillow shown at left,
for example, plays up the warmth of the color
scheme. A blue slipcover would make the blue
elements in the fabrics appear more prominent.

pillow with tie-on slipcover

The creative possibilities are nearly endless with easy-to-sew covers. Make pillows with covers that coordinate to take advantage of layering, or stitch covers to perk up the knife-edge pillows you keep around all year.

To freshen dated-looking pillows, choose fabric in a color that coordinates or contrasts with the pillow fabric, or bring a sense of the changing seasons indoors. For spring and summer, choose white

cotton or linen. For winter, create a cozy look with dark plaids, deep paisley patterns, or rich solids in felt, wool, and flannel. And for the holidays, make pinafores from velvet, organdy, or holiday-print fabrics for festive, elegant accents.

FAST FACTS ON FUSIBLE WEB

■ You don't need a sewing machine to make pillow pinafores. Simply use paper-backed fusible adhesive tape and an iron to secure the hems. Tack ribbon ties to the slipcover with a few hand stitches.

■ Paper-backed fusible web makes easy work of many home decorating projects. Use it to bond fabric to porous materials such as paper lampshades.

■ It generally takes two steps to fuse fabrics. First, apply the paper-backed fusible web to one fabric with a hot iron; remove the paper backing. Next, place the fabric—turn the hem, for example—and fuse the layers together.

■ Read the manufacturer's instructions for fabric suitability. Some recommend different weights of fusible web depending on the fabric weight or finish.

materials

14"-square pillow form
$^1/_2$ yard 54"-wide decorator
    fabric
$^1/_2$ yard 54"-wide
    complementary fabric

sewing tools

Sewing machine
Iron and ironing board
Vanishing fabric marker
Pins
Needle and thread
Scissors
Tape measure
Liquid ravel preventer

skill level: beginner
time required: 3½ hours

1 Cut two squares, each 15", from fabric for the front and back panels. If the fabric has a prominent design, match the pattern from the front panel to the back panel on as many edges as possible.

2 With right sides together, raw edges aligned, and patterns matching, stitch the front panel to the back, using a $^1/_2$" seam allowance. Pivot the stitching at the corners and stitch all corners, leaving an opening in one side for turning. Clip the corners and press the seam. Turn the cover to the right side and press the seam.

3 Insert the form into the cover. Turn the raw edges of the opening to the inside. Using a needle and thread, hand-stitch the opening closed.

4 To make the slipcover, cut two 15$^1/_2$×18" pieces from complementary fabric for the front and back panels. Cut four 2×12" ties. Set the ties aside.

5 With right sides together and raw edges aligned, pin the front panel to the back panel on both 18" sides and on one 15$^1/_2$" side. Using a $^1/_2$" seam allowance, stitch the panels on the pinned edges. Clip the corners and press the seam. Turn to the right side and press the seam.

6 On the open edge of the cover, turn under the raw edges $^1/_4$" twice. Press. Edgestitch along the fold to finish the edge. Measure and mark a line 2$^1/_2$" from the finished edge. Fold the fabric to the right side along the marked line (Figure 1). Press to crease. Set aside.

7 With wrong sides together, fold each tie in half, matching the long edges. Press to crease, then open the fold. On one short end, turn under $^1/_2$" and press (Figure 2). Turn each long edge to meet the center crease. Press. Refold the center crease. Topstitch through all layers along the folded short end and the long edge of the tie. Press.

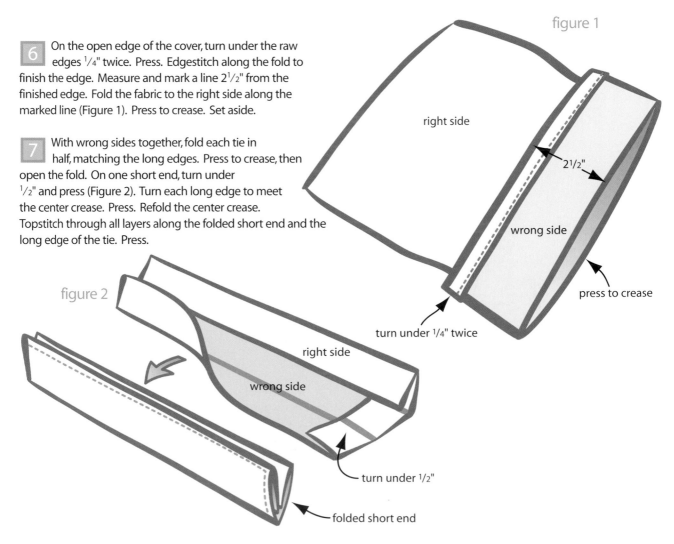

figure 1

right side

2½"

wrong side

press to crease

turn under ¼" twice

figure 2

right side

wrong side

turn under ½"

folded short end

8 On the open edge of the cover, measure $3^1/_2$" from each side seam, marking a point on both the front and back panels. At each marked point, insert the raw end of one tie into the fold on the open edge of the cover (Figure 3). Stitch $^1/_2$" from the fold of the open edge, catching the ties in the stitching line.

9 Press the seam and open the fold. Press. Turn the finished edge of the opening to the inside of the cover to make the facing. Place the seam with the ties on edge and match the side seams of the cover and facing. To secure the facing on the open edge, stitch in the ditch along each side seam.

10 Insert the finished pillow into the cover. Make bows with the pairs of ties to close the slipcover opening.

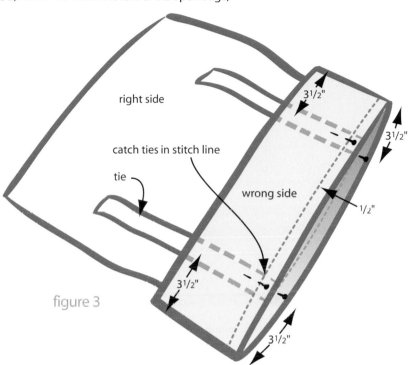

right side

catch ties in stitch line

tie

$3^1/_2$"

$3^1/_2$"

wrong side

$^1/_2$"

$3^1/_2$"

$3^1/_2$"

figure 3

MORE GOOD IDEAS

creative closures Add style and personality to pillow slipcovers by choosing unusual closures.

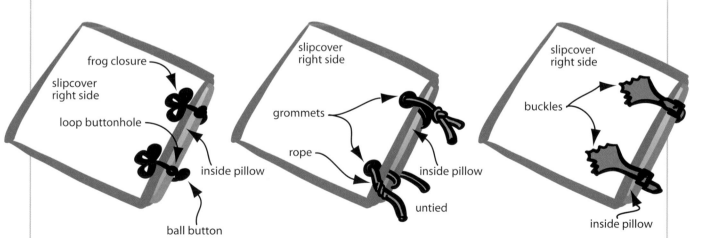

frog closure

slipcover right side

loop buttonhole

inside pillow

ball button

slipcover right side

grommets

rope

inside pillow

untied

slipcover right side

buckles

inside pillow

Frog closures give slipcovers a look of formal elegance. Stitch the loop to the back panel and the three-looped closure to the front panel, making sure the two pieces are perfectly aligned so the slipcover lies straight on the pillow when you insert the button through the loop.

For a casual look, use **large grommets and rope, twine, or leather thongs**. This type of closure would suit a slipcover made of canvas or muslin and would work well for pillows used outdoors on a porch or deck, or even in a child's room or informal family room.

Use **buckles** to secure a slipcover made from wool plaid, corduroy, or canvas to use in a child's room, den, or playroom. These buckles are actually kilt tabs; check the notions aisle at fabric centers to find them. Secure the buckle ends with fabric glue or machine-stitch them in place.

Staples of traditional window dressings, handmade pleats work comfortably in both formal and informal rooms. Hang the draperies on weighty curtain rings slipped onto overscaled rods for an updated look that suits casual settings. For more conservative formality, pair pleated draperies with hard cornices (see pages 104 and 184).

For a window treatment that is elegant but not too formal, opt for shapely handmade pleats. Choose a sturdy medium-weight fabric and trim the long sides of each panel with tassel fringe for a custom-finished look. Remember that a pair of draperies should be wide enough to cover the window when drawn, even if you never intend to close them. Hang the draperies from boldly scaled rods and curtain rings to give the treatment importance. In the room shown at left, the fluted wood rod mounts outside and above the window moldings. This placement fills the narrow wall space between the window frame and the wide crown moldings.

See page 48 for pillow instructions.

MATCHING FABRIC REPEATS

1 Join fabric lengths to make up a required width by first measuring the fabric repeat. To make this easy, look at the selvage for the registration marks; the length between any two identical marks is the fabric repeat.

2 Consider how the length and width of the fabric repeat will affect the amount of fabric needed for each panel. When cutting more than one fabric length for a window treatment, be sure to start each piece at the same point in the repeat. If this results in a short length of fabric left over between the two cuts, use it to make pillows.

3 The registration marks on the left and right selvages match. Use these marks to match the pattern across seam lines. With right sides together, align the marks and pin the fabric sections together. Trim the selvages and stitch the lengths together.

54"-wide decorator fabric*
Lining fabric*
Tassel fringe*
2 drapery tiebacks with
   tassel ends
12 curtain pins
Wood rods with mounting
   hardware
12 wood curtain rings
Stiff paper or file folder

tools
Electric drill and drill bits

sewing tools
Sewing machine
Iron and ironing board
Scissors
Tape measure
Pins
Needle and thread

skill level: intermediate
time required: 2 days
*Purchase materials after
taking measurements.

4 Turn the drapery to the
   right side. Lay the
drapery lining side up. Center
the lining over the drapery
front, turning 1" of drapery
fabric to the lining side on
each side. Press the folds
and seams.

5 Turn the top edge of
   the lining back away
from each drapery front. Turn
the top edge of the drapery
front under 4", mitering the
corners. Press. Turn under
the top edge of the lining
1¼". Turn under the
unstitched side edges of the
lining (the top 8") ½". Press.
Using a needle and thread,
stitch the linings to the
drapery fronts along all
folded edges. Also, stitch the
mitered folds of the
drapery fronts.

handmade pleats

1 Measure the width of the window frame from the outside edges. Mount
   the rod and place the curtain rings on the rod. Measure the distance from
the bottom of the rings to the floor (this is the drapery length). Add 10" to this
measurement to determine the cut length of the panels. Cut each panel as wide
as the total window width. Consider the length of the fabric repeat when
making calculations.

2 Trim the selvages from the fabric and lining. Cut two front panels the
   measured window length from fabric. Be sure each piece starts at the same
point in the fabric repeat. Cut two panels the measured window length plus
4" from the lining.

3 Lay each front panel right side up. With right sides together, place the top
   edge of the lining 3" below the top edge of the panel. Smooth the lining
down the length of the panel. Trim the lining 2" narrower than the front panel.
Slide the lining to one side edge. Measure and mark 8" from the top edge and
12" from the bottom edge. Using a ½" seam allowance, stitch the front and lining
together between the marks. Slide the lining to the opposite side edge of the
drapery front. Stitch the front and lining together between the top and bottom
marks. Press the seams open.

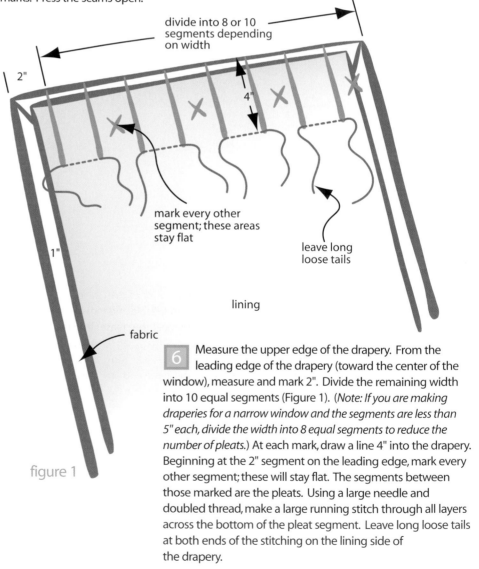

divide into 8 or 10
segments depending
on width

2"

4"

mark every other
segment; these areas
stay flat

leave long
loose tails

1"

lining

fabric

figure 1

6 Measure the upper edge of the drapery. From the
   leading edge of the drapery (toward the center of the
window), measure and mark 2". Divide the remaining width
into 10 equal segments (Figure 1). (*Note: If you are making
draperies for a narrow window and the segments are less than
5" each, divide the width into 8 equal segments to reduce the
number of pleats.*) At each mark, draw a line 4" into the drapery.
Beginning at the 2" segment on the leading edge, mark every
other segment; these will stay flat. The segments between
those marked are the pleats. Using a large needle and
doubled thread, make a large running stitch through all layers
across the bottom of the pleat segment. Leave long loose tails
at both ends of the stitching on the lining side of
the drapery.

7 Fold each pleat, lining sides together, matching the marked lines. Topstitch through all layers at the lines. Working from the lining side, center each pleat behind the seam. Press flat. Pull both tails of the running stitches to gather the lower edge of the pleat. Knot the thread ends together. Finger-press each pleat to resemble the bowl of a water goblet.

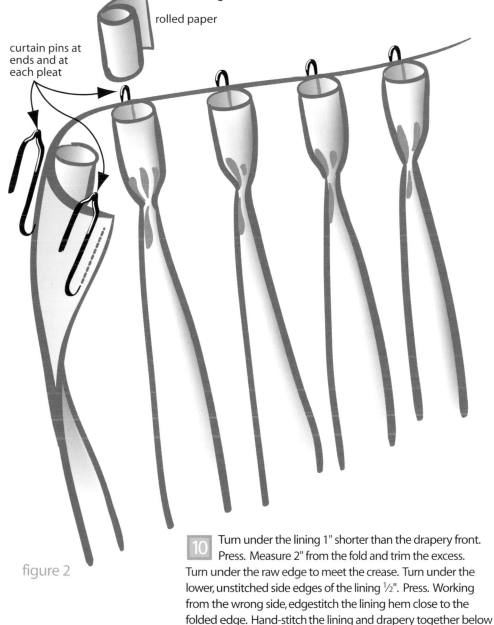

rolled paper

curtain pins at ends and at each pleat

figure 2

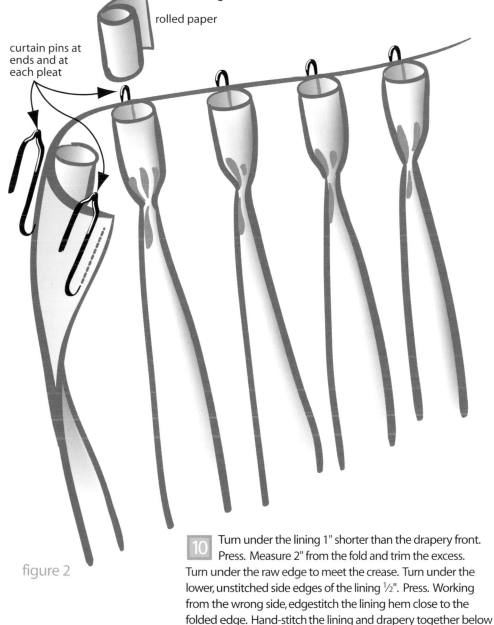

8 Insert curtain pins into the back of each pleat and at the top corners of each drapery (Figure 2). Hang the curtain hooks in the screw eyes on the wooden rings. To keep well-formed pleats, slip a rolled strip of stiff paper into each pleat.

9 Turn under the drapery hem so that the lower edge meets the floor. Pin. Remove the draperies from the rod. Press the fold; open. Keep the lining edge free. Measure 6" from the fold and trim the excess. Turn the raw edge of the drapery front to meet the folded hem edge. Press. Refold the hem, mitering the corners similar to those at the drapery top. Hemstitch the folded edge.

10 Turn under the lining 1" shorter than the drapery front. Press. Measure 2" from the fold and trim the excess. Turn under the raw edge to meet the crease. Turn under the lower, unstitched side edges of the lining ½". Press. Working from the wrong side, edgestitch the lining hem close to the folded edge. Hand-stitch the lining and drapery together below the side seams.

11 Measure the fringe with the leading and outside edges of each drapery. Add 1" at each end. Apply ravel preventer to the braid portion of the fringe. Let dry. Cut through the braid at the ravel preventer. Apply more ravel preventer to the cut ends. Let dry. Place the braided edge of the fringe on the drapery. Turn under the ends 1". Using a long stitch length, topstitch the fringe in place along each edge of the braid. Hang the draperies.

curtain pins and slide hooks

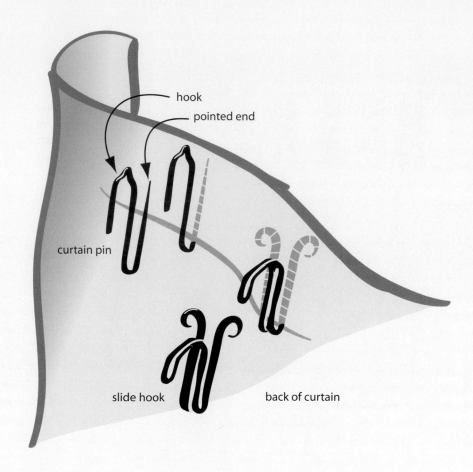

hook

pointed end

curtain pin

slide hook   back of curtain

curtain pins

almost invisibly attach draperies or curtains to the curtain rings. To use the pins successfully, the drapery should have a closed heading. The sharp pin portion of the device is inserted into the back or lining side of the drapery. One pin is inserted $1/2$" to 1" from each end, and the rest are evenly spaced along the width between. For a pleated heading, insert one pin into the back of each pleat. Place the pin so that the tallest portion extends $1/4$" above the drapery front. Place all pins at the same level. Just one pin out of line can cause the drapery to hang crooked.

slide hooks

are used in the same manner as curtain pins, except they are intended for draperies or curtains with an open or folded heading. Fold under the drapery heading the same depth as the back portion of the slide hook. Slip the back portion of the hook into the heading as you would a paper clip. The slide hook is hidden behind the drapery because the top of the hook is not as high as the back portion.

CHOOSING LININGS

Asking for lining at the fabric store can elicit a number of questions from the sales associate, the most important being what type of lining you need: basic, thermal, or blackout. Here are some fast facts to help you answer those questions.

basic lining adds body to draperies and provides some protection against sun damage. In tightly woven cotton or cotton-blend fabric, it is available in white or off-white.

thermal lining is basic lining with a synthetic coating applied to one side. The coating makes the fabric less air permeable, increasing the warming values of closed draperies. Take care in pressing to avoid marring the coated surface. The fabric is easy to find in white, while off-white thermal lining may be more difficult to find.

blackout lining is also basic lining with a synthetic coating applied to one side. The coating is thick, often gray, and is used to block sunlight. In windows with a western or southern exposure where harsh light is a factor, blackout lining can preserve the beauty of the drapery fabric. Care should be taken when pressing to avoid marring the coated surface. This lining is easy to find in white, while off-white blackout lining may be more difficult to obtain.

interlining is not a lining, but a thin flannel-like fabric used between the drapery front and the lining. It adds fullness to the drapery fabric, helps to absorb sound, and provides some insulating benefits. It is ivory in color.

wood poles easily fit into almost any decorating scheme. Painted white, they have country charm, yet stained dark, they offer traditional elegance. The poles may be smooth or fluted. Most poles rest on brackets mounted on the window frame or on the wall surrounding the window. Finials, the decorative knobs that finish the ends of the pole, come in styles from plain to ornate. Brackets usually come with the screws needed to fasten the bracket to solid wood, such as the window frame or a wall stud. If you choose to mount the bracket in a location where no stud exists, use wall anchors to secure the brackets. For help in choosing the appropriate hardware for mounting in special circumstances, visit the "fasteners" aisle of a hardware store.

This window treatment proves that you can warm a room and soften the architecture without complicated cutting and sewing. Flat panels on curtain rings simply hang from knobs in the window frame. A bamboo pole or plain dowel keeps the lower edge rigid so you can pull back the panel to let in light.

lined flat panels

Privacy and light control are two excellent reasons to cover windows with wood blinds or shutters. But stop there and the window looks cold and unfinished. This fabric treatment, layered over blinds, softens the effect and gives you a chance to reinforce a room's color and texture. Here, two flat panels hang by rings along the top edge of the window frame.

Rather than use white lining to layer window treatments, audition different lining materials for an indoor effect. While the blinds or shutters provide uniform curb appeal, the combination of stripes and checks plays up the vintage charm of this setting.

Bamboo poles weight the hem edge of these panels. You could also use custom-finished dowel rods or clean woodsy branches, depending on whether your room is traditional or rustic.

See page 48 for basic pillow instructions.

FABRICS WITH PERSONALITY

■ This window treatment works well with a variety of decorator fabrics, provided they have enough body or weight. Sheers are too flimsy, but you don't want a stiff upholstery fabric either. A suitable fabric should drape nicely in your hand yet have enough weight to stay in place along the bottom edge.

■ Adapt the window dressing to suit the season with a change of fabrics. Consider using a light-colored cotton print for summer and a dark or heavy fabric for winter. For a child's room, try colorful Polarfleece for a cozy winter look and a cotton novelty print for summer.

■ "Found" fabrics, such as chenille bedspreads, quilts, quilt tops, or vintage tablecloths, could be adapted to this design, as well. To protect the textiles from the sun, back them with a lining and consider adding interlining as well, to enhance the fabric's light-blocking quality.

materials

54"-wide decorator fabric*
54"-wide contrasting
   lining fabric*
10 clip rings
Decorative knobs
Dowel screws
Bamboo poles
Drapery tiebacks

tools

Electric drill and drill bits
Pliers

sewing tools

Sewing machine
Iron and ironing board
Scissors
Tape measure
Needle and thread
Pins

skill level: beginner
time required: 1 day
*Purchase materials after
taking measurements.

1 These curtains mount on the window frame without hiding the decorative molding. To cover one large window as shown on page 42, measure the window width and divide by 2; then add 1" to each measurement to obtain the width of each curtain panel. For the panel length, measure the window length and add 10". You may need to seam fabric lengths together to achieve the desired width for the fabric panel and lining. Consider the length of the fabric repeat before you purchase fabrics. For the tabs, you will need an additional ¼ yard of fabric or contrasting fabric.

(Note: If you have multiple closely set windows, make one curtain panel for each window. Measure the window width and length inside the frame. The fabric panel width should equal the measured window width plus 1". The panel length should equal the measured window length plus 10".)

2 Trim the selvages from the fabrics and cut the fabric and lining to the size determined in Step 1. Be sure each piece of fabric starts at the same point in the repeat. With right sides together and using a ½" seam allowance, stitch the fabric and lining together along the side edges. Press the seams open. Stitch the top edge. Press the seam open. Turn the curtain to the right side. Place the seams on edge and press flat.

3 Temporarily catch each top corner of the curtain in a clip ring. Evenly space the remaining clips between the corners. Have a helper hold the curtain in the window to mark the placement of the knobs on the molding (Figure 1).

4 Drill pilot holes at the marks. Using pliers, screw one end of the dowel into the knob. Screw the opposite end of the dowel screw into the molding. Hang the rings on the knobs.

5 At the hem edge of the curtain, position the bamboo pole to determine the finished length of the curtain. Mark the stitching line on the curtain and remove the curtains from the window. Leaving a ½" allowance, trim the excess length from the curtain front and lining. Remove the clips from the curtains; set the curtains and the clips aside.

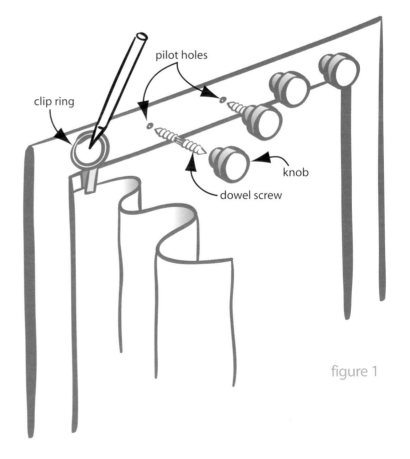

pilot holes

clip ring

knob

dowel screw

figure 1

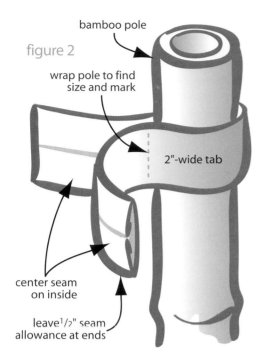

figure 2

bamboo pole

wrap pole to find size and mark

2"-wide tab

center seam on inside

leave ¹/₂" seam allowance at ends

6 From the remaining fabric or lining, cut four 5×8" pieces for the tabs. Fold the tabs in half, right sides together, matching the long edges. Using a ¹/₂" seam allowance, stitch the long edges together. Press the seam open. Turn the tab to the right side. Center the seams on the back and press flat. Wrap the tab around the pole to determine the required size (Figure 2). The tab should fit snugly but allow the bamboo to be removed. Trim the tabs to size, leaving a ¹/₂" seam allowance at each end.

7 Fold the tabs in half, matching the raw edges with the seam inside. Turn the curtain inside out. On the right side of the curtain at the lower edge, place one tab at each corner and evenly space the remaining tabs. Match the raw edges. Place the lining over the tabs. Stitch the edges together, using a ¹/₂" seam allowance and leaving an opening in the seam between two of the tabs. Press the seam open.

8 Turn the curtain right side out. Position the seams on edge and press flat. Turn the seam allowances at the opening to the inside. Press flat. Hand-stitch the opening closed. Insert the bamboo pole.

9 At each top corner, catch the edge of the curtain in a clip ring. Evenly space the remaining clips between the corners. Hang the rings on the knobs. Lift the bottom edge of the curtain to determine drapery tieback placement. Install the tieback.

HARDWARE MADE EASY

clip rings are trendy, as well as vintage-inspired, and are at home in both contemporary and cottage-style settings. Their straightforward function is easy to see. A small and somewhat decorative clip hangs below a metal ring. The clip catches the curtain fabric, eliminating the need to sew on rings or place drapery hooks. The ring glides over poles or hangs on knobs or hooks. For the flat panels in this project, the rings can hang over or behind the knob, depending on the size of the knob compared to the diameter of the ring.

o-rings, made of metal or plastic, provide a less expensive option for hanging window treatments like these flat panels. Because there is no metal clip dangling from the ring, add an extra 1" to the curtain length before you cut the fabric. Sew the O-rings to the top edge of the curtain. Hang each ring over a knob.

knobs or drawer pulls let you show your personality in window dressings. Visit a hardware store to see the options. Many specialty home shops also sell an eclectic range of knobs. To mount most knobs directly into the window molding use a double-ended dowel screw. Ask for these in the "fasteners" aisle at a hardware store. Take the knob along to help in finding the right size screw.

dowel screw

tiebacks do just as the name states: they hold back curtains. Generally, use a tieback to drape a curtain across a window. Look for decorative tiebacks in wood or metal alongside curtain rods in the window-treatment section of department stores and home decorating shops. When installing tiebacks, remember that they will need to bear weight from the fabric. If the drapery fabric is heavy and the curtains are full, install the tieback in a wall stud or use wall anchors to secure the screws.

lined flat panels how to

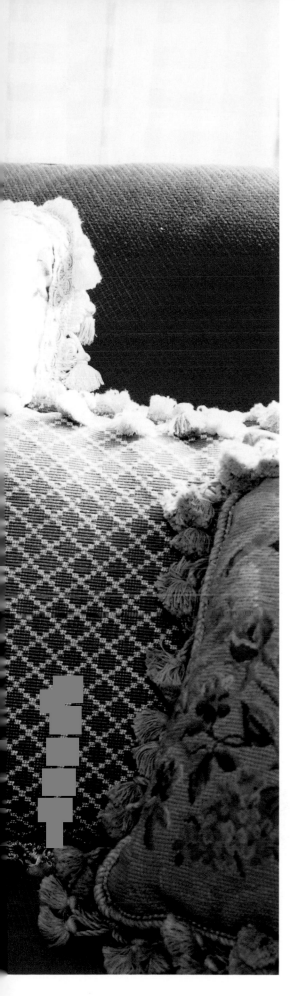

Fringe, welting, and other trims add personality and panache to basic pillows. Trims are usually sewn into the seam, but certain types may be applied to the surface for a rich effect.

basic pillow

Pillows offer one of the easiest ways to accent the color scheme in a room. To play up a theme, use leftover fabric from draperies or upholstery to make two or three pillows; then choose two or more coordinating fabrics, such as checks, solids, and smaller or larger scaled prints, to make additional cushions. To avoid a too-perfectly matched effect, toss in one or two antique pillows that repeat the color theme.

Selecting a palette of coordinating fabrics is the first step. Next, add interest to your pillow collection with trims. Some trims, such as welting, cording with a lip, or moss fringe, are sewn into the seam. Other braids and fringes are applied to the surface of the pillow along the edge (for more information, see pages 50 and 51).

To unify a variety of fabrics, use the same color trim on all of the pillows. The red check pillow at left is trimmed in short brush fringe sewn into the seam. Tassel fringe applied to the front finishes the floral pillow. The green pillow is edged with a pairing of welting and tassel fringe in the seam.

basic pillow

1 Cut two 19" squares from fabric for the front and back panels. Also cut enough $1^1/_2$"-wide bias strips to equal $2^1/_4$ yards. Stitch the bias strips together at the short ends to make one continuous length.

2 To make welting, fold the bias strip, wrong sides together, around the filler cord, matching the long raw edges. Using the zipper foot and a long stitch length, baste close to the cord, encasing the cord in the fabric (Figure 1).

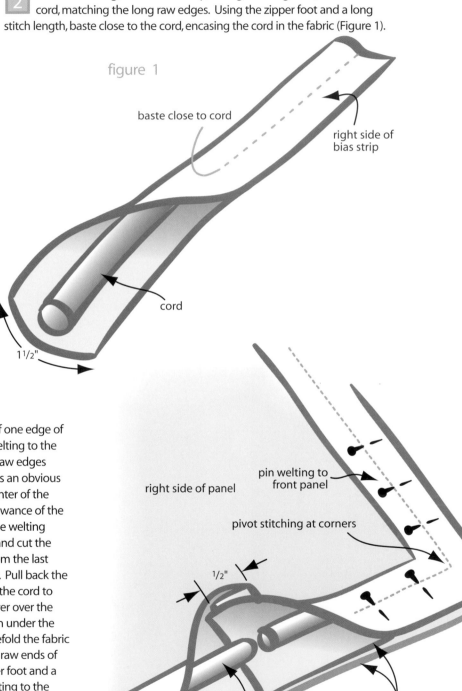

figure 1

baste close to cord

right side of
bias strip

cord

$1^1/_2$"

3 Beginning at the center of one edge of the front panel, pin the welting to the right side of the panel, aligning raw edges (Figure 2). If the fabric design has an obvious top and bottom, begin at the center of the bottom edge. Clip the seam allowance of the welting at the corners. Where the welting ends meet, overlap the ends 1" and cut the welting. Remove the stitches from the last $1^1/_2$" on each end of the welting. Pull back the fabric cover and cut the ends of the cord to meet. Refold one end of the cover over the cord. On the remaining end, turn under the raw edge of the cover $^1/_2$" and refold the fabric around the cord, concealing the raw ends of the fabric cover. Using the zipper foot and a long stitch length, baste the welting to the front panel, pivoting the stitching at the corners.

right side of panel

pin welting to
front panel

pivot stitching at corners

$^1/_2$"

raw edges aligned

cord

figure 2

4 With right sides together and raw edges aligned, pin the front panel to the back panel (Figure 3). Using the zipper foot and a normal stitch length, stitch the back to the front along the basting line, pivoting the stitching at the corners. Leave a long opening in one side for turning. If the fabric has a one-way design, leave the opening in the bottom edge of the pillow. Clip the corners. Grade the seam allowances, except at the opening. Press the seam.

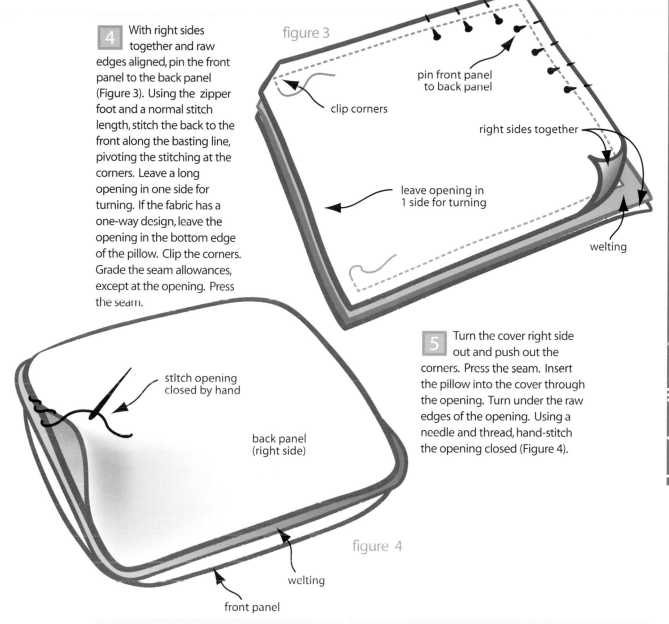

figure 3

pin front panel to back panel

clip corners

right sides together

leave opening in 1 side for turning

welting

stitch opening closed by hand

back panel (right side)

welting

front panel

figure 4

5 Turn the cover right side out and push out the corners. Press the seam. Insert the pillow into the cover through the opening. Turn under the raw edges of the opening. Using a needle and thread, hand-stitch the opening closed (Figure 4).

PICKING THE PERFECT PILLOW FORM

■ Pillow forms provide the easiest way to create an evenly stuffed cushion. Purchase these prestuffed cushions at fabric centers, discount stores, and home decorating fabric stores. The forms come in a range of standard sizes, the most common being 14", 16", 18", and 24" squares. Specialty shapes, such as neckroll and boudoir pillow forms, are also available.

■ The forms generally have a white or off-white cotton cover and are filled with one of a variety of materials. Down-filled cushions are extremely soft and sumptuous, but down does not hold its form well with heavy use. Feather/down-filled forms mimic the softness of down-only forms, but provide more stability and hold their shape better. The material in the feather/down pillow is usually 95 percent feather and 5 percent down. The feather content supports the pillow shape under day-to-day use, and the down provides the slouchy softness.

■ Fiber-filled pillow forms create firm, springy pillows. These are usually the least expensive forms available. The polyester filling is distributed evenly inside the cotton cover for a smooth shape with no lumps or bumps. Choose fiber-filled pillows for use in children's rooms or any location where you need a pillow that can take heavy use. To make a rectangular or round pillow or a square in a size other than the standard ones, stitch a cover from muslin and stuff it with polyester fiberfill.

PASSEMENTERIE

■ Fringe, braid, cording, and welting are all types of *passementerie*, a French term for fancy trims that add texture and color to pillows, draperies, and upholstery. Whether you choose a tassel fringe over a ball fringe is a matter of personal taste, but the material from which the trim is made does affect its character. Ball fringe in brightly colored cotton has a playful look, for example, while the same type of fringe in richly hued rayon is formal and elegant.

■ Trims designed for application to the surface of a pillow have a decorative braid or band that holds the fringe or trim elements together. Other types of trim, intended to be stitched into the seam in the same manner as welting, have a plain braid or lip. The lip is inserted into the seam and stitched in place as you assemble the pillow. Ball fringe, cording with a lip, many styles of tassel fringe, and brush or moss fringe fit this category.

TECHNIQUES MADE EASY

surface application of trims
Monofilament thread is the key to stitching trims to pillow fronts.

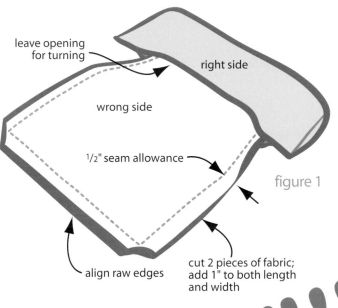

leave opening for turning

right side

wrong side

¹/₂" seam allowance

figure 1

align raw edges

cut 2 pieces of fabric; add 1" to both length and width

3 Using monofilament thread on the top of the machine and conventional thread in the bobbin, topstitch the trim to the front panel only. If you are unable to stitch into the corners, lockstitch to secure the thread ends. Remove the pillow cover from the machine and hand-stitch the trim in the corners with monofilament thread.

4 Complete the pillow as directed on page 49.

1 For the front and back panels, add 1" to the measured length and width of the pillow form. Cut two pieces from fabric to this size for the front and back panels. With right sides together and raw edges aligned, stitch the panels together with a ¹/₂" seam allowance, leaving an opening in one side for turning. Pivot the stitching at the corners. Clip the corners and press the seams, then turn right side out and press (Figure 1).

2 On the front panel, pin the trim along the edge, gently easing it around the corners. Overlap the trim ends 1". Apply liquid ravel preventer to the cut ends. Let dry. Turn under each end ¹/₂" (Figure 2).

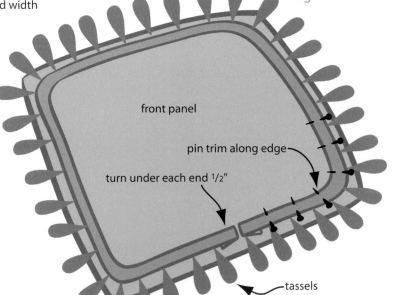

figure 2

front panel

pin trim along edge

turn under each end ¹/₂"

tassels

in-seam application of trims

Stitching trim into the seam is the most common way of accenting a pillow's edges.

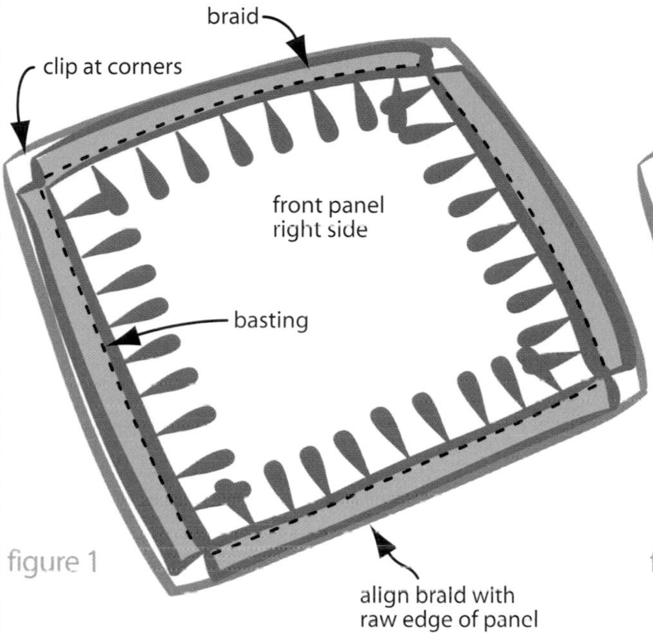

braid

clip at corners

front panel
right side

basting

figure 1

align braid with
raw edge of panel

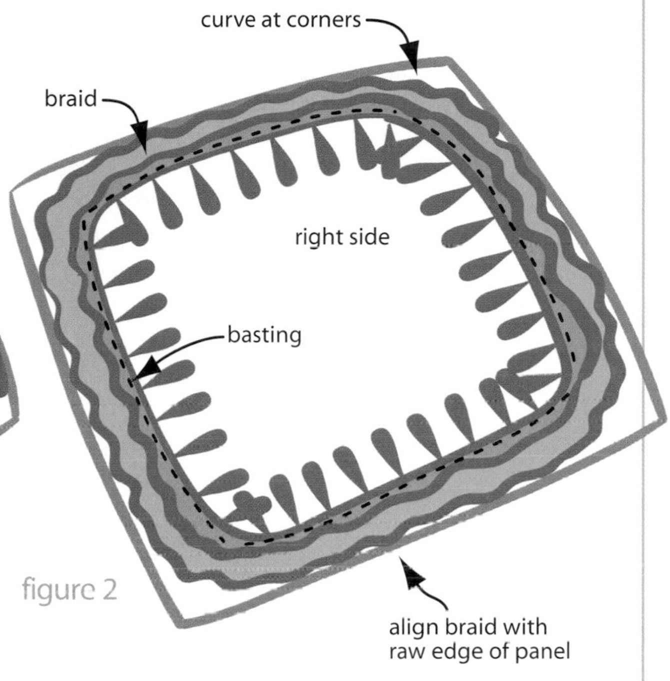

curve at corners

braid

right side

basting

figure 2

align braid with
raw edge of panel

1️⃣ Measure the width of the braid or lip on the trim. Double this measurement and add it to the width and length of the pillow form. Cut two pieces from fabric this size for the front and back panels.

2️⃣ On the right side of the front panel, align the braid or lip with the raw edges of the panel so the fringe or cording extends toward the center of the panel. Pin in place, clipping the braid or lip at the corners. Apply liquid ravel preventer to the cut edges. Let dry. (Although not shown in the drawing, the trim ends should overlap ¹/₂".) Using a long stitch length, baste the trim to the panel along the inside edge of the braid or lip (Figure 1).

3️⃣ For thick or heavy trims, such as brush fringe, gently round each corner. (Although not shown in the drawing, the trim ends should overlap ¹/₂".) Turn the final few

sections of fringe into the seam allowance. Baste the fringe to the panel along the inside edge of the bound edge of the fringe (Figure 2).

4️⃣ With right sides together and raw edges aligned, follow the basting line to stitch the front panel to the back panel, catching the lip in the stitches. Stitch the panels together on three sides; stitch all corners, pivoting at square corners and working in a continuous curve on rounded corners. Leave an opening in one side for turning. Grade the seams and clip the corners. Press the seams and turn to the right side. Press the seams.

5️⃣ Insert the pillow form as directed on page 49. Turn the raw edges of the opening to the inside and hand-stitch the opening closed.

adding buttons
Add a button to the center front panel of a pillow for a stylish look.

After making the front pillow panel, cover one or two buttons with fabric. Thread a tufting needle with a double length of buttonhole thread and knot the ends. Insert the needle through one button shank and secure the thread to the shank. Push the needle through the pillow center from front to back. Insert the needle through the shank of the second button and push the needle through the pillow from back to front. Pull the thread tightly to sink the buttons into the pillow. Pass the needle through the pillow several times to secure both buttons, then knot the thread behind one button and cut the thread.

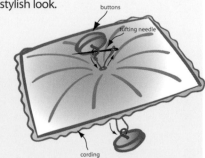

buttons

tufting needle

cording

kitchens & dining rooms

While living rooms are often the conversational centers of homes, kitchens are most often where people tend to gather. And if your dining room is comfortable, guests will linger long after the meal, enjoying the conversation.

See the following pages for instructions: page 84 (window treatment); page 88 (box cushion); page 94 (chair cushion); and pages 96 and 100 (pillows).

Breezy cafe curtains are ideal for kitchens

or breakfast nooks, where you want to admit light but preserve privacy. Paired with chair covers in boldly patterned fabric, cafe curtains perk up an entire room.

cheery kitchen

Depending on your fabric choice, cafe curtains can have a retro look or evoke country cottage charm. For either look—and the best results—choose crisp fabrics. If the hand of the fabric is somewhere between dress shirting and lightweight canvas, it's a perfect choice.

To further dress up your kitchen, make chair covers. Although creating them may seem like a daunting task, those shown are designed to be easy: The back and seat pieces are sewn separately, so fitting the covers is quick. Matching the fabric and pattern unifies the cover so the separate pieces are not immediately evident.

cafe curtains

materials
54"-wide decorator fabric*
Spring tension or cafe rod
  and mounting hardware*
Cafe curtain rings

tools
Electric drill and drill bits
Screwdriver

sewing tools
Sewing machine
Iron and ironing board
Tape measure
Pins
Needle and thread
Scissors

skill level: beginner
time required: 1/2 day
*Purchase materials after
taking measurements.

1 Measure the window height and width inside the frame (Figure 1). The valance and curtains hang on rings that slide along the tension rod, which is purchased to fit the window's inside width. The finished valance width is twice the measured window width. You may need to seam together fabric widths to create adequate fullness in the valance. Each curtain panel equals the measured window width. In general, you need a length of fabric two times the measured height of the window for both the valance and curtains.

figure 1

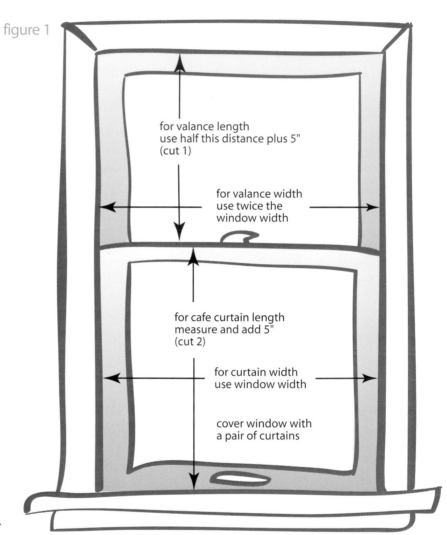

for valance length
use half this distance plus 5"
(cut 1)

for valance width
use twice the
window width

for cafe curtain length
measure and add 5"
(cut 2)

for curtain width
use window width

cover window with
a pair of curtains

2 Trim the selvages from the fabric. For the curtains, measure from the top of the window sash to the windowsill and add 5". Measure the window width; cut two curtain panels this size. If you choose a floral or similarly patterned fabric, be sure each piece begins at the same point in the fabric repeat.

3 For the valance, measure from the top of the sash to the upper inside edge of the window frame. Divide this measurement in half and add 5". Measure the window width and double it. Cut one piece to this size. For wide windows, you may need to seam together fabric widths to achieve the desired fullness. Be sure each piece of a floral or patterned fabric begins at the same point in the repeat.

4 On the side edges of each curtain and the valance, turn under 1½" twice. Press. Working on the wrong side, edgestitch the hem in place. Using a wide stitch width and a short stitch length, zigzag the top raw edge of the curtain. Fold the top under 2" to make a facing. With a needle and thread, tack the facing to each side hem by hand.

5 Clip the cafe rings to the top edge of the curtains and valance. Place one ring at each corner, spacing the remaining rings evenly along the edge, not more than 6" apart. Insert the tension rod through the rings. Fit the valance (or cafe) rod into the top of the window. Fit the curtain tension rod into the window at the sash. Mark the hems. Remove the curtains and valance from the window.

6 Turn under the hem along the marked line and press. Open the fold and turn under the raw edge to meet the crease. Press. Refold the hem and hemstitch the folded edge. Slip the curtains and valance on the rods and return them to the window.

rubber tip →

tension rods are narrow, two-part, spring-
loaded poles with rubber tips at each end. These rods are held in position
inside the window frame by an outward force at both ends. You'll find rods of
different lengths to fit a variety of windows. They can be adjusted a few inches in length by
twisting the two parts of the rod. In the kitchen on page 54, tension rods support the cafe curtains
and valance, and the white rods blend with the crisp white molding. In general, tension rods are
not intended to be a feature, but rather to serve a utilitarian function in window treatments. A
similar but smaller, flatter rod, a sash rod, is often used in pairs to hold shirred curtains in place close
to the window glass.

mount →

cable wire rods are the new generation of
tension rods. These high-tech curtain rods consist of two anchors or mounts
with a tight cable wire stretched between the two. Anchors are available in several styles
to mount inside or outside the frame.

finial →

cafe rods are the classic choice for
charming half-curtains and valances. Traditional
polished-brass cafe rods feature knoblike finials. The rod rests on
matching brackets that attach to the window frame or to the wall just
outside the frame. Because cafe rods intersect the window frame, this hardware
is considered a feature of the overall window treatment.

bracket

rod

cafe rings clip onto fabric with a pinching
action. Because they are easily removed on
laundry day, this may be why cafe curtains are
so widespread in bistros around the world.
When using rings with a rod other than that
for which they were manufactured, such as
with tension rods, be sure to check the fit.
Cafe rings should slide freely along the rod.

cafe curtains how to

seat aprons

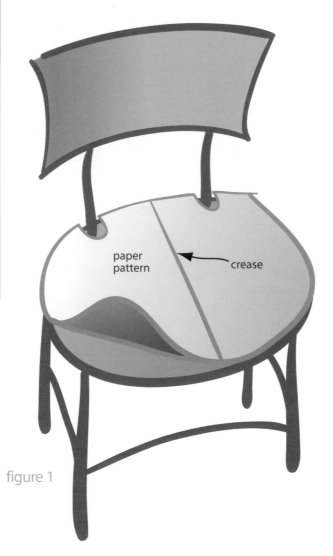

figure 1

1. Place the paper on the chair and mark the seat edges. For aprons, extend the pattern slightly over the edge of the seat. Mark the cutouts for the chair stiles on the pattern. If the seat does not have stiles that interrupt the chair seat, mark the chair legs on the back edge of the pattern. Cut out along the marked lines to make a pattern and adjust as necessary to conform to the seat shape. Crease the pattern from center front to center back (Figure 1).

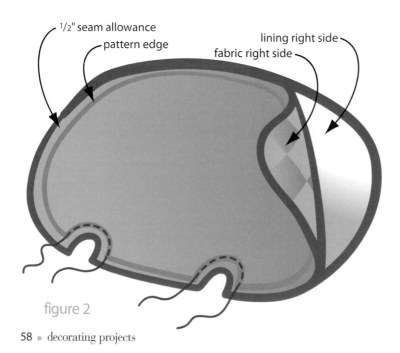

figure 2

2. Place the seat pattern on the right side of the fabric, positioning the pattern to make the best use of the fabric design. Align the crease with the straight grain of fabric. Add a ½" seam allowance to each pattern edge. Cut one seat panel from fabric and one from lining. With right sides together and raw edges aligned, stitch the seat panel to the lining along each cutout, using a ½" seam allowance (Figure 2). (These cutouts allow for the stiles. If the seat back doesn't rise from the seat, there are no cutouts.) Stitch the edge between pairs of marks for each leg. Clip the seam allowance around the curves and grade the seam allowances. Press the seam. Turn right side out, press the seam on edge, and press the seat cover flat.

3 For welting, measure the raw edges of the seat panel and add 6". Cut enough 1½"-wide bias strips from fabric to equal this measurement. Stitch the strips together at the narrow ends to make a continuous length. To make welting, fold the bias strip around the filler cord, matching the long raw edges. Handle bias strips carefully to avoid stretching and distorting the fabric. Using the zipper foot and a long stitch length, baste close to the cord, encasing it in the fabric.

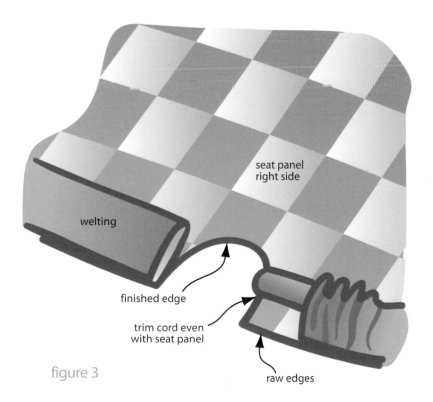

seat panel
right side

welting

finished edge

trim cord even
with seat panel

raw edges

figure 3

4 Pin the welting to the right side of the seat panel, treating the fabric and lining as one. At each end, where the back edge of the seat panel is finished, cut the welting 1" longer than the raw edge of the seat panel. Slide the casing back to expose the cord and trim the cord even with the seat panel (Figure 3). Pull the casing over the cord end and fold it over the seam allowance. Clip the welting seam allowance at the corners and around the curves. Using the zipper foot and a long stitch length, baste the welting to the seat, pivoting the stitching at the corners.

5 Cut four 5×24" strips for ties from fabric. If desired, adjust the width to accent a portion of the fabric. Fold each strip in half lengthwise with right sides together and raw edges aligned. Cut one narrow end of each strip at an angle. Using a ½" seam allowance, stitch the angle and the long edge. Clip the seam allowance at the corner. Press the seam and turn each tie right side out. Place the seam on edge, then press flat. Pin the ties to the seat panel on both sides of the cutouts or the stitched section at the legs, overlapping the welting. Baste the ties in place along the previous basting line (Figure 4).

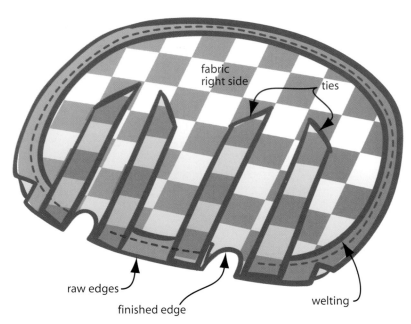

figure 4

6 Measure the seat height from the floor; divide this measurement by 3 and add 1" to the result for the length of the skirt fabric (the length includes ½" seam allowances at the top and bottom edges). Cut one strip to this length from fabric, selvage to selvage, adjusting as necessary to obtain the best pleat arrangement for the apron skirt. Place the seat panel on the chair and pin the skirt fabric to the seat to plan the skirt arrangement. Make a sketch, noting the pleat width, number of pleats, and the width of the folded fabric between pleats. Consider how the pleat arrangement will fit the back edge of the seat panel between the ties.

7 For the apron, the check pattern makes it easy to plan and measure the pleats. Around the front of the chair, there are six pleats three checks wide alternating with seven folds four checks wide behind the pleats (Figure 5). At both ends of the front portion of the apron skirt there are partial pleats one check wide. The back edge of the apron skirt has two pleats two-and-one-half checks wide with one fold four checks wide between the pleats.

8 Cut enough strips from fabric and lining to the measurement of the apron skirt for the required length, plus ½" seam allowances to stitch together the fabric pieces. Allow extra fabric to match patterns. Prepare the strips for the skirt front and back separately.

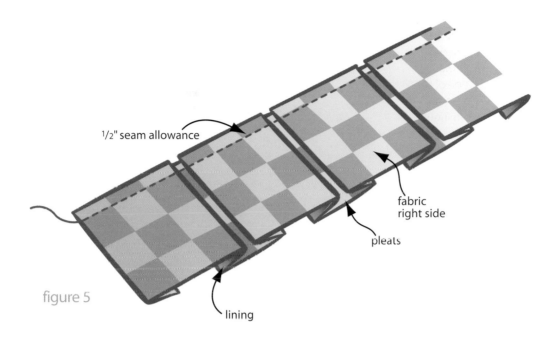

½" seam allowance

fabric right side

pleats

figure 5

lining

9 With right sides together and raw edges aligned, stitch the skirt front to the lining along the bottom and sides, using a ½" seam allowance. Clip the corners, press the seam, and grade the seam allowances. Turn the fabric right side out, placing the seams on edge. Press flat. Stitch the skirt back to the lining in the same manner. Treating the two layers of fabric as one, make pleats in the fabric strip along the raw edge as planned. Press the pleats. Using a long stitch length and a ½" seam allowance, baste through all layers at the raw edge (Figure 5).

10 With right sides together and raw edges aligned, use a ½" seam allowance to stitch the skirt front and back to the seat unit, catching the welting and ties in the stitching. Grade the seam allowances and press the seams. Turn right side out. Place the apron on the chair seat, tying it to the chair back or legs.

DRESSING UP OR DOWN

■ Pillowcase-style slipcovers can change the personality of a room. Sew snappy covers for a casual brunch or everyday use. Consider a cropped version, or trim the lower edge of the skirt with a flirty ruffle instead of a pleat.

■ When the invitation reads "dinner at eight" or the dining room is decidedly formal, dress the chairs in filmy metallic fabrics or soft sheers for glamorous style. Make a fitted apron, rather than pleating or gathering it, and shape the lower edge of the cover into a point and trim it with one exquisite tassel.

chair back covers

1 For the front and back panel, measuring loosely to allow for an easy fit, measure from the seat over the chair back and down to the seat and add 1". Measure the width of the chair back from side to side and add 1". If the chair back has a deep curve, measure from the back side of the chair to include the extra width resulting from the curve (Figure 1).

2 Cut one panel each to these measurements from fabric and lining, positioning the pattern to make the best use of the fabric design or to align with the design on the seat aprons. With right sides together and raw edges aligned, stitch the fabric to the lining at each narrow end, using a $\frac{1}{2}$" seam allowance. Press the seams open. Turn right side out, place the seams on edge, and press the seams flat.

3 Measure the raw edges of the fabric/lining panel and add 6" for the welting length. Cut enough $1\frac{1}{2}$" bias strips from fabric to equal this length. Stitch the strips together at the narrow ends to make a continuous length. Fold the strip around the filler cord, matching the raw edges of the fabric. Handle the bias strips carefully to avoid stretching the fabric. Using the zipper foot and a long stitch length, baste close to the cord to encase the cord in the fabric.

figure 1

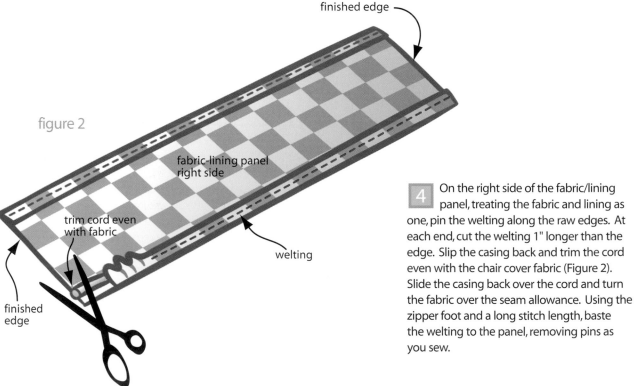

finished edge

figure 2

fabric-lining panel
right side

trim cord even
with fabric

welting

finished
edge

4 On the right side of the fabric/lining panel, treating the fabric and lining as one, pin the welting along the raw edges. At each end, cut the welting 1" longer than the edge. Slip the casing back and trim the cord even with the chair cover fabric (Figure 2). Slide the casing back over the cord and turn the fabric over the seam allowance. Using the zipper foot and a long stitch length, baste the welting to the panel, removing pins as you sew.

5 For the gusset, measuring loosely to allow for an easy fit, measure the chair back depth from front to back at the widest point and add 1". Measure the chair back height and add 1" (Figure 3). Cut two pieces each from fabric and lining to these measurements. As a design detail, the gussets on this cover are cut on the bias to emphasize the red checks. If you cut the fabric on the bias, also cut the lining on the bias. Handle both carefully to minimize stretching and distortion. With right sides together and raw edges aligned, stitch one gusset and one lining together along one narrow end only, using a ½" seam allowance. Press the seams, turn the fabric right side out, place the seam on edge, and press it flat. Repeat for the remaining gusset and lining.

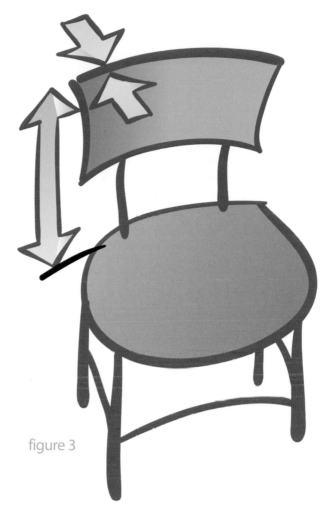

figure 3

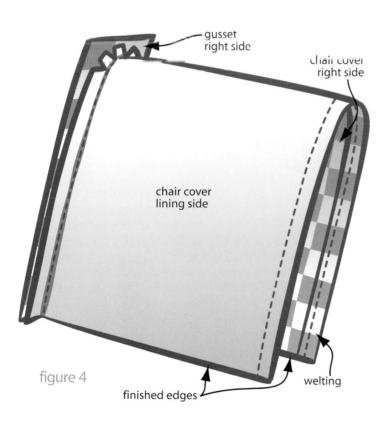

gusset right side

chair cover right side

chair cover lining side

figure 4

finished edges

welting

6 With right sides together and raw edges aligned, pin one gusset between the front and back of the chair cover, starting at the finished ends of the pieces. Make sure the front and back are an equal length. Clip the seam allowance of the cover and welting to form a curve at the top of the cover (Figure 4). The seam allowances of the cover and gusset are different widths and will not align in the curve. Using a ½" seam allowance and a long stitch length, baste the gusset to the cover. At the curve, use the chair cover to determine the ½" seam allowance. Attach the remaining gusset in the same manner.

7 Turn the cover right side out and fit it on the chair back. Check each seam from the right side; the fabrics should fit together smoothly without puckers. The curves on each side of the chair back should drape evenly; if necessary, remove stitches and restitch to make smooth seams. Set the stitch length at a normal setting and sew each gusset to the cover along the basting lines. Grade the seam allowances and press the seams. Turn the cover to the right side.

You may not need to cover
patio doors for privacy, but a simple valance across

the top, paired with a bracket-mounted shelf, softens and dresses up a functional architectural feature. The shelf is easy to make using wooden brackets and lumber from a home improvement center. Cable wire, the high-tech version of a tension rod, holds the valance.

patio door valance

This shelf offers an ideal opportunity to add color and personality to a room by showcasing a favorite collection. In a breakfast area, for example, choose bowls, plates, pitchers, and vases in a variety of shapes and sizes. Select colors that coordinate with the fabrics used in the room and let one color dominate, such as tints and shades of blue, as shown at left. Add a few items in accent colors such as yellow and lime green to enliven the blues by contrast. If you prefer a clean, monochromatic look, choose vessels in a single color, for instance as an arrangement of ironstone vases and pitchers, or a collection of identical objects, such as transferware plates.

Although this valance-and-shelf treatment is designed for sliding glass doors, you also can adapt it to an ordinary window in any room. In a nursery or child's room, use the shelf to display stuffed toys or dolls. If your child is an athlete, showcase trophies from sporting events. See page 67 for tips on mounting the shelf securely on a wall.

Use the valance fabric for an unexpected accent: the border on an ordinary sisal rug. Cut the fabric to the desired width, plus 1" all around; press all raw edges under $1/2$". Using a hot glue gun and glue sticks, adhere the border strips to the rug, overlapping or mitering the strips at each corner.

patio door valance

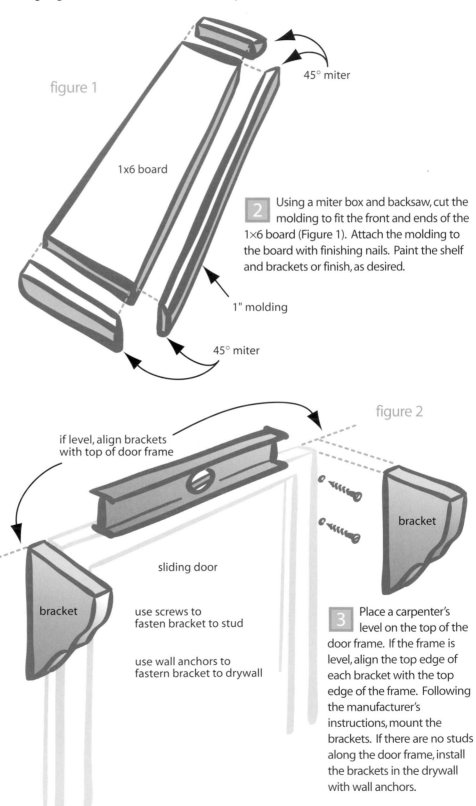

materials

2 (6") decorative wooden
  shelf brackets
1×6 sanded pine, oak,
  or maple board*
1"-wide edge molding*
1" finishing nails or wire brads
Paint
1¼" wood screws and
  wall anchors
Curtain wire
O-rings with clips*
54"-wide decorator fabric*
54"-wide lining fabric*

tools

Electric saw and blades or
  handsaw
Miter box and backsaw
Electric drill and drill bits
Screwdrivers
Hammer
Carpenter's level
Carpenter's square
Paintbrush

sewing tools

Sewing machine
Iron and ironing board
Vanishing fabric marker
Pins
Needle and thread
Scissors
Tape measure
Liquid ravel preventer

skill level: intermediate
time required: 1 day
*Purchase materials after
taking measurements.

1 Measure the door or window width outside the frame. Determine the desired length of the shelf to obtain the cut length of the board. Most lumber is sold in cut lengths of 4', 6', 8', and 10', but a home improvement center or lumberyard may cut the board for you. Purchase edge molding to fit one long edge and two short ends of the board plus 12" for miter cuts.

figure 1

45° miter

1x6 board

2 Using a miter box and backsaw, cut the molding to fit the front and ends of the 1×6 board (Figure 1). Attach the molding to the board with finishing nails. Paint the shelf and brackets or finish, as desired.

1" molding

45° miter

if level, align brackets
with top of door frame

figure 2

bracket

sliding door

bracket

use screws to
fasten bracket to stud

use wall anchors to
fastern bracket to drywall

3 Place a carpenter's level on the top of the door frame. If the frame is level, align the top edge of each bracket with the top edge of the frame. Following the manufacturer's instructions, mount the brackets. If there are no studs along the door frame, install the brackets in the drywall with wall anchors.

wall anchors

The walls in most homes are constructed on a 2×4 frame with drywall covering the structure. In the frame, boards that run from floor to ceiling are called studs. These studs, by industry standards, are placed in the frame every 16½" on center. To hang a picture, mirror, or shelf on a wall, drive the nail or screw into a stud to ensure that the mounting will be secure.

Small devices known as stud finders, available at hardware stores and home improvement centers, can help you locate the position of studs in your wall.

Sometimes, however, the stud isn't where you need support. To mount brackets securely, you need to use wall anchors. Install the anchor in the drywall and insert the screws in the anchor. The wall anchor distributes the weight over a larger area in the drywall and holds the screw in place. Screws used alone in drywall, sooner or later, will pull out of the drywall, bringing your shelf crashing down.

Anchors are rated for the total weight they will support. Determine what you will display and approximate the combined total weight of the items. Include the weight of the fabric valance. Because the shelf shown on page 64 has two brackets, it needs anchors that will support half the total weight. For a securely mounted shelf, err on the side of larger wall anchors or ones with a higher rating.

Manufacturers develop types of anchors to be used on different types of walls: Some can only be used on drywall, while others can be used to anchor screws in wood paneling or masonry. Read the package instructions to find the anchor ideal for a specific job.

universal expanding anchor

As implied by the name, this wall anchor is suitable for use in a wide variety of materials, including masonry. The universal expanding anchor accepts a range of screw sizes. To mount a valance shelf, use a minimum of No. 8 screws and heavier weight screws for larger or heavier boards.

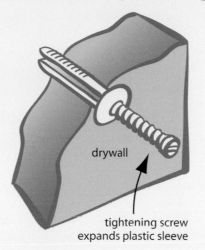

drywall

tightening screw expands plastic sleeve

self-drilling wall anchor

This is only for use in drywall. The only tool you need is a screwdriver, and no pilot hole is required. The anchor accepts specific-size screws; the anchors and screws are packaged together.

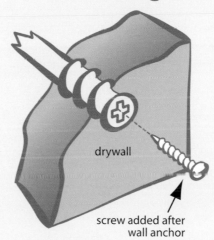

drywall

screw added after wall anchor

expansion bolt

The screw and sleeve in an expansion bolt are a single unit. The sleeve spreads out behind the wall to anchor the screw. Use in drywall only. Blunt-tip expansion bolts require a pilot hole; refer to the packaging for the appropriate-size drill bit to use. A self-tapping expansion bolt has a nail-like point and does not require a pilot hole. Simply drive the screw and sleeve through the wall with a hammer, then tighten the screw to expand the sleeve behind the wall.

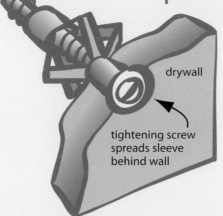

drywall

tightening screw spreads sleeve behind wall

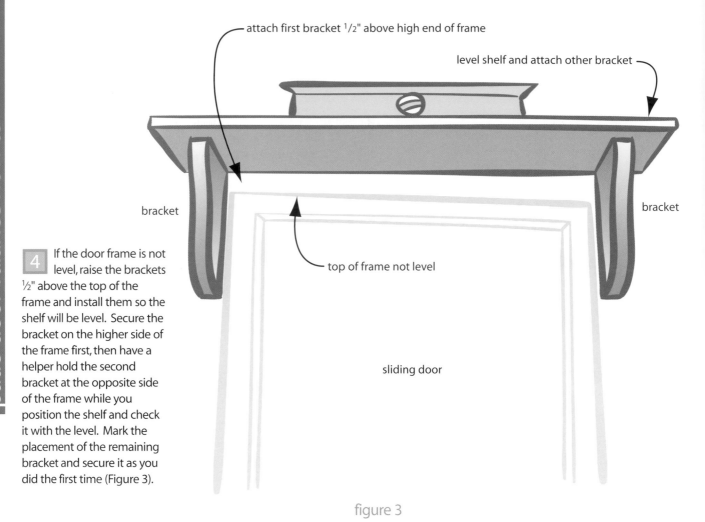

attach first bracket ¹/₂" above high end of frame

level shelf and attach other bracket

bracket

bracket

top of frame not level

sliding door

figure 3

4 If the door frame is not level, raise the brackets ¹/₂" above the top of the frame and install them so the shelf will be level. Secure the bracket on the higher side of the frame first, then have a helper hold the second bracket at the opposite side of the frame while you position the shelf and check it with the level. Mark the placement of the remaining bracket and secure it as you did the first time (Figure 3).

5 Center the shelf on the brackets. Using an electric drill, make pilot holes through the shelf into the top edge of each bracket. Secure the shelf to the brackets with screws.

6 Follow the manufacturer's instructions to install the cable wire. Remove the shelf while you install the wire, if necessary, for easier access to the brackets. If you're using closed O-rings, be sure to thread them onto the wire before installation. The rings used on the valance shown have an opening that allows them to be placed on the wire after it has been installed.

7 For the valance, double the width of the measurement between the shelf brackets and add 1". Determine the desired drop of the valance and add 1" (the drop should be no less than 8"). Cut a piece of fabric to this size. If necessary, piece fabric to obtain the required size, matching motifs or patterns in the fabric repeat. To join sections, with right sides together and raw edges aligned, pin the edge, matching the fabric design across the seam. Using a ¹/₂" seam allowance, stitch the edges together. Press the seam open, then turn and press on the right side, as well. Cut and piece fabric for the lining in the same manner.

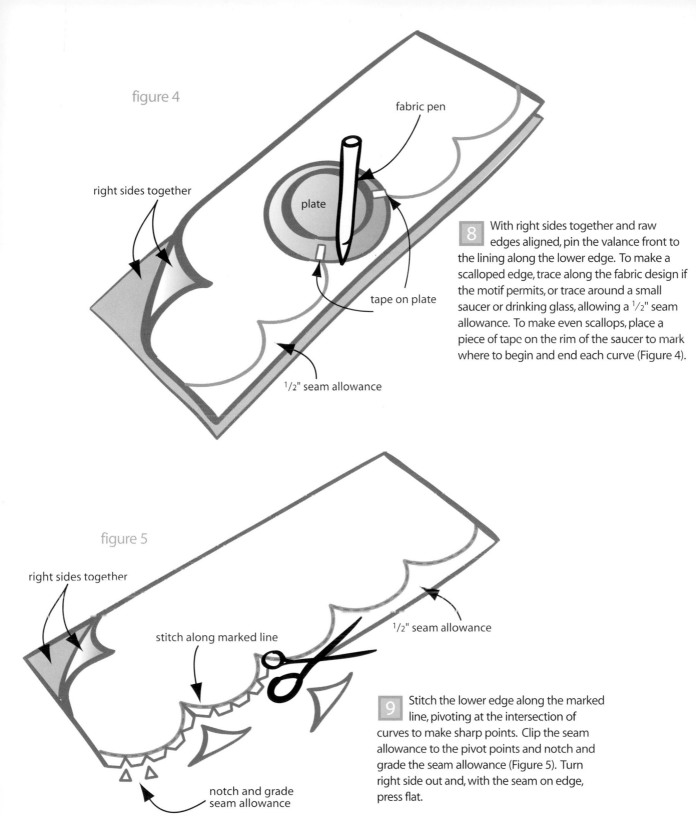

figure 4

right sides together

fabric pen

plate

tape on plate

½" seam allowance

8 With right sides together and raw edges aligned, pin the valance front to the lining along the lower edge. To make a scalloped edge, trace along the fabric design if the motif permits, or trace around a small saucer or drinking glass, allowing a ½" seam allowance. To make even scallops, place a piece of tape on the rim of the saucer to mark where to begin and end each curve (Figure 4).

figure 5

right sides together

stitch along marked line

½" seam allowance

notch and grade seam allowance

9 Stitch the lower edge along the marked line, pivoting at the intersection of curves to make sharp points. Clip the seam allowance to the pivot points and notch and grade the seam allowance (Figure 5). Turn right side out and, with the seam on edge, press flat.

10 Turn the valance again, so right sides are facing. With raw edges aligned, pin the remaining edges. Leave a long opening in the top edge for turning. Using a ½" seam allowance, stitch the edges, pivoting at the corners. Clip the corners and grade the seam allowances. Press the seams open. Turn the valance right side out through the opening in the top edge. Place the seams on the edges and press flat. Turn the raw edges at the opening to the inside and press. Using a needle and thread, hand-stitch the opening closed. Clip the O-rings to the top edge of the valance, spacing them evenly.

A shaped valance is a graceful

topper for gathered panels. To emphasize the window treatment as a single unit, use the same fabric for both the curtains and valance. If you prefer, choose solid fabric for the valance and a coordinating print for the curtains. Repeat the solid color elsewhere in the room, such as in pillows or on a chair.

rod pockets

ADD PERSONALITY TO CURTAINS

Curtains that hang by rod pockets have three parts: the stand, pocket, and drop. The stand is the ruffle that extends above the curtain rod, while the pocket is the casing into which you insert the rod for hanging, and the drop is the length of the finished curtain measured from the bottom of the curtain rod.

Stands can be either decorative or functional. A stand of about 2 inches makes a crisp stand-up ruffle, like the one on the valance at left. Narrow ¼-inch stands keep a curtain from twisting on the rod, giving a neat finished look to the treatment.

The type of curtain rod you choose determines the size—and therefore the decorative appearance—of the pocket. Here, the lined valance hangs on a wide Continental rod, making it a feature of the shirring. Unlined panels hang on a simple adjustable rod mounted behind the Continental rod. The pockets in the curtain panels are functional rather than decorative, so they are just large enough to receive the rod.

■ Combine several bands of sheer and opaque fabrics in curtain panels. Sheer fabrics feature opaque images that range from abstract swirls to floral motifs and flaunt such saucy colors as persimmon, sunflower, lime, and hot pink. Mix in a linen print or luxurious dupioni silk for rich texture.

■ For flair and fun, stitch rows of bead fringe or charms along the seams—or scatter silk flower heads randomly over the curtain panels for a romantic effect.

■ As you plan the curtain, remember to add seam allowances to each band at every seam. If you forget to include the seam allowances, the finished curtain panel may be too short. Also, place the heaviest fabric at the bottom to weight the panel and for a natural appearance.

materials

54"-wide decorator fabric*
54"-wide lining fabric*
2½" Continental rod*
Adjustable rod*

tools

Electric drill and drill bits
Screwdriver

sewing tools

Sewing machine
Iron and ironing board
Tape measure
Pins
Needle and thread
Scissors
Vanishing fabric marker

skill level: intermediate
time required: 1 day
*Purchase materials after taking measurements.

1 Measure the width of the window and purchase curtain rods for the required measurement. Install the adjustable rod just outside the window frame. Position the Continental rod just outside the adjustable rod, allowing ½" to 1" between the mounting hardware for each rod.

2 Measure the window length from the top of the adjustable rod. You will need a fabric piece for each panel that is as wide as the window measurement and as long as the measured length plus 12". For the valance, you will need a fabric piece and lining piece that are each twice as wide as the window measurement and 20" in length. Compare the 20" length of the side edges of the valance to your window; the valance should be one-fourth to one-third the window height. Adjust the valance length to fit your window. It may be necessary to stitch together fabric widths to achieve the desired fullness.

3 Trim the selvages from the fabric and lining. Cut two curtain panels the measured length from rod to floor plus 8". Be sure each piece begins at the same point in the fabric repeat. Use flat-fell seams to stitch together fabric lengths, if necessary, to achieve the required width in the curtain panel. On the long side edges of each curtain panel, turn under 1½" twice and press (Figure 1). Working on the wrong side, edgestitch the hem in place. Turn under the top edge ¼". Press. Turn the edge under 1½". Press. Working from the wrong side, edgestitch close to the first fold, forming the bottom of the rod pocket. Topstitch ¼" from the second fold, forming the top of the rod pocket.

4 Insert the adjustable rod into each pocket. Hang the curtain panels. Turn under the hem so that the edge meets the floor. Pin. Remove the curtain from the rod. Press the fold. Turn under the raw edge to meet the crease. Press. Hemstitch the folded edge to finish the curtain. Hang the curtains.

5 The valance consists of a 2" stand, 3" rod pocket, and 14" drop at the outer edges. Cut pieces twice as wide as the window width and 20" long from the fabric and lining.

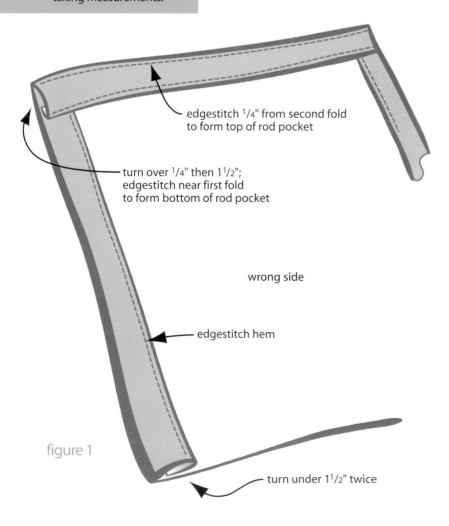

edgestitch ¼" from second fold to form top of rod pocket

turn over ¼" then 1½"; edgestitch near first fold to form bottom of rod pocket

wrong side

edgestitch hem

figure 1

turn under 1½" twice

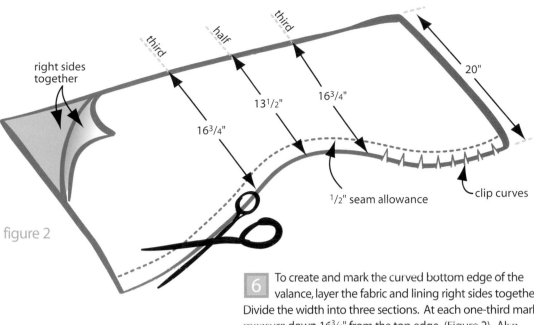

right sides together

third

half

third

16³/₄"

13¹/₂"

16³/₄"

20"

¹/₂" seam allowance

clip curves

figure 2

6 To create and mark the curved bottom edge of the valance, layer the fabric and lining right sides together. Divide the width into three sections. At each one-third mark, measure down 16³/₄" from the top edge (Figure 2). Also measure from the center top edge down 13¹/₂" to mark the highest point of the curve. Draw a gentle curve from each bottom corner, through the 16³/₄" marks to the 13¹/₂" mark. Pin the fabric layers together along this line. Stitch along the marked line. Trim the seam allowance to ¹/₂". Clip into the seam allowance along the curve. Using a ¹/₂" seam allowance, stitch the top edges of the valance together. Press each seam open.

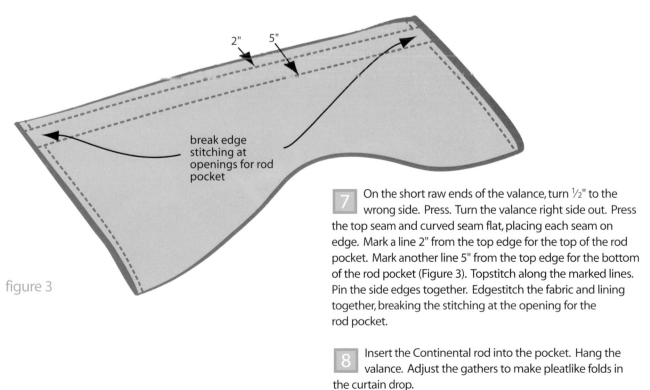

2"

5"

break edge stitching at openings for rod pocket

figure 3

7 On the short raw ends of the valance, turn ¹/₂" to the wrong side. Press. Turn the valance right side out. Press the top seam and curved seam flat, placing each seam on edge. Mark a line 2" from the top edge for the top of the rod pocket. Mark another line 5" from the top edge for the bottom of the rod pocket (Figure 3). Topstitch along the marked lines. Pin the side edges together. Edgestitch the fabric and lining together, breaking the stitching at the opening for the rod pocket.

8 Insert the Continental rod into the pocket. Hang the valance. Adjust the gathers to make pleatlike folds in the curtain drop.

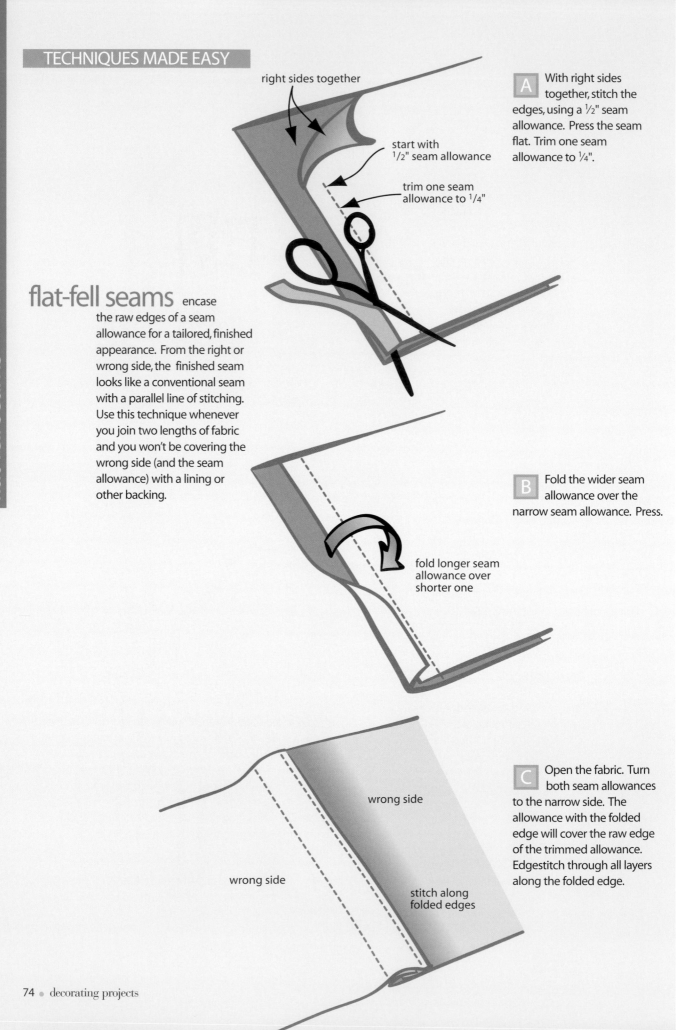

flat-fell seams

right sides together

start with
$1/2$" seam allowance

trim one seam
allowance to $1/4$"

flat-fell seams encase the raw edges of a seam allowance for a tailored, finished appearance. From the right or wrong side, the finished seam looks like a conventional seam with a parallel line of stitching. Use this technique whenever you join two lengths of fabric and you won't be covering the wrong side (and the seam allowance) with a lining or other backing.

A With right sides together, stitch the edges, using a $1/2$" seam allowance. Press the seam flat. Trim one seam allowance to $1/4$".

fold longer seam allowance over shorter one

B Fold the wider seam allowance over the narrow seam allowance. Press.

wrong side

wrong side

stitch along folded edges

C Open the fabric. Turn both seam allowances to the narrow side. The allowance with the folded edge will cover the raw edge of the trimmed allowance. Edgestitch through all layers along the folded edge.

adjustable rods

are the workhorses of window decoration: They are easy to find and install—and are easy on the pocketbook. Adjustable rods, however, are not pleasing to look at; they are best covered with the shirred fabric of a rod pocket or by a valance that completely conceals the rod. Pay attention to the depth of the rod, and the distance the rod projects from the wall, particularly if you hang a valance over curtain panels as shown on page 70.

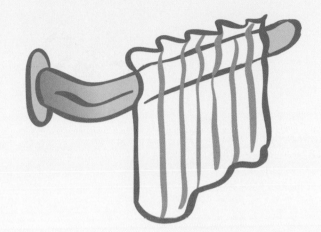

continental rods

create a richly shirred effect for valances and draperies constructed with rod pockets. Like adjustable rods, they are easy to find and install. Rods are available in 2½" and 4" widths. Make sure the width of the rod is in proportion to the size of the window you decorate and the ceiling height of the room (a taller ceiling or larger window calls for the wider rod).

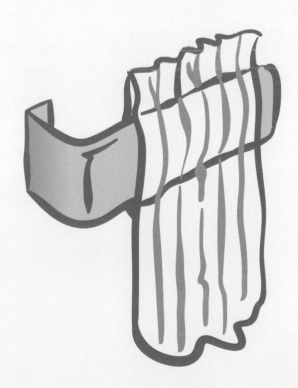

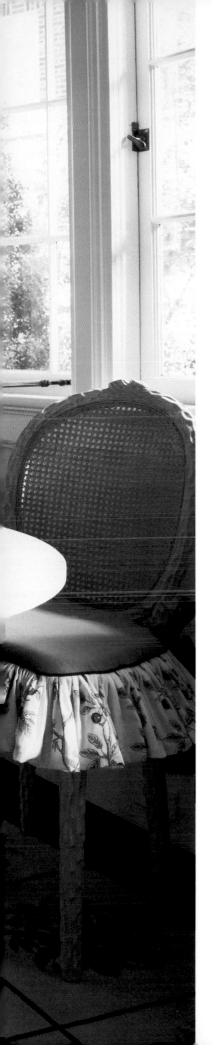

Dressing chairs in ruffles brings romance to a garden-style breakfast room. Solid-color cushions with contrasting piping add a tailored touch to the full, flippy chair skirts and give the eye a place to rest in a room full of pattern.

long ruffle
chair cushion

Bring sunshine into a breakfast nook even on a cloudy day. Sheer window fabrics let in light and expand the view, while bright colors and lighthearted patterns lend a fresh, vibrant attitude to the room. From the meandering wallpaper pattern and the vine design on the table apron to the round chair backs, curves hold the look together.

Gathering the longer chair skirt to maximum fullness creates another curve and makes this seat style the perfect accent for petite chairs. Spots of solid colors—the uncovered tabletop and chair backs and the solid cushions—prevent patterns and curves from overpowering the small space, for a clean, uncluttered look.

Consider fabric weight in determining skirt fullness. The chairs shown are skirted in a sheer fabric that allows the ruffle fullness to be two-and-one-half to three times the edge of the chair cushion from tie to tie. If you choose polished cotton, the skirt may only be one-and-one-half to two times the circumference. Heavy-weight fabrics are not recommended for a ruffled skirt.

See page 38 for drapery instructions.

materials

Paper
3"-thick high-density
    upholstery foam*
1/8"- to 1/4"-loft bonded
    polyester batting*
54"-wide decorator fabric*
54"-wide contrasting fabric
    for welting and skirt ties*
54"-wide complementary
    fabric*
6/32" filler cord*

tools

Electric knife
Permanent marker
Skewer

sewing tools

Sewing machine
Zipper foot
Pins
Needle and thread
Scissors
Tape measure
Vanishing fabric marker
Iron and ironing board

skill level: beginner
time required: 3/4 day
*Purchase materials after
taking measurements.

long ruffle chair cushion

1 Place the paper on the chair seat and mark the edges of the seat on it. Cut the paper to make a pattern; refit the pattern on the chair, adjusting as necessary to conform to the seat shape. Crease the pattern in half from center front to center back.

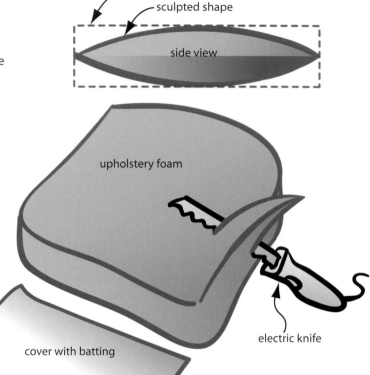

figure 1
— original shape
— sculpted shape
side view
upholstery foam
electric knife
cover with batting

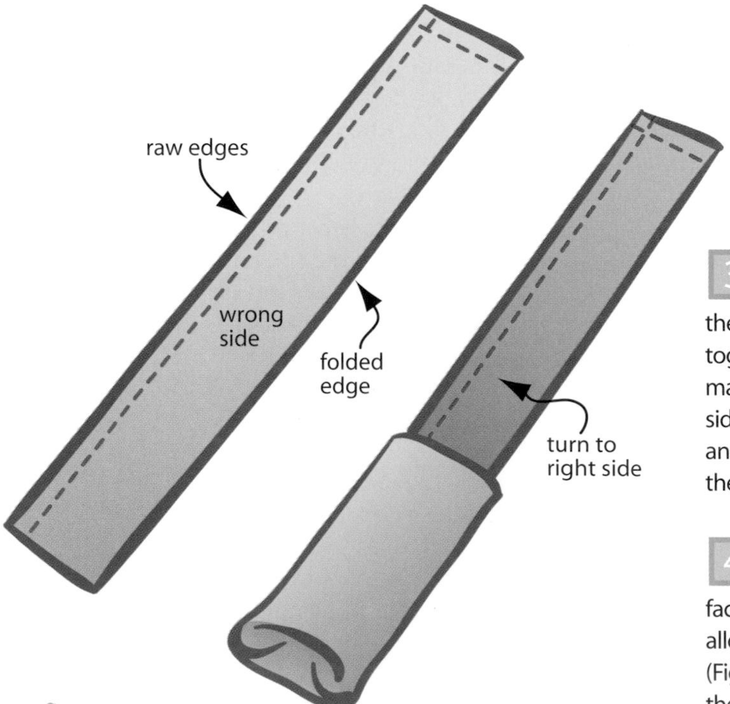

2 Use the pattern to cut one cushion from the foam. Place the cushion on the chair. Determine how much shaping the cushion needs to suit the chair style and mark cutting lines with the permanent marker. With an electric knife held at an angle, slice off the rigid edges of the foam and round the corners (Figure 1). Cut off small amounts at a time to obtain the desired shape. Wrap the cushion in batting. Pin and trim the batting to cover the foam smoothly. Loosely hand-sew the batting edges together.

raw edges

wrong side

folded edge

turn to right side

figure 2

3 Cut enough 1 1/2"-wide bias strips from contrasting fabric to equal the pattern circumference plus 6". Handling the strips carefully to avoid stretching them, stitch the strips together at the narrow ends to make a continuous length. To make the welting, fold the bias strip around the cord with right sides out, matching the long raw edges. Using the zipper foot and a long stitch length, baste close to the cord to encase it in the fabric.

4 Cut four 5×24" straight-grain strips from contrasting fabric for ties. Fold each strip in half, with right sides facing and long raw edges matching. Using a 1/2" seam allowance, stitch the long edges and one narrow end together (Figure 2). Clip the corners and press the seams open. Turn to the right side and press flat, placing the seams on edge. Set the ties aside.

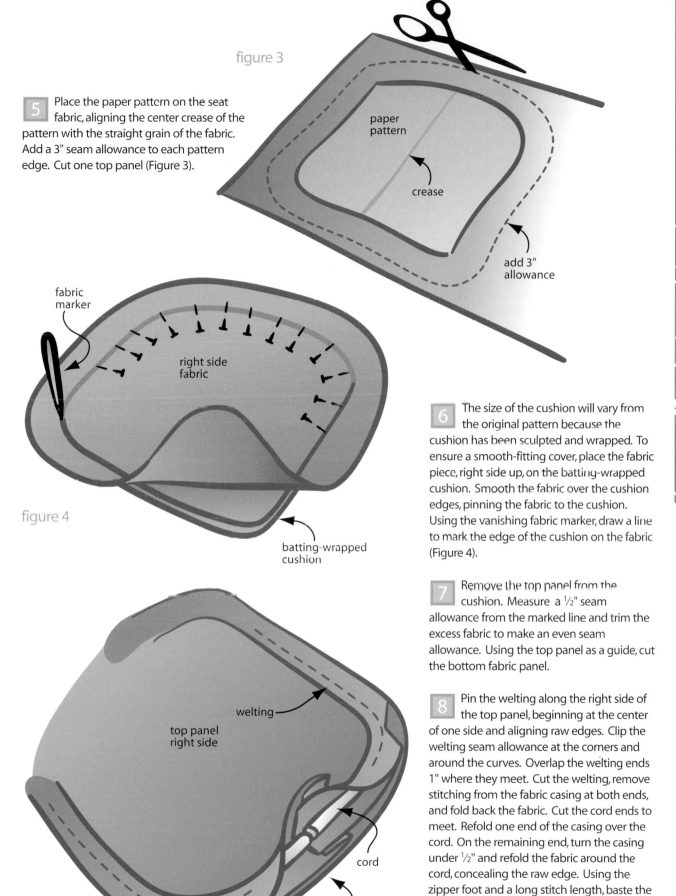

figure 3

5 Place the paper pattern on the seat fabric, aligning the center crease of the pattern with the straight grain of the fabric. Add a 3" seam allowance to each pattern edge. Cut one top panel (Figure 3).

paper pattern

crease

add 3" allowance

fabric marker

right side fabric

figure 4

batting-wrapped cushion

6 The size of the cushion will vary from the original pattern because the cushion has been sculpted and wrapped. To ensure a smooth-fitting cover, place the fabric piece, right side up, on the batting-wrapped cushion. Smooth the fabric over the cushion edges, pinning the fabric to the cushion. Using the vanishing fabric marker, draw a line to mark the edge of the cushion on the fabric (Figure 4).

7 Remove the top panel from the cushion. Measure a ½" seam allowance from the marked line and trim the excess fabric to make an even seam allowance. Using the top panel as a guide, cut the bottom fabric panel.

8 Pin the welting along the right side of the top panel, beginning at the center of one side and aligning raw edges. Clip the welting seam allowance at the corners and around the curves. Overlap the welting ends 1" where they meet. Cut the welting, remove stitching from the fabric casing at both ends, and fold back the fabric. Cut the cord ends to meet. Refold one end of the casing over the cord. On the remaining end, turn the casing under ½" and refold the fabric around the cord, concealing the raw edge. Using the zipper foot and a long stitch length, baste the welting to the top panel (Figure 5).

welting

top panel right side

cord

raw edges

figure 5

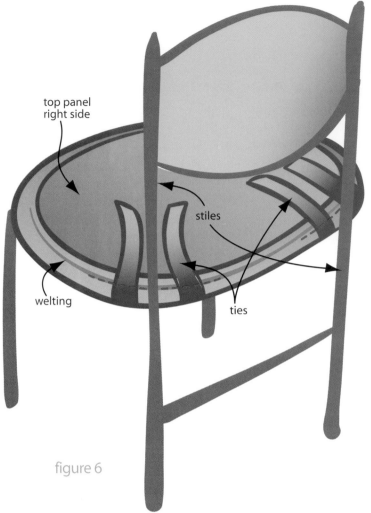

top panel
right side

stiles

welting

ties

figure 6

9 Place the cushion and top panel on the chair; smooth the fabric over the cushion. Determine the placement of the ties, positioning a tie on each side of each stile (Figure 6). You may fold tucks in the ends of each tie to create smaller points of attachment to the panel. Pin the ties to the top panel over the welting, aligning raw edges. Baste in place along the previous basting.

10 To determine the skirt length, measure the height of the chair seat from the floor and divide by 3. To that measurement, add $2\frac{1}{2}$" for the seam allowance and hem. Cut enough straight-grain strips from complementary fabric to create the desired fullness, including $\frac{1}{2}$" seam allowances at both ends of each strip. Also cut enough strips to create the desired fullness for the back skirt, which attaches to the cushion cover between the ties. When working with fabrics that have prominent patterns, match the pattern across the narrow ends. Stitch the narrow ends of the strips together.

11 On the bottom edge of the skirt and back skirt, turn under the raw edge 1" twice for a hem. Edgestitch close to the folded edge or hemstitch. On each narrow end, turn under 1" twice. Edgestitch close to the folded edge or hemstitch. Evenly divide the skirt into four sections, marking each section with pins. Divide the top panel from tie to tie into corresponding quarters. For a finished look, avoid placing the quarter marks at the corners of the top panel (Figure 7).

12 Set the sewing machine for a long stitch length and loosen the upper thread tension. Test the adjustments by sewing gathering stitches on a scrap of skirt fabric. Working from the right side of the skirt, sew four lines of gathering stitches $\frac{3}{4}$", $\frac{1}{2}$", $\frac{3}{8}$", and $\frac{1}{4}$" from the long raw edge. Sew a separate set of stitches for each quarter section of the skirt, stopping and starting at each quarter mark. Repeat on the back skirt.

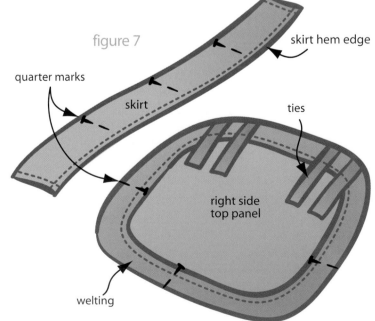

figure 7

skirt hem edge

quarter marks

skirt

ties

right side
top panel

welting

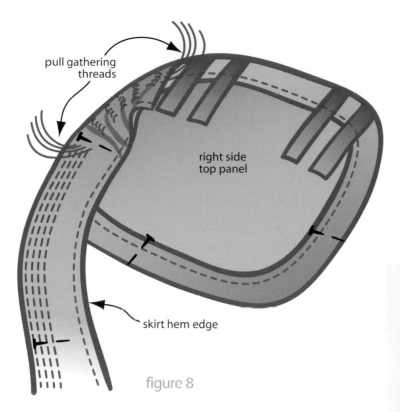

pull gathering
threads

right side
top panel

skirt hem edge

figure 8

13 With right sides together and raw edges aligned, match the quarter marks of the skirt and top panel. Match each skirt end with each pair of ties. One section at a time, gently pull the bobbin thread of all four gathering threads. Adjust the gathers to fit the top panel (Figure 8). Using the zipper foot and a long stitch length, baste the skirt to the top panel along the previous basting stitches. (One line of gathering stitches will be visible in the skirt and will be pulled out later.) Baste each remaining quarter in the same manner. Gather and baste the back skirt section between the ties. Press the seams flat toward the top panel.

14 With right sides together and raw edges aligned, stitch the bottom panel to the top, catching the seam allowances of the skirt, welting, and ties in the stitching and leaving an opening between the ties for turning. Press the seam. Turn the cover right side out. Insert the cushion into the cover through the opening. Turn the raw edges of the opening to the inside and handstitch the opening closed. To remove the visible gathering stitches in the skirt, pull the bobbin thread, then the top thread. Place the cushion on the chair and tie each pair of ties around the stiles.

FOAM BASICS

To find the materials you need, consult your telephone directory for upholstery supply or wholesale dealers that sell to consumers. Fabric stores that carry fashion and home decorating fabric have limited space available for upholstery basics and generally carry only one or two densities of foam in limited widths and thicknesses.

For long-wearing cushions, begin with high-density upholstery foam. The higher the density, the less crushing, and the greater the cushioning, occurs when you sit on the cushion. At the fabric center, sit on a block of foam to see how it holds up under pressure. Over time the foam will compress, so it is important to buy good materials.

When you have to cut or trim a slab of foam to fit your specific need, follow these tips:
■ Mark the cutting line with a permanent felt-tip marker.
■ Use an old electric knife to cut the foam (once you use the knife for this purpose, it won't be suitable for kitchen use).
■ Be aware of the electric cord location when using the knife to avoid cutting into it.
■ For sculpted edges or corners, slice the foam at an angle as if cutting a beveled edge.
■ Trim small amounts at a time. It is impossible to reattach the foam if you have cut off too much.
■ Wrap the finished foam in polyester batting to disguise small inequalities in the cut of the foam and to provide a smooth surface for the fabric cover. Note this will not necessarily provide additional softness.

Turn a bay window into a cozy seating nook

with a collection of trimmed pillows, a ruched box cushion, and unfussy Roman shades and coordinating valance. Further carry the theme through the room with ruched chair cushions embellished with tassels that echo those used on the valance. For a dressy look, choose polished or crisp cottons or medium-weight linens.

tailored collection

With clean, uncluttered lines, Roman shades control light and privacy. As you raise the shade, it pleats, forming flat accordionlike folds that stack at the top of the window. In the window-seat niche shown at left, the shade and valance are mounted outside the frame to cover the whole window wall. This makes the area look larger by downplaying the small strip of wall on each side of the window. Plan for the valance to be one-fourth to one-third the height of the window, but no shorter than 8 inches.

Use the same fabric as the valance for stylish box and chair cushions. The shirred edging on both is a ruche gusset—a gathered fabric that forms the box sides. Such an edging adds rich texture to the cushions; it is a good technique for dressing up seat pads for dining chairs or for adding a luxurious touch to a cushion for a dressing-table bench. A zippered back gusset makes the covers easy to remove when you need to have them dry-cleaned.

Complete this cozy setting with pillows. These examples show the versatility of a few basic techniques. Dress them up with buttons, piping, and different types of fringe for unexpected decorative touches.

54"-wide decorator fabric*
Loop shade tape*
Shade-and-blind cord*
Flat braid or ribbon*
1×2 pine board*
$^1/_2$"-diameter dowel*
Cleat with fasteners
8 (2") No. 8 wood screws
8 (1") No. 8 wood screws
5 screw eyes
4 (3") inside corner braces

tools

Handsaw
Electric drill and drill bits
Screwdriver
Staple gun and $^1/_2$" staples

sewing tools

Iron and ironing board
Pressing cloth
Scissors
Tape measure

skill level: intermediate
time required: 1 day
*Purchase materials after
taking measurements.

basic roman shade

1 Measure the height and width of the window inside the window recess or frame. For the shade, you will need a piece of fabric at least 2" wider and 16" longer than this measurement. You will also need loop tape 4 times the measured height plus 24", cord 8 times the measured height plus 4 times the measured width, and braid $2^1/_2$ times the measured window height. The 1×2 board serves as the mounting board at the top of the shade. The $^1/_2$" dowel will weight the lower edge of the shade. Both the board and dowel must be as long as the measured width.

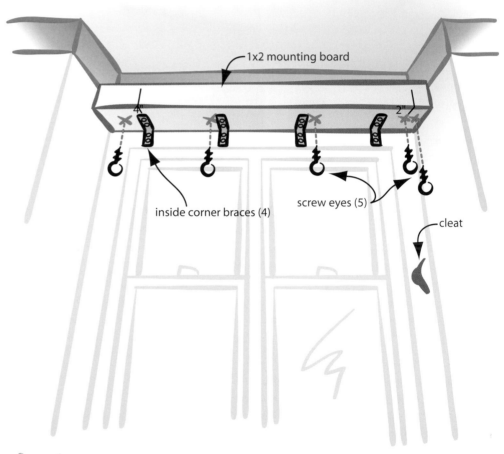

1x2 mounting board

inside corner braces (4)

screw eyes (5)

cleat

figure 1

2 Cut the 1×2 board and dowel to the width measurement. Referring to Figure 1, fit the board into the top of the window frame (or to the wall below the crown molding) with the narrow edge facing into the room. Install one inside corner brace to the wall above the window at each end of the board, using 2" wood screws. Space the remaining two braces evenly between the first two. Place the mounting board on the braces and drill pilot holes through the braces into the board; remove the board. Mark points 2" from each end on the underside of the board for screw eyes. Measure even segments and mark two more points along the board for screw eyes. Drill shallow pilot holes. Drill one additional pilot hole for a fifth screw eye 1" from the right end of the board. Set the board aside.

3 Place the cleat on the right side of the frame or wall about midway between top and bottom. The cleat holds the cords taut. (If you have small children in your home, place the cleat closer to the top of the frame to eliminate the risk of possible entanglement.) Drill pilot holes in the frame or wall. Mount the cleat.

4 Determine the cut size of the fabric for the shade. Add 3" to the width measurement and 13" to the length measurement; cut the fabric. For the shade shown on page 82, fabric lengths were seamed together for the required width. For the most attractive panel, arrange lengths with a wide center panel flanked by two narrow side panels. If applicable, match pattern repeats across seams. In most cases, use a full fabric width for the center panel because fabric patterns are easier to match with full widths. Remember to include $1/2$" seam allowances for your calculations on each section. Topstitch braid or ribbon to the shade front to cover the seams, if desired (Figure 2).

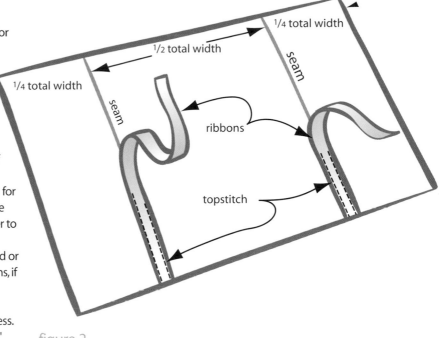

basic roman shade how to

1/4 total width

1/2 total width

1/4 total width

seam

seam

ribbons

topstitch

figure 2

5 Turn under each side edge $1^{1}/2$". Press. On the bottom edge, turn under $1/4$". Press. Turn under $3/4$" for the dowel casing. Press. Working from the wrong side, edgestitch the casing on the bottom edge close to the top folded edge.

6 On the wrong side, measure and mark a line 2" from each side edge. Also measure and mark two more lines to match the spacing of additional pilot holes for screw eyes in the mounting board. Center the loop shade tape along each line, having the first loops at the casing (Figure 3). Also cover the raw edge of the side edges with tape. Sew each line of stitches from the casing to the top.

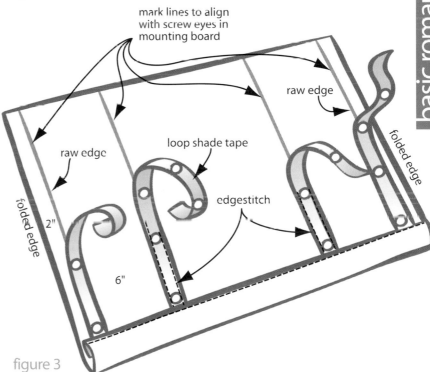

mark lines to align with screw eyes in mounting board

raw edge

loop shade tape

raw edge

folded edge

folded edge

edgestitch

2"

6"

figure 3

7 Center the top edge of the shade, wrong side down, on the narrow front edge of the board with the pilot holes. Staple the fabric to the board (see Figure 6, page 14). Wrap the fabric smoothly around the board, overlapping the first edge. Punch a small hole through the fabric into each pilot hole. Install the board in the window frame with wood screws. (If using the shade with a flat valance, assemble and staple the valance over the shade before installing the mounting board in the window frame.) Install screw eyes. Insert the dowel into the casing.

8 For the two left-hand cords, cut lengths 2 times the measured window length plus the measured width. Tie one end of each cord to the lowest loops on the left side of the blind. For the two right-hand cords, halve the remaining length. Tie one end of each cord to the lowest loops on the right side of the shade. Thread the cords through the column of loops and through the screw eye at the top. Thread all cords through the extreme right screw eye. Pull the cords to take up the slack. Trim the cord ends even. To raise the shade, gently pull the cords, causing the fabric to pleat. Secure the cords to the cleat with a figure-eight motion.

9 To set the pleats, raise the shade to the highest position and secure the cords. Arrange the pleats by hand and leave in place for one week.

materials

1×1 pine board*
54"-wide decorator fabric*
54"-wide lining fabric*
Flat braid*
Frog and tassel
2 (2") No. 8 wood screws
Braces (optional)

tools

Handsaw
Electric drill and drill bits
Screwdriver
Plate or drinking glass

sewing tools

Sewing machine
Thread
Vanishing fabric marker

skill level: intermediate
time required: 1 day
*Purchase materials after
taking measurements.

flat valance

1. Measure the window height and width inside the window recess or frame. The valance should be one-fourth to one-third the measured window height, but no shorter than 8". The finished width is as wide as the measured width. You need a piece of fabric and lining 1" wider and 6" longer than the measurements.

2. If you use the flat valance with the Roman shade as shown on page 82, you will attach the valance to the same mounting board as the shade, layering it over the shade. If you use the flat valance alone, it mounts inside a window recess on a mounting board or inside the window frame on a tension rod. To prepare a separate mounting board, cut the 1×1 board to the width measurement. Fit the board into the top of the window frame or window recess. Measure 4" from each end of the board and drill pilot holes through the board into the frame. Take the board down.

figure 1

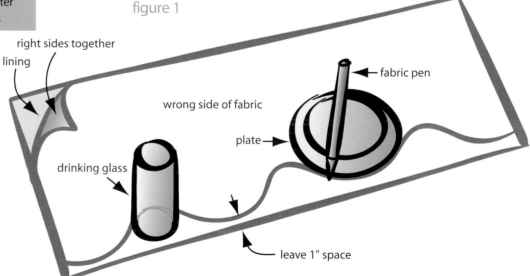

right sides together
lining
fabric pen
wrong side of fabric
plate
drinking glass
leave 1" space

3. Plan the pattern placement on the valance. If necessary, seam together fabric lengths and lining lengths for the required valance width. Plan the shaped edge. Cut one piece each from the fabric and lining the measured window width plus 1" and the finished valance length plus 6". With right sides together, layer the fabric and lining, so you can see the pattern on the wrong side of the fabric. On the lower edge, draw a shaped edge by tracing around a plate or drinking glass, allowing a 1" seam allowance below each curve (Figure 1).

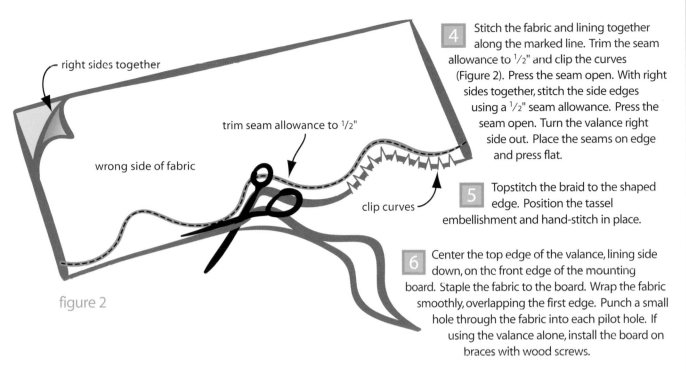

right sides together

wrong side of fabric

trim seam allowance to ¹/₂"

clip curves

figure 2

4 Stitch the fabric and lining together along the marked line. Trim the seam allowance to ¹/₂" and clip the curves (Figure 2). Press the seam open. With right sides together, stitch the side edges using a ¹/₂" seam allowance. Press the seam open. Turn the valance right side out. Place the seams on edge and press flat.

5 Topstitch the braid to the shaped edge. Position the tassel embellishment and hand-stitch in place.

6 Center the top edge of the valance, lining side down, on the front edge of the mounting board. Staple the fabric to the board. Wrap the fabric smoothly, overlapping the first edge. Punch a small hole through the fabric into each pilot hole. If using the valance alone, install the board on braces with wood screws.

TECHNIQUES MADE EASY

planning a shaped edge

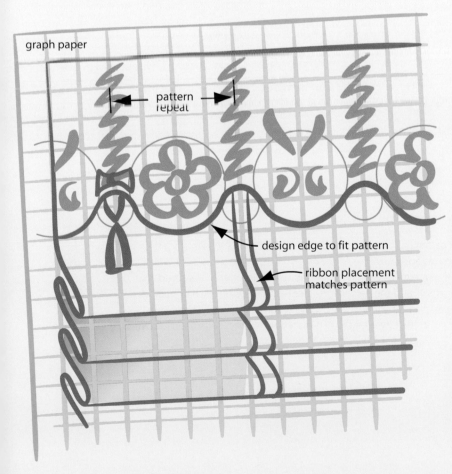

graph paper

pattern repeat

design edge to fit pattern

ribbon placement matches pattern

Although the individual elements of this window treatment are simple, the valance and shade combination requires planning.

1 The striped fabric is centered on the valance so each end has a similar pattern.

2 The scalloped edge of the valance rises at each dark stripe and falls below the dominant flower in every other light stripe. To make these curves, look for plates and glasses with diameters similar to the design.

3 The trim placement further highlights the shaped edge, defining the curve with the braid and accenting the dark stripe with a frog and tassel embellishment.

4 Note that the ribbon-covered seam in the Roman shade is directly below a dark stripe and tassel.

To create a well-planned window treatment, make sketches, loosely penciling in the fabric patterns, to help you see what the overall design will look like. Use ¹/₄" graph paper to keep the drawings in proportion. Buy trims and tassels *after* you finalize a shaped edge.

2"-thick high-density
    upholstery foam*
Polyester batting*
Muslin*
54"-wide decorator fabric*
Zipper*
Medium-weight nonwoven
    interfacing*
Cording with lip*

tools

Electric knife or serrated knife

sewing tools

Sewing machine
Iron and ironing board
Vanishing fabric marker
Pins
Needle and thread
Scissors
Tape measure
Liquid ravel preventer
Zipper foot

skill level: advanced
time required: 9½ hours
*Purchase materials after
taking measurements.

ruche gusset box cushion

1 Measure the window seat from front to back and side to side (Figure 1). For long spans, consider making two cushions for the space instead of one extra-long cushion. When using two cushions, subtract 1" from the side-to-side measurement for ease.

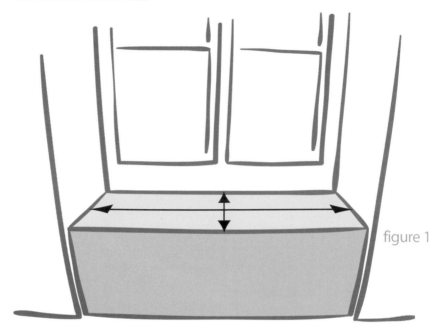

figure 1

2 Cut the foam to the window seat dimensions (less ½" to allow for the batting). Wrap the foam in batting, pinning and trimming the batting to cover it smoothly. Loosely sew the batting edges together by hand.

3 To make a muslin sleeve for the batting-wrapped cushion, measure the girth of the cushion and add 2". Measure the cushion from side to side, including the depth of both ends, and add 2". Cut one piece of muslin to this size. (Muslin is available in extra-wide widths, so you can cut this piece from a single length of fabric. If you must seam fabric to make up the required width, place the seam on a corner of the cushion.)

4 Center the muslin over the cushion and smooth the fabric around it, wrapping tightly. Turn under the raw edges on one long side; align these edges with a corner of the cushion. Using a needle and thread, make tiny hand stitches to secure (Figure 2). Fold each end of the muslin cover as if wrapping a package, minimizing bulk as much as possible. Hand-stitch to secure the folded edges.

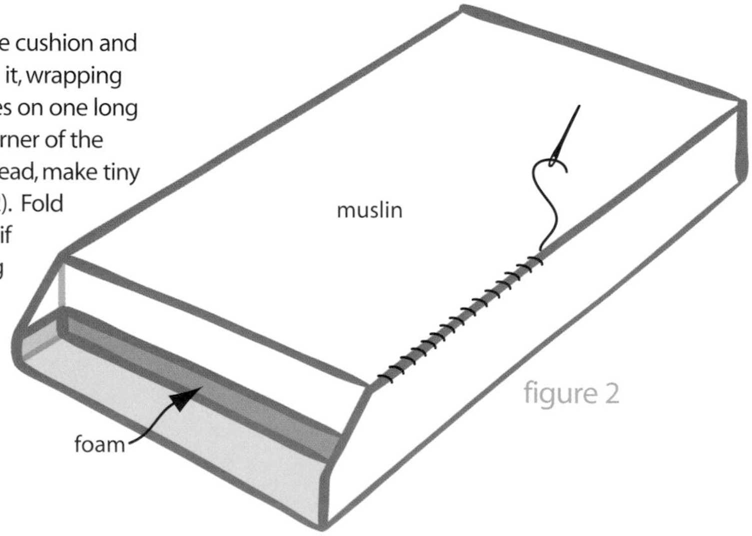

muslin

foam

figure 2

5   Measure the cushion top from side to side and front to back and add 1" to each measurement. Cut two pieces from fabric to this size for the top and bottom panels. If working with stripes or plaids, place them symmetrically on each panel and center any floral motifs or other prominent patterns. To determine the best placement of the fabric design, drape the fabric over the cushion before you cut.

6   Measure the back edge of the cushion and add 9". Cut two 4"-wide strips from fabric to this length, matching the pattern across the long edges for the zippered back gusset. With right sides together, long raw edges aligned, and patterns matching, baste the strips together on one long edge, using a $^3/_4$" seam allowance. Press the seam open. On the wrong side, center the zipper tab side down over the basted seam (Figure 3). Using a needle and thread, hand baste the zipper tapes to the fabric. Turn to the right side. Using the zipper foot, stitch the zipper in place following the manufacturer's instructions for centered zipper installation. Remove all basting stitches. Trim the strip to $3^1/_2$" wide with the zipper at the center.

figure 3

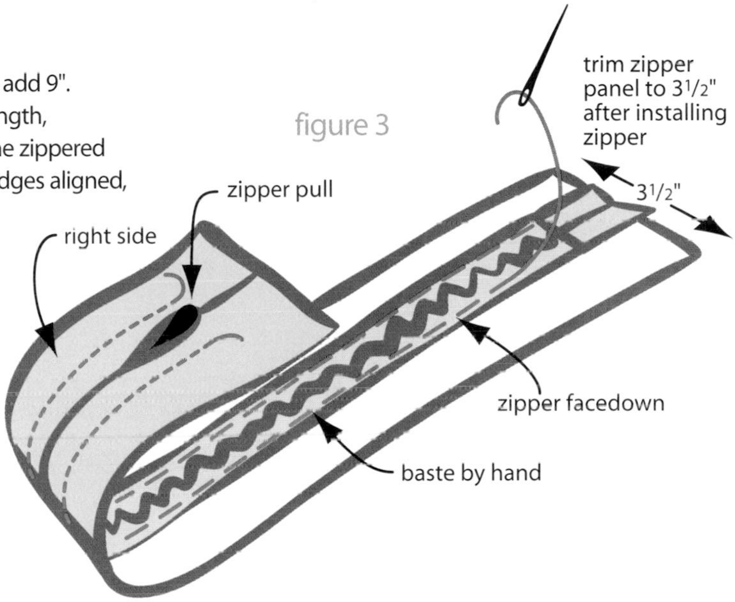

trim zipper panel to $3^1/_2$" after installing zipper

$3^1/_2$"

zipper pull

right side

zipper facedown

baste by hand

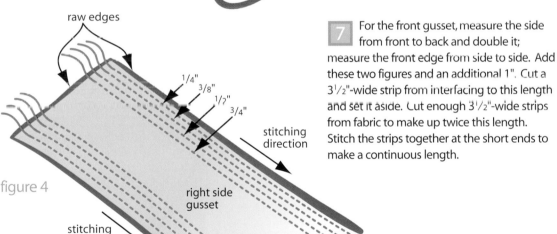

figure 4

raw edges

1/4"
3/8"
1/2"
3/4"

stitching direction

right side gusset

stitching direction

7   For the front gusset, measure the side from front to back and double it; measure the front edge from side to side. Add these two figures and an additional 1". Cut a $3^1/_2$"-wide strip from interfacing to this length and set it aside. Cut enough $3^1/_2$"-wide strips from fabric to make up twice this length. Stitch the strips together at the short ends to make a continuous length.

8   Set the sewing machine for a long stitch length and loosen the upper thread tension. Working from the right side of the long fabric strip for the gusset, sew four lines of gathering stitches on each long side $^3/_4$", $^1/_2$", $^3/_8$", and $^1/_4$" from the raw edge (Figure 4). To create even gathers in the ruche, sew all lines of gathering stitches in the same direction. (Do not sew down one side, flip the strip around, and sew up the second side; this will cause uneven gathering.)

ruche gusset box cushion continued

9 To gather the fabric, pull the bobbin thread of all four stitching lines together on each side of the gusset. Fit the gathered fabric to the length of the interfacing strip. Adjust the gathers evenly along the length. Using both hands, tug each side of the gathered strip to straighten the gathers across the width of the piece. Pin the gathered fabric to the interfacing. Firmly press the gathers along the stitching lines and lightly press the gathers between the stitching lines to set the folds.

10 Using a normal stitch length and thread tension, stitch the fabric to the interfacing on each edge, following the gathering line $1/2$" from the edge (Figure 5). Stitch each edge in the same direction as before.

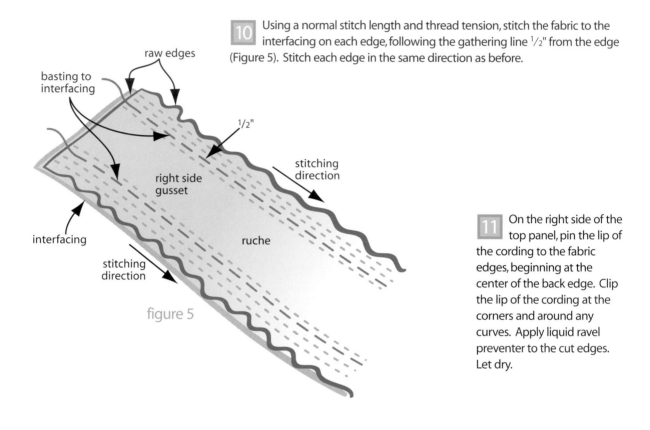

raw edges

basting to interfacing

$1/2$"

stitching direction

right side gusset

interfacing

ruche

stitching direction

figure 5

11 On the right side of the top panel, pin the lip of the cording to the fabric edges, beginning at the center of the back edge. Clip the lip of the cording at the corners and around any curves. Apply liquid ravel preventer to the cut edges. Let dry.

12 Where the cording ends meet, overlap the ends 2". Carefully remove the stitches that hold the cord to the lip for 1" to $1^{1}/4$" on each end (Figure 6).

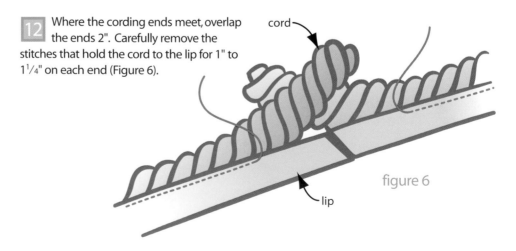

cord

lip

figure 6

ruche gusset box cushion how to

13 At one end, gently unwrap the cords. Apply liquid ravel preventer to the ends of each cord in the trim. Let dry. Turn the raveled cord across the lip, keeping the tension on the twists to maintain the look of twisted cord. Using a needle and thread, hand-stitch the raveled ends of the cord to the lip (Figure 7). Repeat at the opposite end of the cord.

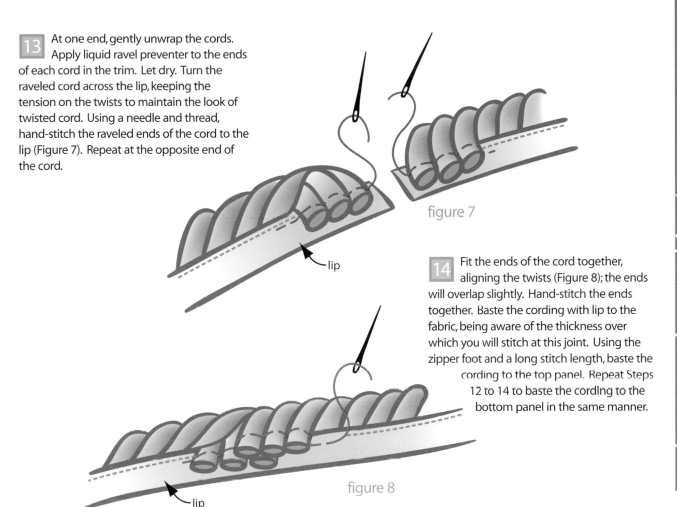

figure 7

lip

14 Fit the ends of the cord together, aligning the twists (Figure 8); the ends will overlap slightly. Hand-stitch the ends together. Baste the cording with lip to the fabric, being aware of the thickness over which you will stitch at this joint. Using the zipper foot and a long stitch length, baste the cording to the top panel. Repeat Steps 12 to 14 to baste the cording to the bottom panel in the same manner.

figure 8

lip

15 With right sides together and raw edges aligned, center the zippered gusset back on the back edge of the bottom panel (Figure 9). Position the pins on the wrong side of the gusset to sew the seam from that side of the fabric. Using the zipper foot and a long stitch length, baste the back gusset to the long back edge, starting and stopping the seam at each corner. Do not sew around the corner. Clip the seam allowances of the back gusset to each corner.

16 With right sides together and raw edges aligned, center the front gusset on the front edge of the bottom panel. Position the pins on the wrong side of the gusset to sew the seam from that side of the fabric. Using the zipper foot and a long stitch length, baste the front gusset to the long front edge, starting and stopping the seam at each corner. Do not sew around the corner; clip the seam allowance of the front gusset to each corner.

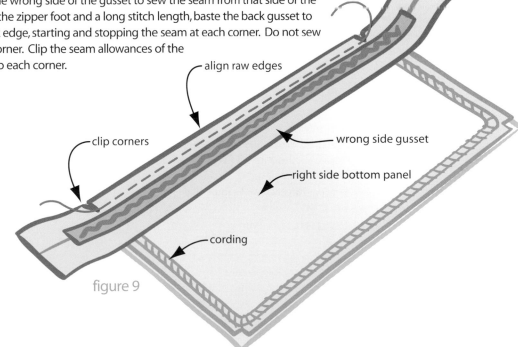

align raw edges

clip corners

wrong side gusset

right side bottom panel

cording

figure 9

ruche gusset box cushion continued

17 With right sides together and raw edges aligned, pin the back gusset (where the zipper stop is located) and front gusset to the side edge of the bottom panel (Figure 10). Bring the short ends of the gussets together, with right sides facing, to the seam line of the back and front gussets. Stitch the back and front gussets together at the top of the zipper (the seam allowances will be differing depths on the front and back gussets). Trim the seam allowance to $1/2$". Trim the interfacing in the seam allowance from the front gusset and press the seam toward the front gusset. Repin the gusset to the bottom panel on that side. Position the pins on the wrong side of the gusset to sew the seam from that side of the fabrics. Using the zipper foot and a long stitch length, baste the gusset to the side edge of the bottom panel, stitching around the corners. Pivot the stitching at the corners.

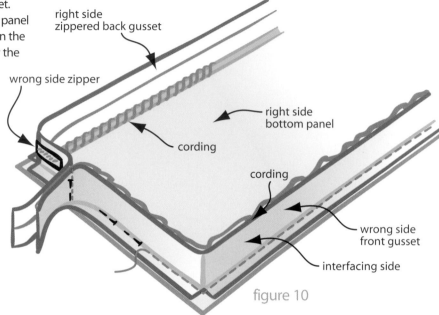

right side zippered back gusset

wrong side zipper

right side bottom panel

cording

cording

wrong side front gusset

interfacing side

figure 10

18 With right sides together and raw edges aligned, pin the back and front gussets to the remaining side edge of the bottom panel. Bring the short ends of the gussets together, with right sides facing. Make a 1"-deep tuck at the end of the gusset front to cover the zipper tab (Figure 11). Trim the end of the front gusset to match the back gusset. Stitch the back and front gussets together at the opposite end of the zipper. Trim the interfacing from the back of the front gusset in the seam allowance. Press the seam toward the front gusset. Repin the gusset to the bottom panel. Position the pins on the wrong side of the top panel to sew the seam from that side of the fabrics. Using the zipper foot and a long stitch length, baste the gusset to the side edge of the bottom panel, stitching around the corners. Pivot the stitching at the corners.

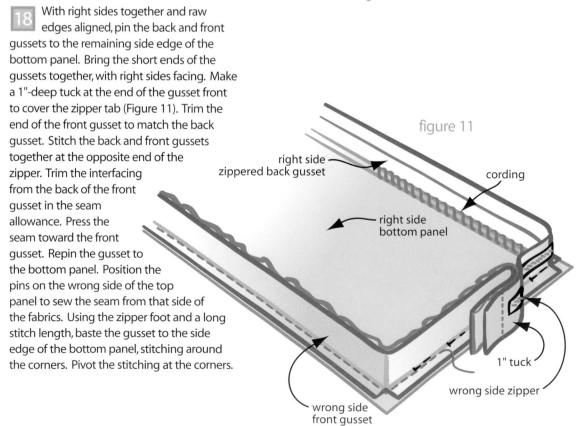

figure 11

right side zippered back gusset

cording

right side bottom panel

1" tuck

wrong side zipper

wrong side front gusset

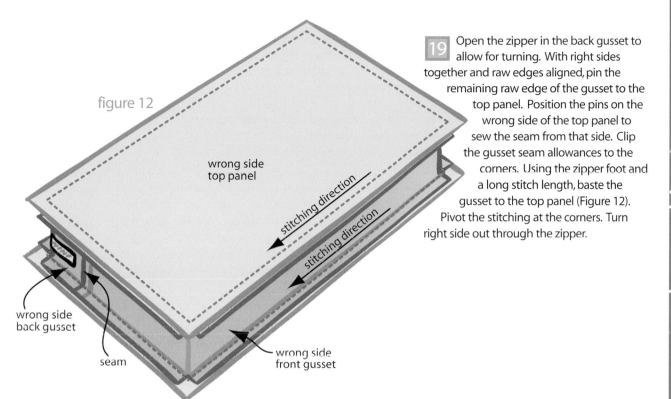

figure 12

wrong side
top panel

stitching direction

stitching direction

wrong side
back gusset

seam

wrong side
front gusset

19 Open the zipper in the back gusset to allow for turning. With right sides together and raw edges aligned, pin the remaining raw edge of the gusset to the top panel. Position the pins on the wrong side of the top panel to sew the seam from that side. Clip the gusset seam allowances to the corners. Using the zipper foot and a long stitch length, baste the gusset to the top panel (Figure 12). Pivot the stitching at the corners. Turn right side out through the zipper.

20 Look at the right side of each seam; the fabrics should fit together smoothly without puckers. If necessary, remove stitches and restitch to make each seam smooth. Return the stitch length to the normal setting. Turn the cushion cover wrong side out again and sew the gusset to the top panel along the basting lines, working with the wrong side of the top panel facing you (Figure 13). Sew the gusset to the bottom panel along the basting lines, working with the wrong side of the gusset facing you. Remove the gathering stitches from the right side of the gusset by pulling the bobbin thread and then the upper thread. Tear or trim the interfacing from the wrong side of the gusset and seam allowances. Press the seams.

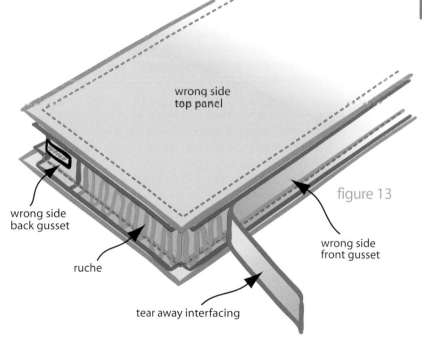

wrong side
top panel

wrong side
back gusset

ruche

figure 13

wrong side
front gusset

tear away interfacing

21 Turn the cover right side out. Insert the cushion in the cover through the opening. Adjust the cushion to match the top and bottom corners at the cording. Close the zipper.

ruche gusset chair cushion

materials

Paper
2"-thick high-density
    upholstery foam*
$1/8$"- to $1/4$"-loft bonded
    polyester batting*
54"-wide decorator fabric*
Medium-weight nonwoven
    interfacing*
Cording with lip or flange*
Liquid ravel preventer
2 cord-and-tassels
    trim pieces

sewing tools

Sewing machine
Needle and thread
Pins
Tape measure
Iron and ironing board
Zipper foot
Scissors

skill level: advanced
time required: $1 1/2$ to
    2 days
*Purchase materials after
taking measurements.

1 Place the paper on the chair seat and trace the edges of the seat onto the paper, adjusting as necessary to conform to the seat shape. Cut the paper along the marked line to make a pattern. Crease the paper pattern from center front to center back.

2 Use the pattern to cut one cushion from foam. Wrap the cushion in batting, pinning and trimming the batting to cover the foam smoothly. Loosely hand-sew the batting edges together. Remove the pins.

3 For the top panel, place the pattern on the fabric, centering any motif or aligning motifs symmetrically. Align the center crease of the pattern with the straight grain of the fabric. Add a $1/2$" seam allowance to each pattern edge and cut one top panel. Reposition the pattern and cut one bottom panel.

4 For the gusset length, measure the pattern circumference and add 1". Cut one $3 1/2$"-wide strip from interfacing to this length; set aside. Cut enough $3 1/2$"-wide strips from fabric to equal twice the length of the interfacing. Stitch the narrow ends of the fabric strips together to make a continuous length. Press the seams open.

5 Set the sewing machine for a long stitch length and loosen the upper thread tension. Working right side up on the gusset, sew four lines of gathering stitches on each long side $3/4$", $1/2$", $3/8$", and $1/4$" from the raw edges. Sew all of the lines in the same direction to ensure even gathering (Figure 4, page 89).

6 To gather the gusset, pull the bobbin thread of all four stitching lines on each side of the gusset. Fit the gathered fabric to the interfacing strip and adjust the gathers evenly along the length. Using both hands, tug sharply at both sides of the gathered strip to straighten gathers across the width of the piece. Pin the gathered fabric to the interfacing. Firmly press the gathers along the stitching lines and lightly press the gathers between the stitching lines to set the folds.

7 Remove each gathering line $3/4$" from the edge by removing the bobbin thread, then the upper thread. Be careful not to disarrange the gathers in the ruche. Using a normal stitch length and thread tension, stitch the fabric to the interfacing on each edge, following the $1/2$" gathering line and stitching each edge in the same direction as the gathering stitches (see Figure 5, page 90). With right sides together and raw edges aligned, stitch the narrow ends together, using a $1/2$" seam allowance. Trim the interfacing from the seam allowance at the narrow ends. Press the seam open.

8 On the right side of the top panel, pin the lip of the cording to the raw edge of the fabric, beginning at the center of the back. Clip the cording lip at the corners. Apply liquid ravel preventer to the cut edges. Let dry. Where the cording ends meet, blend the ends of the twisted cording (see pages 90 and 91, Steps 12 to 14). Using the zipper foot and a long stitch length, baste the cording to the top panel. Remove pins as you sew. Pin and baste the cording to the bottom panel in the same manner.

9 With right sides together and raw edges aligned, pin the gusset to the top panel, placing the gusset seam at the center back of the top panel. Clip the gusset seam allowance at the corners. Position the pins on the wrong side of the top panel to sew the seam from that side (Figure 1). Using the zipper foot and a long stitch length, baste the gusset to the top panel, pivoting the stitching at the corners.

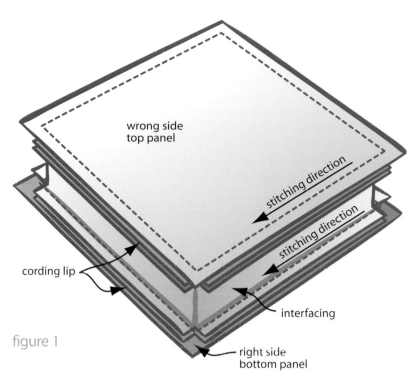

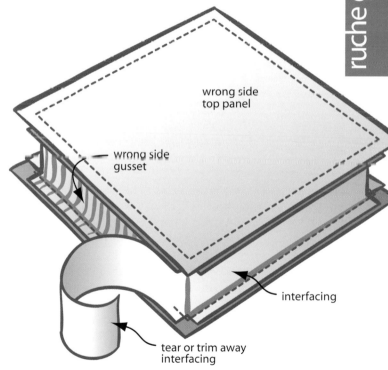

wrong side
top panel

stitching direction

stitching direction

cording lip

interfacing

right side
bottom panel

figure 1

10 With right sides together and raw edges aligned, pin the remaining long raw edge of the gusset to the bottom panel. Clip the gusset seam allowance at the corners. Position the pins on the wrong side of the gusset to sew the seam from that side. Stitch around the cushion in the same direction to alleviate pulling or puckering of the gusset (Figure 1). Using the zipper foot and a long stitch length, baste the gusset to the bottom panel. Stitch all corners, pivoting the stitching at the corners. Leave an opening in the back edge for turning.

11 Check each seam from the right side; the fabrics should fit together smoothly without puckers. If necessary, remove stitches and restitch to make each seam smooth. Set the stitch length at a normal setting and sew the gusset to the top panel along the basting lines, working with the wrong side of the top panel up. Sew the gusset to the bottom panel along the basting lines, working with the wrong side of the gusset up. Carefully tear or trim away interfacing from the wrong side of the gusset and seam allowance (Figure 2). Press the seams.

12 Turn the cover right side out. Insert the cushion through the opening. Adjust the cushion to fill the top and bottom corners of the cover at the cording. Turn under raw edges of the opening and hand-stitch the opening closed.

13 Place the cushion on the chair and determine chair tie placement. Hand-stitch the cording to the cushion.

wrong side
top panel

wrong side
gusset

interfacing

tear or trim away
interfacing

figure 2

pillow with double flange

Paper
1 yard 54"-wide decorator
    fabric
2 yards decorative loop fringe
14"-square pillow form

sewing tools

Sewing machine
Iron and ironing board
Vanishing fabric marker
Pins
Needle and thread
Monofilament thread
Scissors
Tape measure
Liquid ravel preventer

skill level: intermediate
time required: 4 hours

1 Cut a 6" square from paper to make a template for mitered corners. Fold the paper once from corner to corner. Crease the fold. Mark an X on a corner that is not folded. Cut the paper square into two triangles by cutting along the crease; discard one triangle. Mark the paper triangle "Template." *Note: The corner of the triangle marked with an X is a 90-degree angle.*

2 Cut two 24" squares from fabric for the front and back panels. Center any prominent fabric motifs or symmetrically place geometric designs.

3 Place the template on a corner of the wrong side of the front panel (Figure 1). Fit the 90-degree corner of the template into the corner of the panel and align the sides of the template with the raw edges of the panel. Using the vanishing fabric marker, make a line on the panel along the long side of the template. Mark the remaining corners of the front panel and the corners of the wrong side of the back panel.

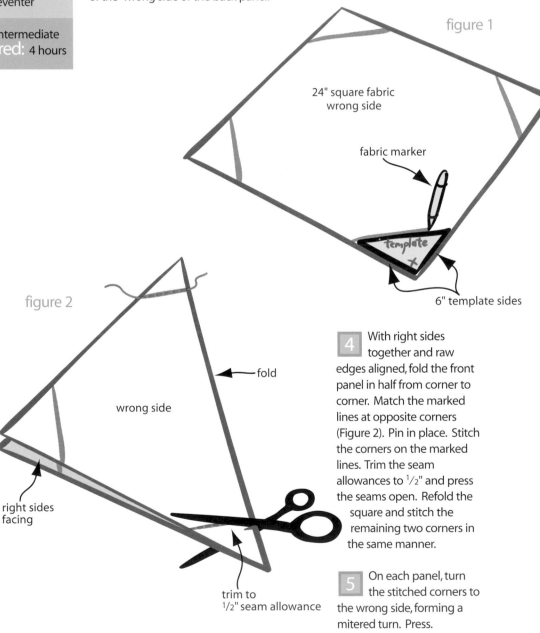

figure 1

24" square fabric
wrong side

fabric marker

template

6" template sides

figure 2

fold

wrong side

right sides
facing

trim to
1/2" seam allowance

4 With right sides together and raw edges aligned, fold the front panel in half from corner to corner. Match the marked lines at opposite corners (Figure 2). Pin in place. Stitch the corners on the marked lines. Trim the seam allowances to 1/2" and press the seams open. Refold the square and stitch the remaining two corners in the same manner.

5 On each panel, turn the stitched corners to the wrong side, forming a mitered turn. Press.

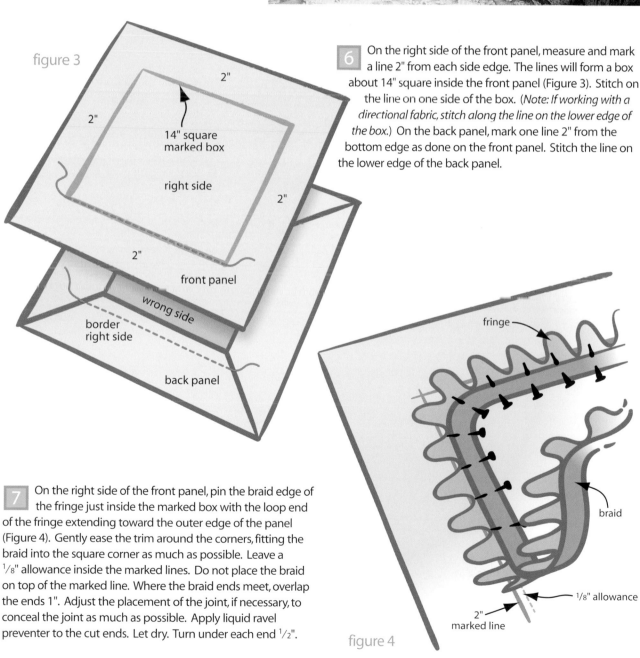

figure 3

2"

2"

2"

14" square
marked box

right side

2"

front panel

wrong side

border
right side

back panel

6 On the right side of the front panel, measure and mark a line 2" from each side edge. The lines will form a box about 14" square inside the front panel (Figure 3). Stitch on the line on one side of the box. (*Note: If working with a directional fabric, stitch along the line on the lower edge of the box.*) On the back panel, mark one line 2" from the bottom edge as done on the front panel. Stitch the line on the lower edge of the back panel.

7 On the right side of the front panel, pin the braid edge of the fringe just inside the marked box with the loop end of the fringe extending toward the outer edge of the panel (Figure 4). Gently ease the trim around the corners, fitting the braid into the square corner as much as possible. Leave a ¹/₈" allowance inside the marked lines. Do not place the braid on top of the marked line. Where the braid ends meet, overlap the ends 1". Adjust the placement of the joint, if necessary, to conceal the joint as much as possible. Apply liquid ravel preventer to the cut ends. Let dry. Turn under each end ¹/₂".

fringe

braid

¹/₈" allowance

2"
marked line

figure 4

8 Thread the machine with monofilament thread on the top and conventional thread in the bobbin. Using a normal stitch length, stitch the braid to the front panel following the edge of the braid next to the fringe. Pivot the stitching at the corners. Working in the same direction, stitch the remaining edge of the braid to the front panel, easing the braid into the corners. To control the stitches in the corners, you may need to shorten the stitch length (when the machine makes more stitches per inch, you have greater control of the placement of each stitch).

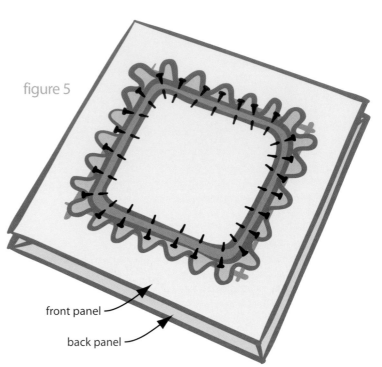

figure 5

9 With wrong sides together and turned edges aligned, layer the front panel on the back panel (Figure 5). Match the stitched lines from Step 6 along the lower edge of each panel; these stitched lines will be at the opening in the bottom of the pillow cover to insert the pillow form. Lift the fringe to reveal the marked line on the front panel and pin the panels together along the marked line.

front panel

back panel

10 Using the zipper foot, beginning 1" from the corner, and following the line of stitches on the bottom edge of the marked box, stitch to the corner. Keep the fringe free and pivot the stitching at the corners. Stitch the remaining sides to make a pocket for the pillow form. Stop stitching 1" into the line of stitches on the lower edge. Leave the center section of the lower edge of the pocket open.

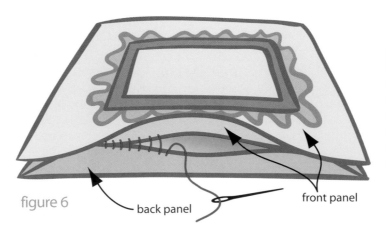

11 Insert the pillow form into the pocket through the opening. Using a needle and thread, make small hand stitches between the front and back panels along the lines of stitches to close the opening (Figure 6).

figure 6

back panel

front panel

double flange with contrast facing

Create interest by facing the edges of the panels in the double flange pillow with a boldly contrasting fabric (Figure 1). Follow these instructions to make a cover for a 14"-square pillow.

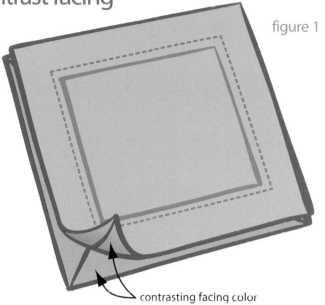

figure 1

contrasting facing color

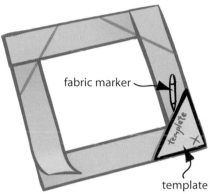

fabric marker

template

figure 2

1 Make the template as described in Step 1, page 96.

2 Cut two 19" squares from fabric for the front and back panels. Cut eight facing strips 3×24" from contrasting fabric.

3 Lay out four facing strips wrong side up; set the remaining strips aside. With raw edges aligned, layer one end of two adjacent strips to form the corner. Place the template made in Step 1 on the corner of the layer. The long edge of the template will cross the inside corner of the facings (Figure 2). Mark the stitching line on the facings by tracing along the long edge of the template. Mark one pair of facing strips at a time. Repeat with the remaining four facing strips.

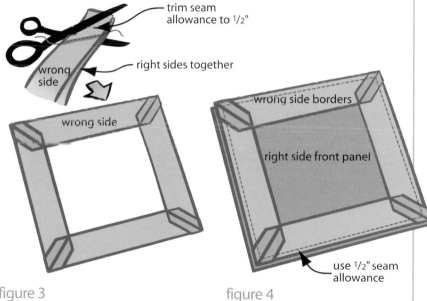

trim seam allowance to 1/2"

right sides together

wrong side

wrong side

wrong side borders

right side front panel

use 1/2" seam allowance

figure 3

figure 4

4 With right sides together, raw edges aligned, and matching marked lines, stitch the facings on the marked line. Trim the seam allowance to 1/2" (Figure 3). Press the seam open. Mark and stitch the remaining facing strips in the same manner.

5 With right sides together and raw edges aligned, pin the front panel to one facing square. Using a 1/2" seam allowance, stitch each edge. Pivot

the stitching at the corners. Clip the corners and press the seam open (Figure 4). Attach the remaining facing square to the bottom panel in the same manner.

6 Turn each facing to the wrong side, placing the seams on edge. Press flat. Follow the instructions from Step 9, page 98 (disregarding reference to fringe).

pillow with double flange how to

1 yard 54"-wide decorator
  fabric
2 yards $^6/_{32}$" filler cord
Scraps of complementary
  fabric
3 (1$^1/_4$"-diameter) buttons
  to cover
1 yard tassel fringe
14×17" pillow form

sewing tools

Sewing machine
Iron and ironing board
Vanishing fabric marker
Pins
Needle and thread
Monofilament thread
Scissors
Tape measure
Liquid ravel preventer
Zipper foot

skill level: intermediate
time required: 4 hours

button-front pillow

1 Cut one 18×15" back panel, one 16×15" front panel, and one 6×15"
side front panel from fabric. Cut 2 yards of 1$^1/_2$"-wide bias strips. Stitch
the strips together at the short ends to make a continuous length.

2 To make welting, fold the bias strip around the cord, matching the long
raw edges. Using the zipper foot and a long stitch length, baste close to
the cord, encasing the cord in the fabric. Set the welting aside.

3 On the front panel, turn under 2" along one 15" edge. Press. Cover
the buttons with scraps of complementary fabric, following the
manufacturer's instructions. Evenly space the buttons on the front of the panel
along the turned edge (Figure 1). With the right side of the fabric up, lap the
button-trimmed edge of the front panel over the side front panel. Position the
panels to make an 18×15" panel. Using a long stitch length, baste the
lapped panels along the raw edges.

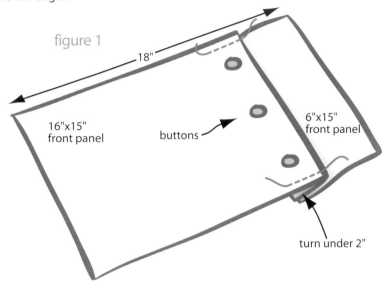

figure 1

18"

16"x15"
front panel

buttons

6"x15"
front panel

turn under 2"

4 On the right side of the front panel,
place the braid edge of the fringe inside
the $^1/_2$" seam allowance so the tassel fringe
extends over the raw edges of the panel.
Thread the machine with monofilament thread
in the top and conventional thread in the
bobbin. Using a long stitch length, baste the
braid portion of the fringe to the front
panel on each short edge. Stitch
each edge of the braid in the same
direction (Figure 2) to prevent
puckering in the finished front panel.
(Do not stitch down one edge and up
the other; this will cause puckering.)
Turn the panel to the wrong side and
press the stitching.

figure 2

braid

stitching direction

fringe

$^1/_2$" gap

5 On the right side of the front panel, pin the welting, aligning raw edges (Figure 3). Begin at the center of the side edge to conceal the joint in the welting under the tassel fringe and to keep the fringe out of the seam. Overlap the raw ends of the braid at each end with the welting. Clip the welting seam allowance at the corners. Where the welting ends meet, overlap the ends 1". Remove the stitching from the fabric cover on each end. Unfold the fabric and cut the ends of cord to meet. Refold one end of the cover over the cord. On the remaining end, turn the cover under ¹/₂" and refold the fabric around the cord, concealing the raw ends of the fabric. Using the zipper foot and a long stitch length, baste the welting to the front panel. Pivot the stitching at the corners.

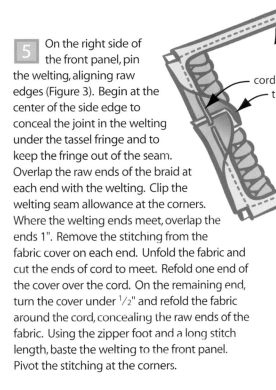

folded edge

cord

turn under ¹/₂"

welting

figure 3

6 With right sides together and raw edges aligned, pin the front panel to the back panel. Using the zipper foot, stitch along the previous basting lines on the front panel. Stitch all corners, pivoting the stitching at the corners. Leave an opening in one side edge for turning. Press the seam and grade the seam allowances. Turn the cover right side out through the opening.

7 Insert the pillow form into the cover through the opening. Turn the raw edges along the opening to the inside of the pillow. Using a needle and thread, stitch the opening closed by hand.

MORE GOOD IDEAS

add personality with buttons

Buttons lend a high-style, fashion-influenced look to pillows and other home decorating projects. You can find buttons for every taste and style.

◼ Fabric-covered buttons suggest a traditional decorating scheme.

◼ Bakelite buttons found at flea markets are perfect accessories for retro-style homes.

◼ Sophisticated shell buttons, such as mother-of-pearl and abalone, suit an elegant setting.

◼ For handmade interest, look for polymer clay pieces sold by artists at large crafts shows. Many of these are miniature works of art. Use them on a pillow and you'll have an interesting conversation piece.

Practical and decorative, cornices conceal

curtain hardware and add architectural importance to windows, making them appear grand. For a cornice that looks custom-designed, shape a lower edge inspired by an element in the room—the curves of a Chippendale chair, for example—or the curtain fabric. Give chairs importance, too, by covering drop-in seats in beautiful prints, tapestries, or pieced solid fabrics.

dining in style

A cornice box mounts above the window frame and should extend at least 8 inches over the window. Cornices are made from plywood and usually consist of a front or face board, a top or dust board, and two sides. To give the cornice a custom-designed look, create a shaped edge, drawing inspiration from objects or motifs in the room or using drapery fabric as a starting point. The crisp harlequin fabric in the curtains shown here sparked the idea for this pennant-shape edge.

Seats of dining room chairs can be just as interesting as other elements in a room, even though they spend most of their time hidden under the tabletop. Use the flat surface to add pattern, tie together diverse colors, or bring a new motif into the room. The chairs shown at left use triangular blocks of color to unify red walls and yellow draperies.

When choosing fabrics for drop-in seats, look for tightly woven fabrics that won't distort when stretched over the seat and that are lightweight enough to fit into the frame of the chair and fold into sharp corners.

materials

³/₈" plywood*
2×4 pine board*
11 (1") No. 6 wood screws
3 (3") No. 8 wood screws
2 (2") No. 8 wood screws
Spray adhesive
Clear-drying fabric glue
54"-wide decorator fabric*
54"-wide lining fabric*
Cording*
Tassels*
Adjustable rod
Curtain pins*

tools

Electric drill and drill bits
Electric saw
Screwdrivers

sewing tools

Sewing machine
Iron and ironing board
Tape measure
Upholstery or
   tapestry needle
Pins
Vanishing fabric marker

skill level: advanced
time required: 2 days
*Purchase materials after
taking measurements.

1 Install the 2×4 pine board and adjustable rod and drill pilot holes through the top of the cornice box into the 2×4 as directed in Steps 4 and 5 on page 107. Remove the cornice box from the window.

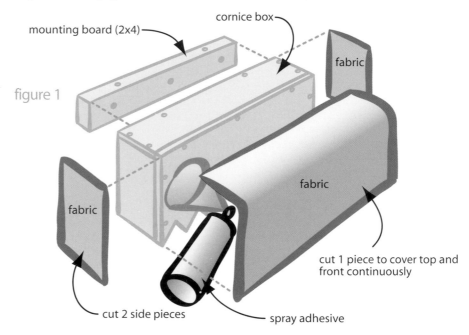

mounting board (2x4)
cornice box
fabric
figure 1
fabric
fabric
cut 1 piece to cover top and front continuously
cut 2 side pieces
spray adhesive

2 Cut two side pieces from fabric to fit the cornice box sides. Cut one continuous piece to fit the cornice box top and front. Do not cut the lower edge of the fabric to match the edge of the box front at this time. Following the manufacturer's instructions, apply spray adhesive to the box front. Place the fabric to match the pattern with the custom cuts on the lower edge of the box front. Smooth the fabric onto the box and wrap it over the box top (Figure 1). Apply spray adhesive to the ends of the box. Let dry. Matching the pattern at the corners, smooth the fabric onto both box ends. Punch small holes through the fabric into the pilot holes on the box top.

3 Trim the fabric at the bottom edge of the front to match the custom-cut box edge (Figure 2).

4 Using fabric glue, attach cording to the custom edge of the box, covering the raw edge of the fabric. With an upholstery needle, stitch one tassel to the cord at each point in the custom edge.

5 Measure the window length from the top of the adjustable rod. Trim the selvages from the fabric and the lining. Cut two front panels the measured window length plus 10" from fabric. Be sure each piece starts at the same point in the fabric repeat. Cut two panels the measured window length plus 4" from lining. If necessary, make up the required widths by cutting additional fabric and lining lengths and seaming the panels together.

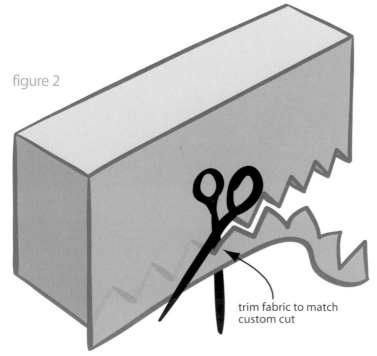

figure 2

trim fabric to match custom cut

6 Lay each front panel right side up. Place the top edge of the lining 3" from the top edge of the panel. Trim the lining 1" narrower on each side than the front panel (Figure 3). Slide the lining to one edge. Measure and mark 8" from the top edge and 12" from the bottom edge. Using a $1/2$" seam allowance, stitch the front and lining together between the marks. Slide the lining to the opposite side of the curtain front; stitch the front and lining together in the same manner. Press the seams open.

7 Turn the curtain right side out. Lay the curtain with the lining side up. Center the lining so 1" of curtain fabric is turned to the lining side on each side. Press the folds and seams.

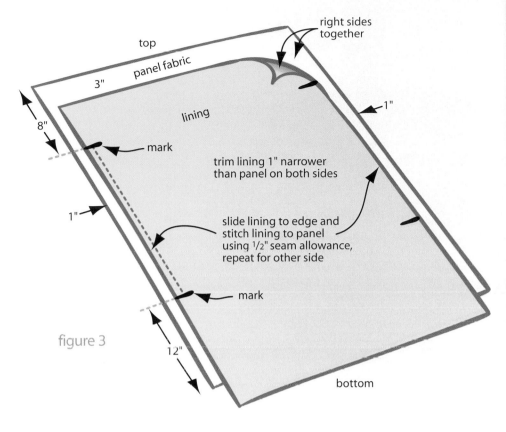

right sides together

top

panel fabric

3"

8"

lining

trim lining 1" narrower than panel on both sides

mark

1"

1"

slide lining to edge and stitch lining to panel using $1/2$" seam allowance, repeat for other side

mark

figure 3

12"

bottom

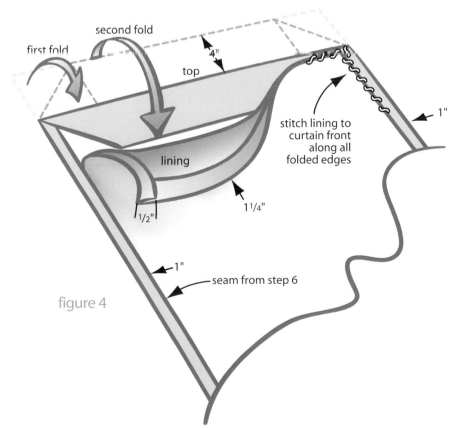

second fold

first fold

top

4"

stitch lining to curtain front along all folded edges

1"

lining

$1/2$"

$11/4$"

1"

seam from step 6

figure 4

8 Turn the top edge of the lining back away from each curtain front. Turn under the curtain front 4", mitering the corners. Press. Turn under the top edges of the lining $11/4$" and the side edges $1/2$". Press. Using a needle and thread, stitch the lining to the curtain front along all folded edges and the miters of the curtain fronts (Figure 4).

9 At the top corners of each curtain, insert curtain pins into the curtain back. Evenly space the remaining pins between the corners. Hang the hook portion of the pins on the rod.

hard cornice and curtain panels continued

10 Turn under and pin a hem for each curtain front so the edge just meets the floor. Remove the curtains from the rod. Keeping the lining edge free, press the hem fold. Open the fold. Measure 6" from the fold and trim the excess. Turn under the raw edge of the curtain front to meet the crease for the hem. Press, then refold the hem, making miters at the ends. Using a needle and thread, hemstitch the folded edge.

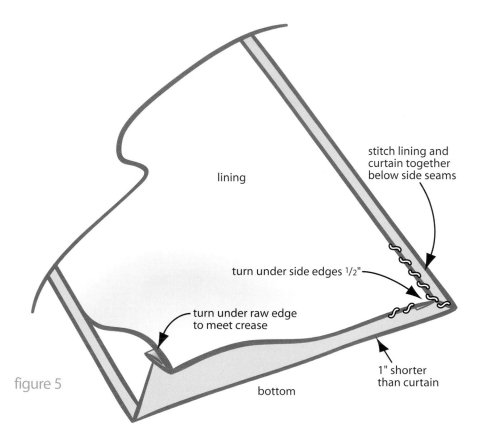

stitch lining and curtain together below side seams

lining

turn under side edges 1/2"

turn under raw edge to meet crease

1" shorter than curtain

figure 5

bottom

11 Turn under the lining 1" shorter than the curtain front. Press. Measure 2" from the fold and trim the excess. Turn under the raw edge to meet the crease and turn under the side edges 1/2". Press. Working from the wrong side, edgestitch the hem close to the folded edge (Figure 5). Using a needle and thread, stitch the lining and curtain together below the side seams. Replace the curtains on the rod.

12 Place the cornice box on the mounting board and install with 2" wood screws through the pilot holes.

making and mounting a cornice box

Cornice boxes are fabric- or wallpaper-covered boxes that serve as a valance treatment for windows. For easy installation, fasten a 2×4 board above the window as a mounting board for any hard cornice box. The weight of the box is then distributed over a wider area than if it were mounted on inside corner braces. It is also much easier to install the final screws from above the box than from inside and below.

1 Measure the width of the window frame. Cut the 2×4 board to the window width less 1". Determine where to place the top of the cornice. Measure from that point to the floor and divide by 4 for the finished height of the box. For pleasing proportions, the box should be at least 8" tall.

2 Cut the following pieces from plywood: the cornice front (the window width by the height of the box), the cornice top (the window width by 5"), and two cornice sides (5" by the height of the box less $^3/_8$"). For the lower edge of the cornice front, make a pattern. Trace the fabric design on paper; transfer the design to one long edge of the cornice front.

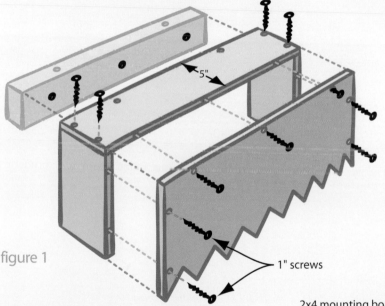

5"

figure 1

1" screws

3 Place the cornice top on the edge of each cornice side. Make sure the corners are flush and square. Drill pilot holes and attach the pieces with 1" screws. Place the cornice front on the front edge of the sides and top. Make sure the edges are flush and square. Drill pilot holes and attach with 1" screws (Figure 1). Paint the inside of the box and all edges, as well as the 2×4 board, in a color to match the curtain fabric.

4 Hold the cornice board above the window to determine placement. Lightly mark the top edge on the wall. Center the 2×4 board over the window $^1/_2$" below the mark, placing the wide side of the board against the wall. Drill pilot holes and install with 3" screws (Figure 2). Install the adjustable rod just outside the window frame.

5 Set the cornice box on the board. Drill pilot holes through the top of the box into the 2×4 board. Remove the box from the window and cover with fabric as directed on page 104.

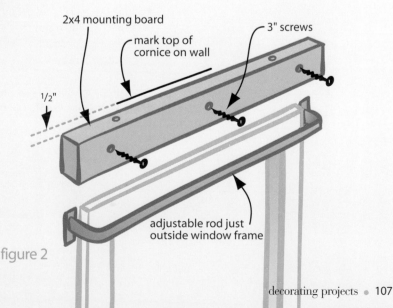

2x4 mounting board

mark top of cornice on wall

3" screws

$^1/_2$"

adjustable rod just outside window frame

figure 2

materials

High-density upholstery foam*
1"-loft bonded polyester batting*
45"-wide muslin*
54"-wide decorator fabric*
54"-wide complementary or contrasting fabric*
Paper
45"-wide interlining*
Spray fabric protector

tools

Screwdriver
Wood filler
Spray adhesive
Flat screwdriver
Staple gun and ¼" light-duty staples
Chair hardware

sewing tools

Sewing machine
Needle and thread
Pins
Scissors
Tape measure
Iron and ironing board

skill level: beginner
time required: ½ day
*Purchase materials after taking measurements.

1. Turn the chair upside down and remove the screws that secure the seat. Remove the seat and use a flat screwdriver to pry out the staples that hold the fabric in place. Carefully remove the original cover to use as a pattern.

2. Inspect the wood seat board; if the screw holes appear stripped, fill them with wood filler, following the manufacturer's instructions. Inspect the foam and padding; if they are compressed or stained, replace them. To replace foam and padding, use the original pieces as patterns to cut the new materials. Using spray adhesive, fasten new foam and batting to the wood seat, following the manufacturer's instructions.

3. Place the original seat cover on muslin and cut one panel. To cover the seat with one fabric, also cut the fabric from the original seat cover.

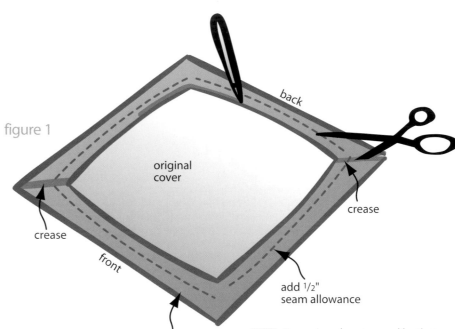

figure 1

original cover

back

crease

crease

front

add ½" seam allowance

paper pattern

4. For a pieced seat cover like that on page 102, place the original seat cover on a piece of paper and trace around it. Fold the paper diagonally from corner to corner and cut the paper on the fold (Figure 1). Place half of the pattern on the main fabric and the remaining pattern half on the complementary or contrasting fabric. Add ½" seam allowances around the patterns. Cut out each panel. With right sides together and raw edges aligned, stitch the fabrics together along the diagonal edge, using a ½" seam allowance. Press the seam open.

5. Place the pieced cover right side up on the muslin. Pin the seam to the muslin. Lift one fabric half. Topstitch the seam allowance to the muslin, positioning the stitches close to the seam (Figure 2). Lift the opposite fabric half and topstitch the seam allowance to the muslin.

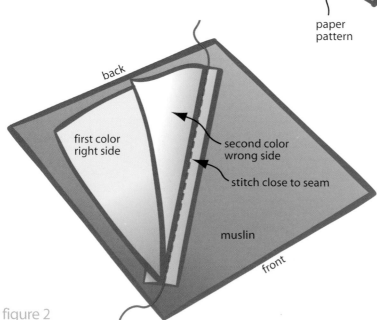

back

first color right side

second color wrong side

stitch close to seam

muslin

front

figure 2

6 Place the pattern pieces on the interlining and cut one from each pattern. Slip matching interlining under both halves of the pieced cover, placing the diagonal edge of the interlining directly on the seam (Figure 3). Smooth the fabric layers away from the seam.

7 Position the pieced cover, interlining, and muslin right side up on the chair padding with the diagonal running from seat corner to corner. Turn the seat upside down. At the center of each side, pull the fabric to the underside and staple it to the board. Check the right side of the seat for fabric placement.

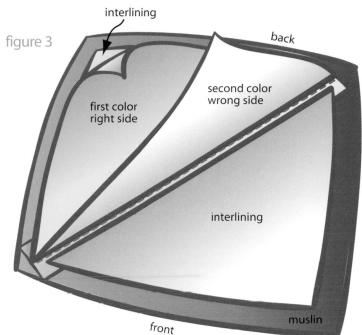

figure 3

interlining

back

second color wrong side

first color right side

interlining

front

muslin

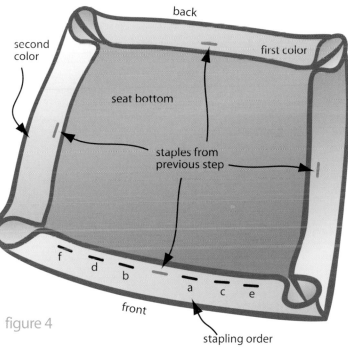

back

second color

first color

seat bottom

staples from previous step

f d b a c e

front

figure 4

stapling order

8 Turn the seat upside down again. Working on the front edge, pull the fabric and staple it on both sides of the center staple. Work across the front edge from side to side, leaving the corners free (Figure 4). Repeat to staple the back edge and then the side edges.

9 At each corner, open the fabric to pull it over the corners. Place the diagonal seam directly on the corners and staple it in place. Pull and fold the resulting fabric ears to make small pleats on both sides of each corner and staple them in place (Figure 5).

10 Trim the excess fabric beyond the staples. Following the manufacturer's directions, apply spray fabric protector to the top of the seat. Let dry. Place the seat on the chair and secure it with screws.

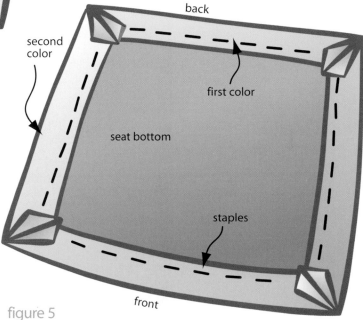

back

second color

first color

seat bottom

staples

front

figure 5

bedrooms

Your bed is—or should be—your refuge. You can create snuggly duvets and pamper yourself with piles of pillows, but don't stop there: Add tailored bed skirts, canopies, and window treatments to make your bedroom the ultimate retreat.

See the following pages for instructions: page 140 (canopy); page 144 (bedspread); page 150 (roller blind); page 152 (knotted swag); and page 154 (bolster pillow).

Bedding accessories reach far beyond

sheet sets and comforters. In fact, they almost run to laundry list lengths with custom-made headboards, bed curtains, dust ruffles, duvets, shams, and every shape and size of pillow. A little overwhelming? Perhaps, but this cottage-style setting puts it into perspective with an easy offering of accessories that you can add one element at a time.

cottage-style bedding

Building a cozy, relaxing space is doable when you start with a plain slate—white walls and a matching coverlet. Simply brush on color and pattern with each new accessory.

The headboard design (concealed behind pillows in the photo, but shown on page 115) can be a padded version or stitched as a slipcover to fit over an existing headboard. Make yours reversible with a second fabric for the back to give the bed a fresh look when the seasons change.

For a snug retreat, nestle your bed between panels of sheers. Cut from gauzy floral print, these floor-length sweeps frame the head of the bed with enough color and light to bring it into focus. Fastened with tab ties, the pair falls from painted dowels suspended from ceiling hooks.

To dress the bed completely, slip a ruffled skirt over the box springs and bed frame. The repetition of gathers sets up a lovely contrast against a lightweight coverlet, so don't scrimp on the fullness! To minimize wasted yardage for matching seams, choose a fabric with a small repeat. In some cases, if the motifs aren't directional, you may be able to cut the skirt panels the length of the fabric.

For lush comfort, arrange oversize pillows at the head of the bed. Here, a pair of European squares in ruffled shams leans against the headboard. Instead of a zipper, the shams feature a lapped opening, or French back, into which each pillow is inserted.

fabric chart

Estimated yardage assumes a maximum headboard height of 48" and fabric with no discernible pattern repeat. Purchase additional yardage to match repeats.

Twin	Full	Queen	King	California King
4 yards	8 yards	8 yards	8 yards	8 yards
40×24" foam	55×24" foam	62×24" foam	74×24" foam	78×24" foam

1 This headboard will be bolted to a metal bed frame. It should extend at least 12" above the mattress and rest on the floor for stability. Using a single sheet of plywood for a full-size or larger bed, the maximum height possible (floor to top of headboard) is 48".

2 Cut the plywood to equal the width of the metal bed frame, then round off the top corners using the jig saw. Remove the mattress and box springs and position the headboard against the bed frame. Transfer the bolt openings in the frame to the headboard (Figure 1). Plan at least two points of attachment on each side of the headboard. Using the electric drill and a drill bit of appropriate diameter, drill holes in the headboard at each mark. To check the fit and determine whether additional mounting or bracing is necessary, temporarily bolt the headboard to the bed frame.

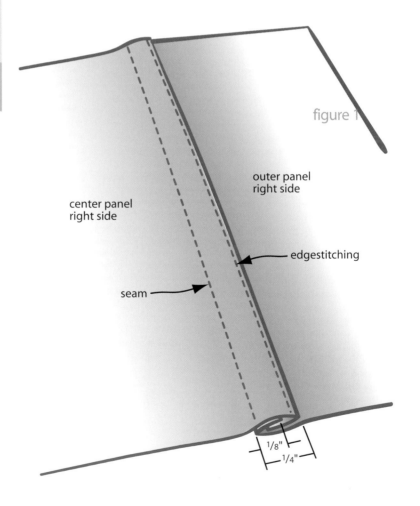

figure 1

outer panel
right side

center panel
right side

edgestitching

seam

1/8"

1/4"

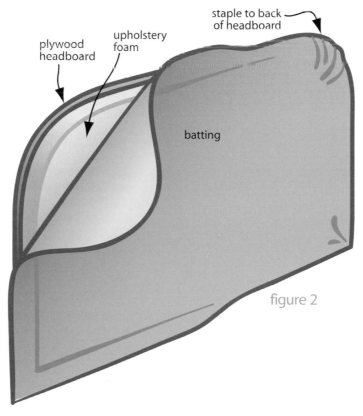

staple to back
of headboard

plywood
headboard

upholstery
foam

batting

figure 2

3 Remove the headboard from the bed frame. Trace the headboard onto paper to make a pattern, then trace the headboard onto upholstery foam with a permanent marker. Cut out the foam along the marked line. Apply spray adhesive to the headboard and adhere the foam. Center batting over the foam and pull the batting edges to the back of the headboard (Figure 2). Staple the batting in place. Trim the excess batting close to the staples.

simple padded headboard continued

4 Drape the fabric over the headboard before cutting it to determine the best pattern placement. Place stripes or plaids symmetrically and center any floral motifs or other prominent patterns. For full-, queen-, king-, and California king-size beds, join fabric widths to make a panel that fits the headboard. Match fabric repeats across the seams. Place the pattern on the right side of the fabric. Draw a 1½" seam allowance around the pattern (Figure 3). Cut out the front panel on the marked line; cut out a matching back.

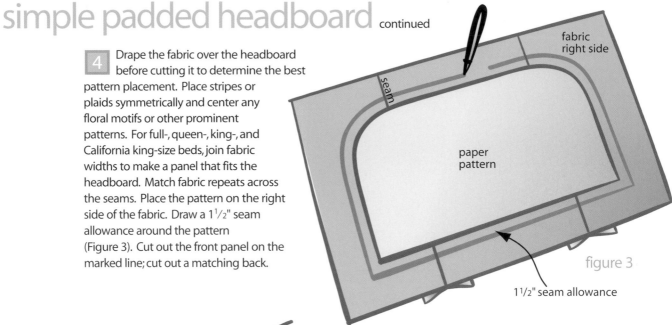

figure 3

1½" seam allowance

5 Cut enough 1½"-wide bias strips from fabric to equal 5 yards. Stitch the short ends of the strips together to make a continuous length. To make welting, fold the bias strip around the cording, matching the long raw edges. Using the zipper foot and a long stitch length, baste close to the cording.

6 On each rounded corner of the front and back panels, ease-stitch around the curve with a ½" seam allowance (Figure 4). Fit each panel to the padded headboard, pulling the bobbin thread slightly to shape, but not gather, the curves.

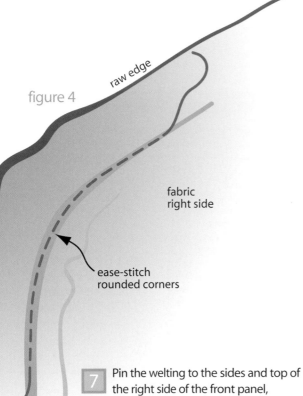

figure 4

raw edge

fabric right side

ease-stitch rounded corners

7 Pin the welting to the sides and top of the right side of the front panel, aligning the raw edges. Using the zipper foot and a long stitch length, baste the welting to the front panel. Measure from the floor to the top of the metal bed frame and add 1". Transfer this measurement to each side of the front panel for side vents. With right sides together and raw edges aligned, stitch the back panel to the front panel along the basting stitches, stitching between the marks. Clip into the seam allowances along the curves. Press the seam open. Turn right side out and press.

HEADBOARD SLIPCOVERS

If you have an old-fashioned cast-iron bed or your bed already has a plain wooden headboard, give the bed a new look with a headboard slipcover. Measure the headboard from side to side to determine the required width; measure from the top of the headboard to the floor to determine the required length of one panel. Add 1½" to 2" to each measurement for seam allowances and ease of fit. Cut two pieces of fabric to these measurements, joining widths as necessary. Make welting as directed in Step 5. Assemble the welting and front and back panels as directed for the headboard cover and slip the cover over the existing headboard.

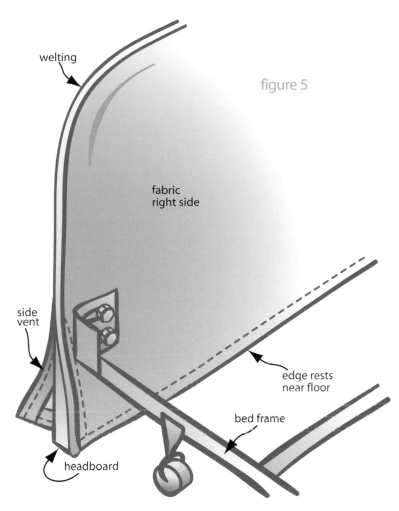

welting

figure 5

fabric
right side

side
vent

headboard

edge rests
near floor

bed frame

8 On the bottom edges of the headboard cover, turn under ½" twice. Press, then edgestitch close to the folded edge. Turn under the edges of the vents once and topstitch close to the fold. Slip the cover over the padded headboard. Pierce small holes in the fabric over the drilled holes in the headboard. Install the bolts through the bed frame, front fabric, and headboard (Figure 5).

PERFECT MATCHES

To match a fabric design across a seam, check the selvage edge of the fabric. A registration mark in the selvage indicates the start of a repeat. By matching the registration marks from panel to panel, you can easily match designs. For floral or all-over designs, you may need to purchase additional yardage to accommodate the repeat.

The legend provides additional information. An arrow, for example, indicates pattern direction, which is helpful for allover prints that may not appear to have a one-way design.

A row of color-filled circles identifies the colors in the fabric design. When you select paint or other fabrics for the room, this color legend helps to coordinate color choices; for example, it makes it easier to coordinate individual colors in a floral design with those in a plaid.

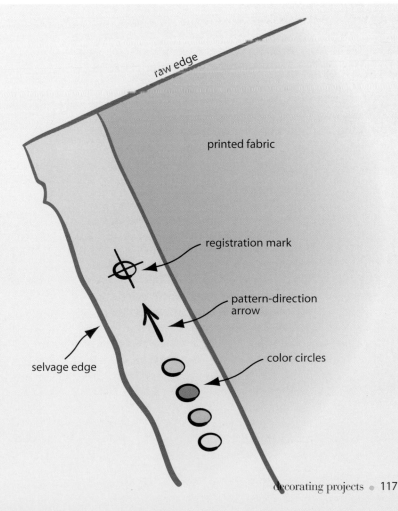

raw edge

printed fabric

registration mark

pattern-direction
arrow

color circles

selvage edge

bed draperies

materials

13 yards 54"-wide
  decorator fabric
2 ($^1/_2$"-diameter) dowel
  poles, 20" long
2 wood finials
4 ($^1/_4$×4") eyebolts with 4 ($^1/_4$")
  toggle bolts (drywall
  installation) *or*
4 (#0) $3^{15}/_{16}$" ceiling hooks
  (ceiling joist installation)
2 cup hooks
Paint

tools

Electric drill and drill bits
Stud finder

sewing tools

Sewing machine
Iron and ironing board
Vanishing fabric marker
Pins
Needle and thread
Scissors
Tape measure

skill level: beginner
time required: $^1/_2$ day

note Yardage is estimated for bed draperies to be hung in a room with 9-foot ceilings. Yardage does not include fabric required to match pattern repeats.

1 The draperies will hang at each side of the headboard. On the ceiling, measure and mark 2", then 18" from the wall against which the headboard will be placed; align marks with each side of the headboard. Drill pilot holes at the marks. To mount in beams or a ceiling joist, use ceiling hooks to hold the dowel poles. To install in paneling or drywall, use eyebolts with toggle mechanisms. Following the manufacturer's instructions, install the hardware. Paint the hardware, poles, and finials the same color for a custom look. Slip the poles into the hooks or eyebolts and install finials on each pole end (Figure 1).

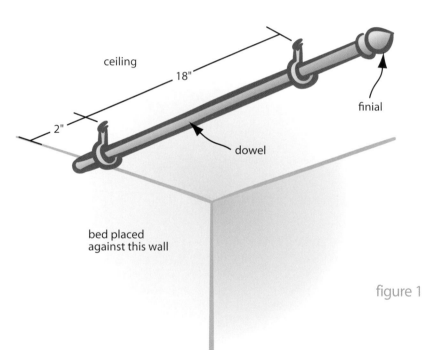

ceiling

18"

finial

2"

dowel

bed placed
against this wall

figure 1

2 Measure from the top of the pole to the floor for the cut length of the draperies. Trim the selvages from the fabric, then cut four panels from a full width of fabric to the measured length and 18 strips, each 4×26", for tabs.

3 With wrong sides together, press each tab in half lengthwise, making a center crease. Open the fold, then press under ¹/₂" on the short ends (Figure 2). Fold the long edges of the tab to meet the center crease. Press. Refold each tab on the center crease and edgestitch the long edge. Fold each tab in half crosswise and press.

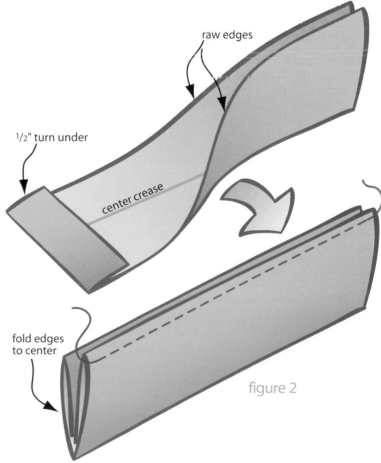

raw edges

¹/₂" turn under

center crease

fold edges to center

figure 2

decorating projects • 119

4 On the right side of one panel, place a tab $1/2$" from each side edge, aligning the tab fold with the top raw edge of the panel. Evenly space six tabs between the two end tabs (Figure 3). Using a $1/2$" seam allowance and a long stitch length, baste the tabs to the panel. In the same manner, baste eight tabs to one of the remaining panels. Set aside the last two tabs for tiebacks.

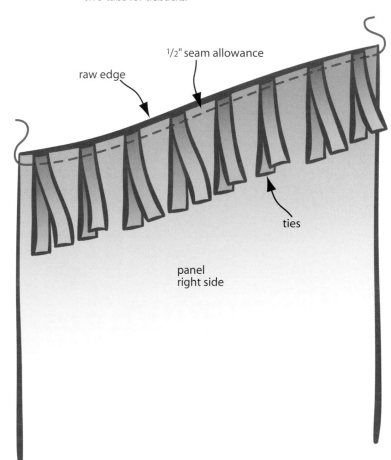

$1/2$" seam allowance

raw edge

ties

panel
right side

figure 3

5 With right sides together and raw edges aligned, pin each tabbed panel to a plain panel along the sides. Using a $1/2$" seam allowance, stitch the panels together. Press the seams open. Turn right side out, place the seam on edge, and press flat.

6　Turn the panel wrong side out. Pin the top panel edges together with the side seam allowances turned toward the center of the fabric (Figure 4). Pin the bottom panel edges together. Using a $1/2$" seam allowance, stitch the top edge. Stitch the bottom edge, leaving a long opening for turning. Press the seams open. Turn right side out through the opening. Slipstitch the opening closed. Press the panel flat.

7　Topstitch $3/8$" from the top edge of each panel. Knot the tab ends over the poles to hang the draperies (Figure 5).

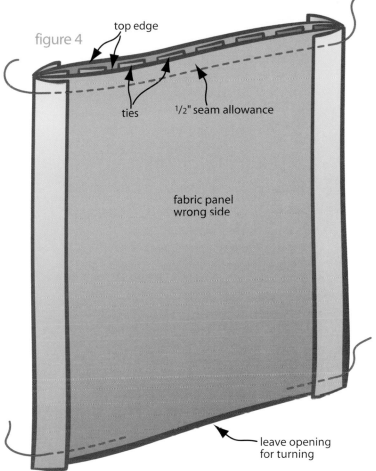

figure 4

top edge

ties

$1/2$" seam allowance

fabric panel
wrong side

leave opening
for turning

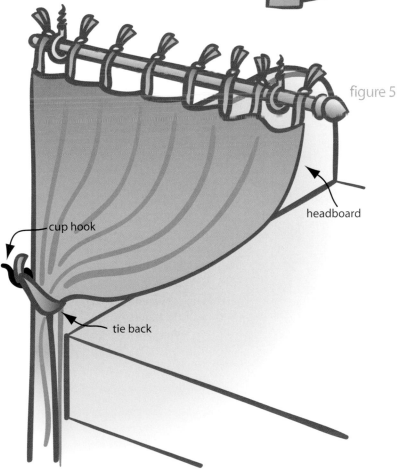

figure 5

cup hook

tie back

headboard

8　To install cup hooks for the tiebacks, measure 18" above the mattress at each side of the headboard. Adjust the height as necessary to complement the headboard: For a low headboard, place the hooks higher so the draperies pull back to the top of the headboard; for a tall headboard, install the hooks lower so the draperies pull back to the center of the headboard. Wrap each drapery panel with one tieback tab and knot the ends. Catch the tieback loop on the hook (Figure 5).

materials

54"-wide decorator fabric
54"-wide lining fabric
Paper-backed fusible
  adhesive tape

sewing tools

Sewing machine
Iron and ironing board
Vanishing fabric marker
Pins
Needle and thread
Scissors
Tape measure

skill level: beginner
time required: ¹/₂ day

gathered bed skirt

fabric chart
Estimated yardage is for solid fabric. Purchase additional yardage to match repeats. Pieces for skirt panels are cut from selvage to selvage.

	Twin	Full	Queen	King/California King
Lining	2¹/₄ yards	2¹/₄ yards	2¹/₂ yards	2¹/₂ yards
14" drop	3¹/₄ yards	3³/₄ yards	4¹/₄ yards	4¹/₄ yards
18" drop	4 yards	4³/₄ yards	5¹/₄ yards	5¹/₄ yards
fusible tape	10¹/₂ yards	11¹/₂ yards	12¹/₄ yards	13¹/₂ yards

1 Cut a piece, or pieces, for the platform cover (which covers the box springs) from lining fabric. For twin-size beds, cut one 39×76¹/₂" piece. For full-size beds, cut one 54×76¹/₂" piece. For queen-size beds, cut three 21×81¹/₂" pieces. For king-size beds, cut three 26¹/₂×81¹/₂" pieces. For California king-size beds, cut three 25×85¹/₂" pieces. For queen-, king-, and California king-size beds, pin two pieces together along one long edge with wrong sides together and raw edges aligned. Stitch together, using a ¹/₂" seam allowance. To make a flat-fell seam, trim the seam allowance on one panel to ¹/₈". On the remaining seam allowance, press under ¹/₄". Turn the folded seam allowance over the trimmed seam allowance. Working from the right side of the fabric, topstitch close to the folded edge. Press. Stitch the remaining panel to the seamed panel in the same manner.

2 Remove the mattress from the box springs. Place the lining panel on top of the box springs with 1" extending beyond the head of the bed and ¹/₂" on each side (Figure 1). Pin the panel to the box springs to temporarily hold it in place. Add the length of two sides and the width of the box springs and divide this figure into four equal sections: 47" sections for a twin-size bed, 50³/₄" sections for a full-size bed, 55" sections for a queen-size bed, 59" sections for a king-size bed, and 60" sections for a California king-size bed.

3 Measure from the top edge of the box springs to the floor and add 2¹/₂" for the cut depth of the skirt pieces. For a twin-size bed, cut 10¹/₂ yards of skirt panels to this depth. For a full-size bed, cut 11¹/₂ yards. For a queen-size bed, cut 12¹/₄ yards. For a king-size bed, cut 13¹/₄ yards. For a California king-size bed, cut 13¹/₂ yards. Stitch the short ends together with right sides facing and using a ¹/₂" seam allowance. Press the seams open.

4 Along one long edge of the skirt, press under 2". Open the fold. Following the manufacturer's instructions, apply paper-backed fusible adhesive tape to the raw edge of the hem. Remove the paper backing and fuse the hem in place. On each short end of the skirt, turn under ¹/₂" twice. Press, then edgestitch close to the fold.

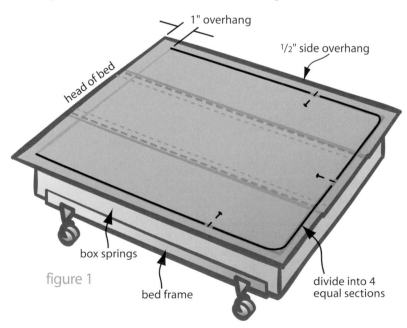

1" overhang
¹/₂" side overhang
head of bed
box springs
figure 1
bed frame
divide into 4 equal sections

5 Divide the raw edge of the skirt into four equal sections, marking each quarter with pins. Set the machine for a long stitch length and loosen the upper thread tension. Starting and stopping the stitching at each quarter mark, make four rows of gathering stitches ³/₄", ¹/₂", ³/₈", and ¹/₄" from the edge; leave long thread tails (Figure 2). To create even gathers in the skirt, sew all rows in the same direction and with the right side of the fabric faceup.

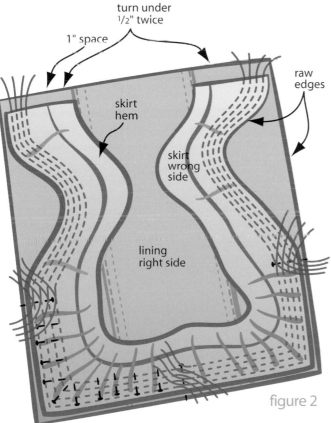

turn under
1/2" twice

1" space

raw edges

skirt hem

skirt wrong side

lining right side

figure 2

6 With right sides together and raw edges aligned, match quarter marks on the skirt to the quarter marks on the lining panel. Pin the ends of the skirt 1" from the top edge (Figure 2). On the skirt, evenly pull the bobbin thread on all four stitching rows to fit the skirt to the lining panel. Adjust the gathers, placing them closer together around the corners. Using a long stitch length, baste the skirt to the lining panel. Check that the gathers are even; if necessary, remove the basting, adjust the gathers, and rebaste. Press the seam allowance flat. Using a regular stitch length, stitch the skirt to the lining panel along the basting stitches. Finish the raw edges of the lining and skirt together.

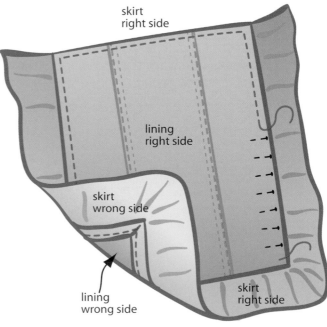

skirt right side

lining right side

skirt wrong side

lining wrong side

skirt right side

figure 3

7 Turn the seam allowances toward the lining panel and pin them in place. At the top edge of the lining, press under 1/2" twice. Topstitch around the lining panel 1/4" from the seam lines and the top folded edge (Figure 3). To remove any visible gathering stitches, pull the bobbin thread, then the top thread.

materials
54"-wide decorator fabric
54"-wide complementary fabric
54"-wide accent fabric
Cording

sewing tools
Sewing machine
Iron and ironing board
Vanishing fabric marker
Pins
Needle and thread
Scissors
Tape measure
Zipper foot

skill level: beginner
time required: 1 day

fabric chart

	Standard	Queen	King	European Square
Fabric	1$\frac{1}{4}$ yards	1$\frac{1}{4}$ yards	1$\frac{1}{4}$ yards	1$\frac{3}{4}$ yards
Ruffle	1$\frac{1}{2}$ yards	1$\frac{1}{2}$ yards	1$\frac{1}{2}$ yards	1$\frac{1}{2}$ yards
Accent	$\frac{1}{2}$ yard	$\frac{1}{2}$ yard	$\frac{1}{2}$ yard	$\frac{1}{2}$ yard

1 For each pillow sham, cut one front panel and two back panels from decorator fabric. For a 20×26" standard bed pillow, cut one 21×27" front and two 20×21" backs. For a 20×30" queen bed pillow, cut one 21×31" front and two 20×22" backs. For a 20×36" king bed pillow, cut one 21×37" front and two 21×25" backs. For a 26"-square European square pillow, cut one 27×27" front and two 20×27" backs.

2 Cut 5"-wide bias strips for the ruffle from complementary decorator fabric. For a standard bed pillow ruffle, cut 5$\frac{1}{4}$ yards. For a queen bed pillow ruffle, cut 5$\frac{3}{4}$ yards. For a king bed pillow ruffle, cut 6$\frac{1}{4}$ yards. For a European square pillow ruffle, cut 6 yards. Using a $\frac{1}{2}$" seam allowance, stitch the strips together at the short ends to make a loop. Press the seams open.

3 Cut 3$\frac{1}{4}$ yards of 1$\frac{1}{2}$"-wide bias strips from accent fabric. Join the strips at the narrow ends to make one continuous length. For welting, fold the strip around the cording, matching long edges. With the zipper foot and a long stitch length, baste close to the cording.

figure 1

welting

clip the welting seam allowance

front panel right side

$\frac{1}{2}$"

raw edges aligned

cording

4 Pin the welting to the right side of the front panel, aligning raw edges and beginning at the center of one panel edge (Figure 1). For a directional fabric, begin at the center of the bottom edge of the panel. Clip the welting seam allowance at the corners. Where the welting ends meet, overlap the ends 1" and cut the excess. Remove the stitches from the welting fabric on each end. Unfold the fabric and cut the cording ends to meet (Figure 1). Refold one end of the welting fabric over the cord. On the remaining end, turn the fabric under $\frac{1}{2}$" and refold around the cording, concealing the raw end of the welting fabric. Using the zipper foot and a long stitch length, baste the welting to the front panel.

5 Fold the ruffle in half lengthwise with the wrong sides facing and press. Divide the ruffle into quarters and mark with pins (Figure 2). Set the machine for a long stitch length and loosen the upper thread tension. Starting and stopping the stitching at each quarter mark, make four lines of gathering stitches $\frac{3}{4}$", $\frac{1}{2}$", $\frac{3}{8}$", and $\frac{1}{4}$" from the open edge. To create even gathers in the ruffle, sew all lines of gathering stitches in the same direction and from the same side of the ruffle. Label this side of the ruffle as the right side.

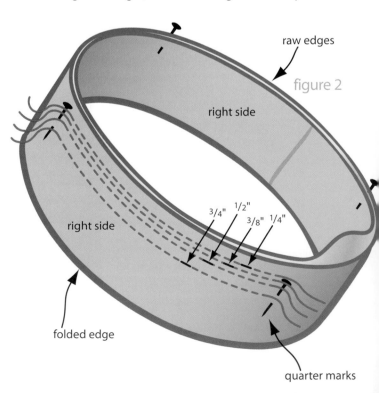

raw edges

figure 2

right side

right side

$\frac{3}{4}$" $\frac{1}{2}$" $\frac{3}{8}$" $\frac{1}{4}$"

folded edge

quarter marks

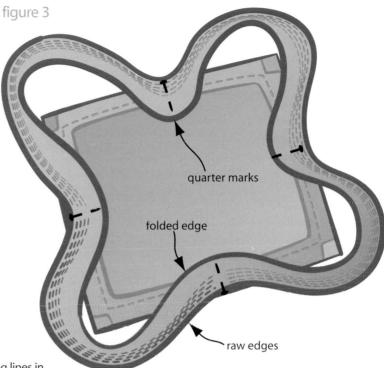

figure 3

quarter marks

folded edge

raw edges

6 On the front panel, mark the center of each side with a pin, dividing the panel edges into quarters (Figure 3). With right sides together and raw edges aligned, match the quarter marks on the ruffle to the quarter marks on the front panel.

7 Pull up the bobbin thread on all four stitching lines in the ruffle. Fit the ruffle to the edge of the front panel. Adjust the gathers, placing them closer together around the corners. Using the zipper foot and a long stitch length, baste the ruffle to the front panel along the basting line in the front panel. Check that the gathers are even. If necessary, remove the basting, adjust the gathers, and rebaste. Press the seam allowance. Press the seam from the wrong side of the ruffle.

8 On the narrow edges of each back panel, press under ¹/₂", then 3". Edgestitch close to the folded edge through all layers.

9 With right sides together and raw edges aligned, pin the back panels to the front panel, overlapping the hemmed edge of the back panels (Figure 4). Using the zipper foot, stitch the back panels to the front panel along the basting lines. Finish the seam allowances and press the seams. Turn the pillow right side out through the opening in the back. Press. To remove visible gathering stitches, pull the bobbin thread and then the top thread.

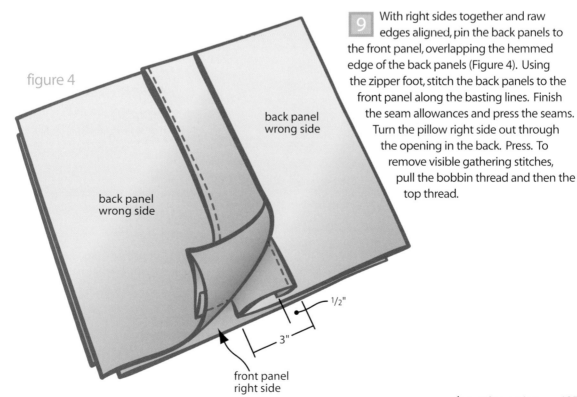

figure 4

back panel wrong side

back panel wrong side

¹/₂"

3"

front panel right side

Perhaps your ready-made comforter is beginning to show its age. Maybe you just want to put a new face on a guest room. Ready to play dress up? A duvet cover as easy to sew as this one is ready in a snap with envelope-styling and easy ribbon ties.

simple embellishment

A duvet cover sends a comforter to bed with lots of color, texture, and pattern—or less, if that's what you want. That's the beauty of this embellishment. With fabric and straight seaming, you can completely change your bedspread and your room scheme in a day. The basic construction is accomplished with a front, back, and bottom flap, and is assembled like an envelope. You maneuver the comforter under the flap between the front and back layers, then tie it as a pretty package with ribbon bows. A contrasting band adds a pattern accent.

Use leftover fabric to dress up throw pillows for the bed and a nearby chair. If you have extra fabric, hem a large square to fashion a quick table cover. To completely coordinate the bed, trim pillowcases and purchased knife-edge pillows with ribbon or fabric appliqués. A bed skirt hides the box springs and bed rails for a tailored, finished appearance.

WHAT IS A DUVET COVER?

In the last 15 or 20 years, duvets have become popular additions to well-dressed beds. *Duvet* is French for comforter. Usually made of plain cotton and filled with down or down and feathers, a comforter is slipped inside a decorative cover that can be removed for laundering. European-style duvets are plumper and more luxurious looking than ordinary bedspreads or coverlets, but they may not extend as far down the side of the bed as American-style comforters do.

materials

Down- or polyester-filled
  comforter to fit bed
54"-wide decorator fabric
54"-wide complementary
  lining fabric
10½ yards of cording
1"-wide ribbon

sewing tools

Sewing machine
Ironing board and iron
Vanishing fabric marker
Pins and safety pins
Needle and thread
Scissors
Tape measure
Liquid ravel preventer
Zipper foot

skill level: intermediate
time required: 1 day

fabric chart

Fabric chart estimates are for solid fabric. Purchase additional yardage to match pattern repeats.

	Twin	Full/Queen	King
Fabric	5½ yards	5½ yards	5½ yards
Complementary fabric	6¼ yards	6¼ yards	6¼ yards
Ribbon	5 yards	7 yards	9 yards

1 The duvet top and lining are pieced from three panels of fabric. For the top, cut the panels from the decorator fabric. For the lining, cut the panels from the complementary fabric. To match patterns across the seams, be sure to measure each piece from the same point in the pattern repeat. Trim the selvages from the fabric before measuring the panel width. Cut the panels as follows:

Twin-size duvet: Cut one 40×97" center panel and two 11½×97" side panels from fabric. Cut one 40×88" center panel, two 11½×88" side panels, and one 7×62" strip for the lapped edge of the lower panel from complementary fabric.

Full/queen-size duvet: Cut one 53×97" center panel and two 18×97" side panels from fabric. Cut one 53×88" center panel, two 18×88" side panels, and one 7×88" strip for the lapped edge of the lower panel from complementary fabric.

King-size duvet: Cut one 53×97" center panel and two 26×97" side panels from fabric. Cut one 53×88" center panel, two 26×88" side panels, and one 7×104" strip for the lapped edge of the lower panel from complementary fabric. If necessary, stitch several shorter sections of 7"-wide strips to make the required length. Match patterns across the seams.

2 For the welting, cut 7 yards of 1½"-wide bias strips from the remaining complementary fabric. Stitch the strips together at the narrow ends to make a continuous length. Fold the bias strip around the cording, matching the long raw edges. Using the zipper foot and a long stitch length, baste close to the cording. Cut the welting into two equal lengths.

3 To assemble the duvet top, pin one side panel to each long edge of the center panel with wrong sides facing and raw edges aligned. Match the patterns across the seams. Join the panels with flat-fell seams (Figure 1). Assemble the duvet lining in the same manner.

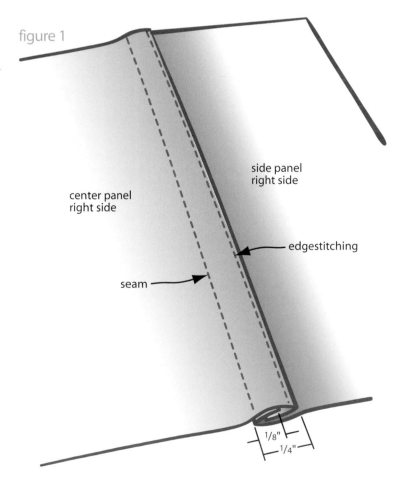

figure 1

side panel
right side

center panel
right side

edgestitching

seam

1/8"
1/4"

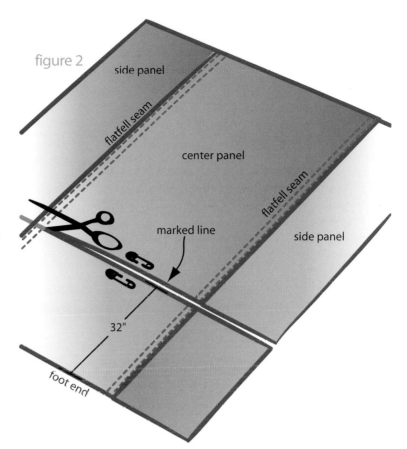

figure 2

side panel

flatfell seam

center panel

flatfell seam

side panel

marked line

32"

foot end

4 Beginning at the foot end of the duvet top, measure 32" and mark a line from side to side (Figure 2). Fasten a safety pin in the fabric on both sides of the marked line; the pinned edges will become the lapped opening in the finished duvet. Cut the duvet top along the marked line. On the larger section, press under 1" twice on the pinned edge. Edgestitch close to the folded edge.

5 Cut the ribbon into 18" lengths as follows: For twin-size, cut five pairs; for full/queen, seven pairs; for king, nine pairs. Apply ravel preventer to the cut ends, if desired. Let dry. On the wrong side of the smaller section of the duvet top, evenly arrange half of the ribbon lengths across the pinned edge (Figure 3). Begin and end 4" from each end and align the raw edge of each ribbon with the raw edge of the fabric. Using a ½" seam allowance and a long stitch length, baste the ribbons to the duvet top.

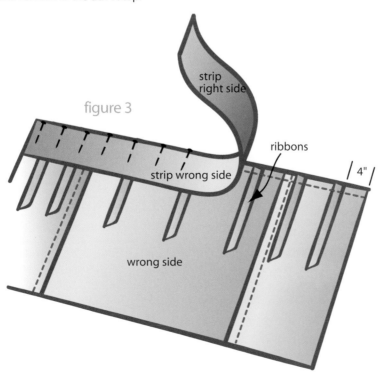

figure 3

strip right side

strip wrong side

ribbons

4"

wrong side

6 Lay the strip of complementary fabric (cut in Step 1) right side down over the ribbon edge of the smaller section, aligning the raw edges (Figure 3). Pin in place.

bow-tied duvet continued

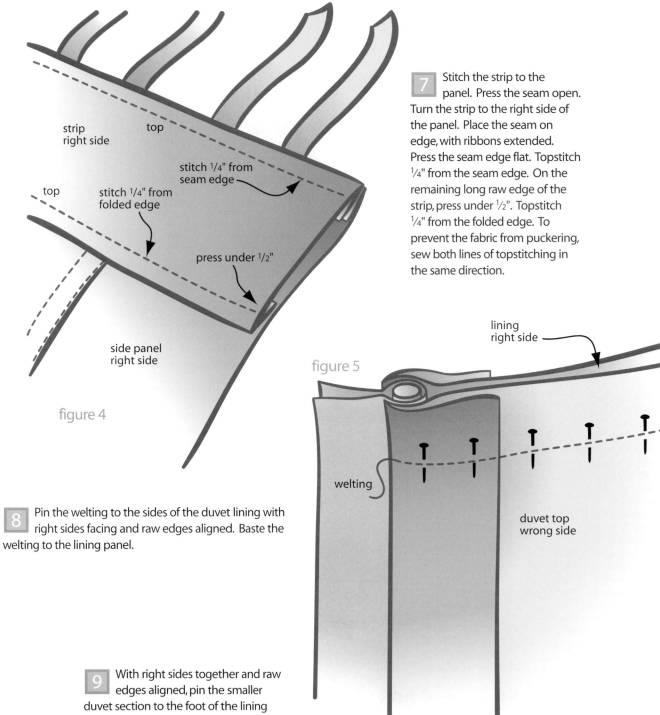

strip
right side

top

top

stitch ¹⁄₄" from
seam edge

stitch ¹⁄₄" from
folded edge

press under ¹⁄₂"

side panel
right side

figure 4

7 Stitch the strip to the panel. Press the seam open. Turn the strip to the right side of the panel. Place the seam on edge, with ribbons extended. Press the seam edge flat. Topstitch ¹⁄₄" from the seam edge. On the remaining long raw edge of the strip, press under ¹⁄₂". Topstitch ¹⁄₄" from the folded edge. To prevent the fabric from puckering, sew both lines of topstitching in the same direction.

figure 5

lining
right side

welting

duvet top
wrong side

8 Pin the welting to the sides of the duvet lining with right sides facing and raw edges aligned. Baste the welting to the lining panel.

9 With right sides together and raw edges aligned, pin the smaller duvet section to the foot of the lining panel along the sides. In the same manner, pin the larger duvet section to the top portion of the lining panel along the sides, lapping the hemmed edge over the ribboned edge. Using the zipper foot, stitch the top and lining together on each side. Finish the seam allowances. Press the seams open.

10 Pin the top and bottom edges of the duvet top to the lining. Turn the side seam allowances to the center of the duvet, leaving the seam allowance of the welting extended from the seam (Figure 5). Using the zipper foot, stitch the top and bottom edges. Press the seams open. Turn the duvet cover right side out through the lapped opening. Place the seams on edge. Press flat.

11 Press under ½" twice on one end of each remaining ribbon length. Pin the ribbons to the larger duvet section, aligning them with the ribbons on the smaller section (Figure 6). Machine-stitch the ribbons in place, being careful to keep the lining fabric away from the stitches.

12 Insert the comforter into the duvet through the lapped opening. Shake to distribute the comforter inside the duvet cover. Tie the ribbon ends in bows.

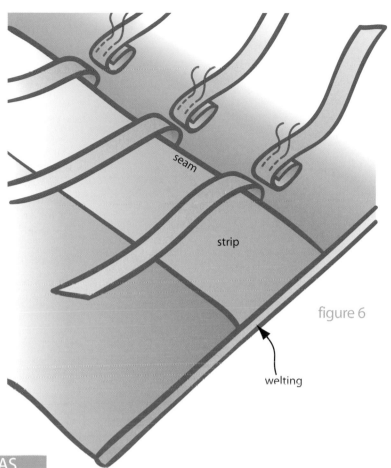

seam

strip

figure 6

welting

MORE GOOD IDEAS

creative closures
Instead of ribbons, fasten the duvet with closures that suit your decorating style.

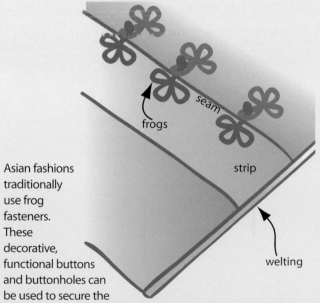

seam

frogs

strip

welting

Asian fashions traditionally use frog fasteners. These decorative, functional buttons and buttonholes can be used to secure the lapped opening in the duvet cover. Trim the smaller section of the duvet top with a band of oriental-inspired fabric. Sew the button half of the frog on top of the band. Evenly space the fasteners in the same manner as you would the ribbons. Sew the buttonhole half to the larger portion of the duvet top.

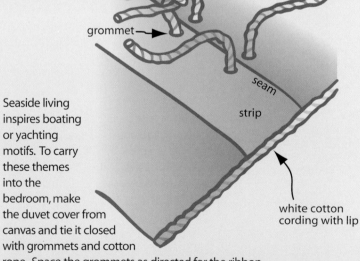

grommet

seam

strip

white cotton cording with lip

Seaside living inspires boating or yachting motifs. To carry these themes into the bedroom, make the duvet cover from canvas and tie it closed with grommets and cotton rope. Space the grommets as directed for the ribbon placement. Lace 18" lengths of cotton rope though each pair of grommets. Tie the rope ends together in a square knot. To keep the rope ends from fraying, bind each with sewing thread and apply ravel preventer to the cut ends.

materials

54"-wide decorator fabric
54"-wide lining fabric
2"-wide grosgrain ribbon

sewing tools

Sewing machine
Iron and ironing board
Vanishing fabric marker
Pins
Needle and thread
Scissors
Tape measure
Liquid ravel preventer

skill level: beginner
time required: 1 day

fabric chart

Fabric chart estimates are for solid fabrics. Purchase additional yardage to match pattern repeats.

	Lining	18" Drop	14" Drop
Twin	2¼ yards	4 yards	3¼ yards
Full	2¼ yards	5¼ yards	4¼ yards
Queen	4¾ yards	5¼ yards	4¼ yards
King	4¾ yards	5¼ yards	4¼ yards
California king	4¾ yards	5¼ yards	4¼ yards

1 The platform cover (which covers the box springs) is cut from lining fabric. For a twin-size bed, cut one 39×76½" panel. For a full-size bed, cut one 54×76½" panel. For a queen-size bed, cut three 21×81½" panels. For a king-size bed, cut three 26½×81½" panels. For a California king-size bed, cut three 25×85½" panels.

2 For queen-, king-, and California king-size beds, join the panels with flat-fell seams (Figure 1). Edgestitch close to the folded edge of the seam allowance.

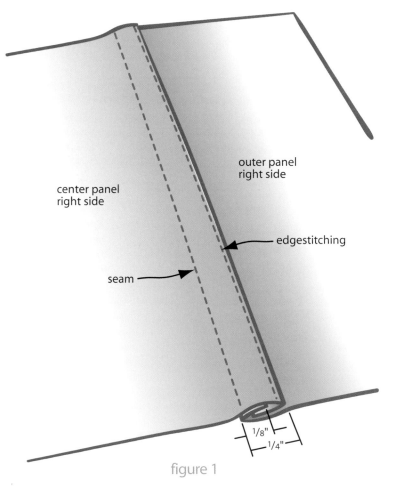

center panel
right side

outer panel
right side

edgestitching

seam

1/8"
1/4"

figure 1

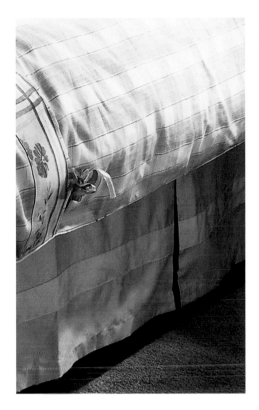

3 Place the lining panel over the box springs, allowing 1" at the top edge and ½" on the other edges. Pin the panel to the box springs temporarily. Measure the bed skirt drop from the surface of the box springs to the floor and add 2½". For the bed skirt, cut panels to this width and to the following lengths. Also cut the ribbon to the panel skirt lengths provided.

Twin-size bed: Cut five skirt panels 42" long and four insert panels 24" long.

Full-size bed: Cut two skirt panels 31" long, four skirt panels 42" long, and five insert panels 24" long.

Queen-size bed: Cut two skirt panels 34" long, four skirt panels 44" long, and five insert panels 24" long.

King-size bed: Cut two skirt panels 42" long, four skirt panels 44" long, and five insert panels 24" long.

California king-size bed: Cut two skirt panels 40" long, four skirt panels 46" long, and five insert panels 24" long.

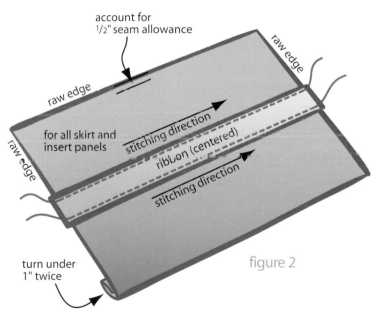

account for ½" seam allowance

raw edge

raw edge

raw edge

for all skirt and insert panels

stitching direction

ribbon (centered)

stitching direction

turn under 1" twice

figure 2

4 On each skirt and insert panel, press under one long edge 1" twice for the hem. Allowing a ½" seam allowance on the remaining long edge, center and pin the ribbon lengthwise on each panel. Edgestitch the ribbon in place, stitching each edge in the same direction to avoid puckering (Figure 2). Open the second fold in the hem edge of each skirt panel. Turn the narrow ends of the panels under 1" and press. Refold the lower edge. Turn under each short end 1" again and press. Edgestitch close to the folded edges of all hems.

panel bed skirt continued

5 With right sides together and raw edges aligned, arrange the skirt panels on the lining panel on the box springs (Figure 3). Leave a 1" allowance at the head end of the lining panel. Each side of the bed will have two panels, except for the foot of the twin-size bed, which has one. Pin the panels to the lining.

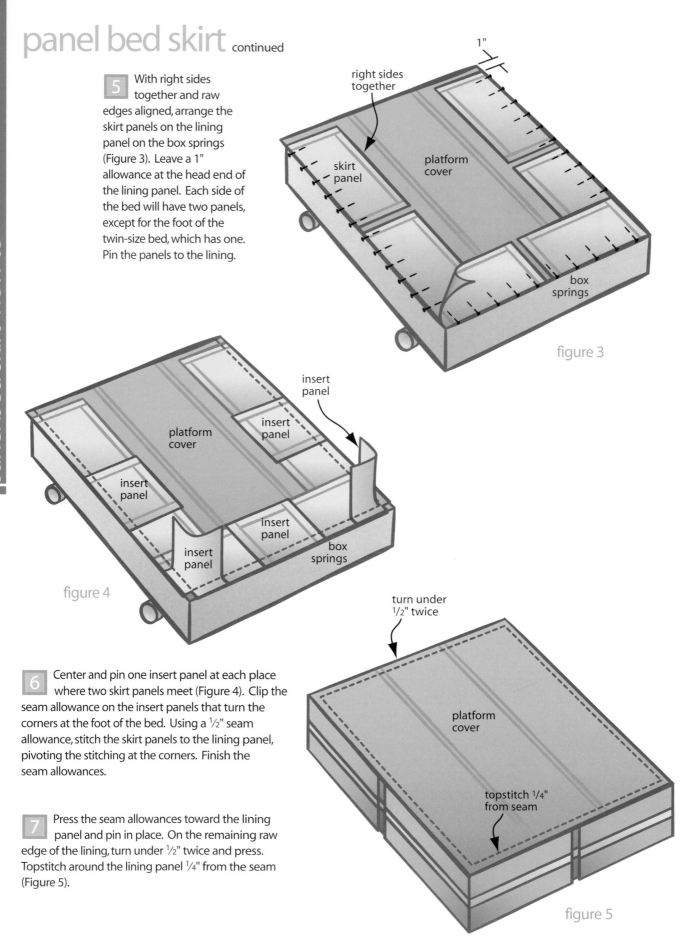

1"

right sides together

right sides together

skirt panel

platform cover

box springs

figure 3

platform cover

insert panel

insert panel

insert panel

insert panel

insert panel

box springs

figure 4

turn under ¹/₂" twice

platform cover

topstitch ¹/₄" from seam

figure 5

6 Center and pin one insert panel at each place where two skirt panels meet (Figure 4). Clip the seam allowance on the insert panels that turn the corners at the foot of the bed. Using a ¹/₂" seam allowance, stitch the skirt panels to the lining panel, pivoting the stitching at the corners. Finish the seam allowances.

7 Press the seam allowances toward the lining panel and pin in place. On the remaining raw edge of the lining, turn under ¹/₂" twice and press. Topstitch around the lining panel ¹/₄" from the seam (Figure 5).

folding screen

To make a simple decorative screen, you will need a wooden or metal folding screen, fabric, thread to match, large grommets and a grommet tool, and coordinating ribbon.

1. Cut the fabric to fit the screen openings, adding 3" at the top and bottom and 1" at each side. Fold all raw edges under, then fold again, making a 1½" hem at the top and bottom and ½" hem on each side. Topstitch the hems in place.

2. Insert grommets evenly across the top and bottom edges, centering them in the hems.

3. Tie the panels to the screen crossbars with ribbon. Let the bottom edges float freely or stretch the fabric panel tightly and tie them in place.

pillow panel

1 Customize a purchased pillow with leftover fabric from other bedroom sewing projects, as shown on page 135. Cut a panel from fabric, leaving a $1/2$" seam allowance on each edge. Turn under the allowance and press. Whipstitch the panel to the pillow front.

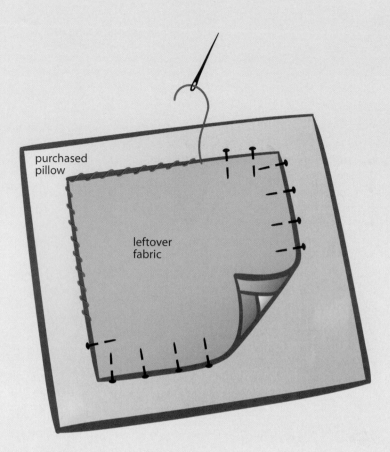

purchased pillow

leftover fabric

beribboned bed pillow
To complete the custom bed ensemble, add ribbons to the edges of ordinary pillowcases, like those on page 135. You'll need $1^{1}/_{8}$ yards of ribbon to trim a standard pillowcase with one row of ribbon.

1 Measure and mark the ribbon placement lines around the hem end of the pillowcase. Pin the ribbons to the lines, positioning the ends at the pillowcase seam. Overlap the ends, turning under the end of the top ribbon. Edgestitch each side of the ribbons, sewing in the same direction to prevent puckering.

2 For a sumptuous look, double-case each pillow. Insert the pillow into the first case. Fold the pillowcase opening over to one side of the pillow. Insert the folded end into a second pillowcase. The bottom of the inner case will show through the opened end of the outer case.

fabric-trimmed pillowcase

1 Sew a cuff of decorator fabric to the open end of a purchased pillowcase (Figure 1). Choose fabrics carefully—the decorator fabric should be similar in weight to the pillowcase. Because decorator fabrics generally require dry cleaning, use this technique for display pillows rather than those you intend to sleep on.

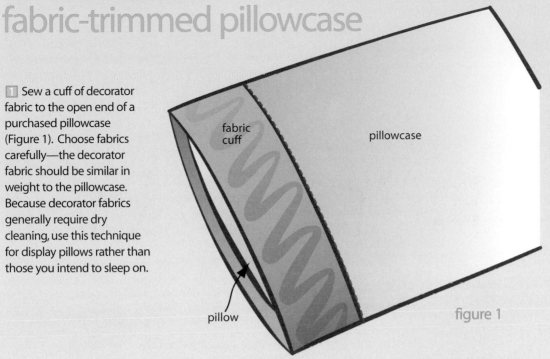

fabric cuff

pillowcase

pillow

figure 1

2 Cut an 11×42" strip from fabric. With right sides together and raw edges aligned, pin the narrow ends together, forming a loop. Use a $1/2$" seam allowance to stitch the short edges together. Press the seam open. Turn under $1/2$" on one long edge and press.

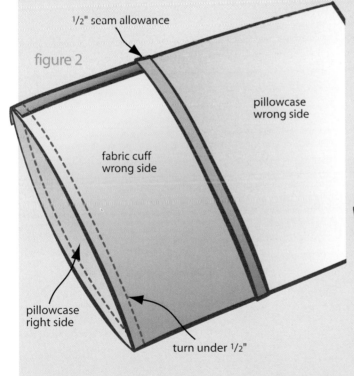

$1/2$" seam allowance

figure 2

pillowcase wrong side

fabric cuff wrong side

pillowcase right side

turn under $1/2$"

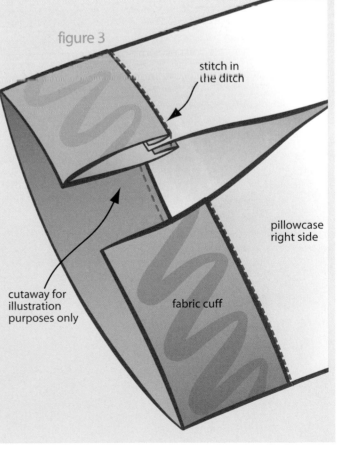

figure 3

stitch in the ditch

pillowcase right side

cutaway for illustration purposes only

fabric cuff

3 Cut the fabric cuff from the pillowcase opening. Turn the pillowcase wrong side out. Pin the fabric loop inside the pillowcase with the right sides facing and raw edges aligned. Stitch together using a $1/2$" seam allowance. Open out the fabric cuff. Press the seam allowance toward the cuff (Figure 2).

4 Turn up the folded edge of the cuff to overlap the seam by $1/8$" and pin in place. Turn the pillowcase right side out and stitch in-the-ditch (Figure 3). Press the cuff.

For decorating romance, it's hard to surpass a canopy: During the day it is a comfortable getaway for lounging, and at night it cloaks the bed in a tent of privacy. To carry this rich feel throughout the room, create a bedspread that echoes the canopy lines, as well as sheer, draped swags for the windows and bolster pillows that provide firm support.

european elegance

Crowning a daybed with a wall-hung swag creates Old World elegance and comfort. To re-create the treatment, position a twin bed on a metal frame along the wall and attach identical headboards to each end of the frame. Cover the bed with a unique valanced bedspread that can be quilted.

To continue the elegant theme, proportion bolster pillows to fit the bed. For a daybed, use a cushion at least 9 inches in diameter and as long as the bed is deep. Finish the bolster ends with deeply inset buttons for a formal look.

To dress the windows, try roller blinds, which offer tailored and traditional styling along with the ease of no-sew construction. Fusible tapes take the place of needle and thread in this project. The blind, named for its form, has a lower edge that rolls up when you pull the cords, which are similar to those in Roman shades. This is the reverse of an old-fashioned roller blind, which snaps in a roll at the top.

The semitranslucence of unlined cotton fabric makes it a fresh choice for a blind, bringing an airy look to a room. To carry out the breezy feeling, create knotted swags from a sheer fabric that coordinates with the blinds.

materials

9½ yards of 54"-wide
  decorator fabric
7 yards of 54"-wide
  complementary fabric
Dinner plate
Mounting pole (see page 142)

tools

Electric drill and drill bits
Wall anchors
Wood screws
Double-sided carpet tape
Rope or heavy twine

sewing tools

Sewing machine
Iron and ironing board
Vanishing fabric marker
Pins
Needle and thread
Scissors
Tape measure
Liquid ravel preventer

skill level: intermediate
time required: 2 days

note Yardage estimates are based on a room with a 9-foot ceiling. The canopy is designed to drape over panels at the ends of a twin-size bed and drop to the floor. Purchase additional fabric to match pattern repeats.

1 Following the manufacturer's instructions, install the canopy pole just below the crown molding or 2" below the ceiling. Drape a length of rope or heavy twine over the pole and over each end of the bed to the floor (Figure 1). Adjust the drape to determine the most pleasing line of the canopy. Measure the rope length and add 1". Cut one piece each from the decorator and complementary fabrics to this measured length. Trim away the selvages.

2 To plan the scallop trim, measure the diameter of the dinner plate and subtract 1". Divide this number into the canopy length to determine the number of scallops. Fold the canopy fabric in half with right sides together and raw edges aligned. Using the vanishing fabric marker and the dinner plate as a template, draw enough circles on the folded fabric to equal half the number of scallops. Pin the fabric layers together in the center of each circle. Cut out the circles.

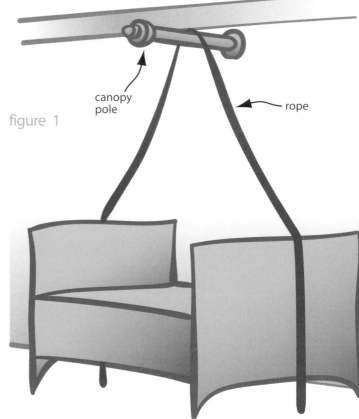

canopy pole

rope

figure 1

figure 2

½" seam allowance

3 Using a ½" seam allowance, stitch around each pair of circles (Figure 2). Cut each stitched circle in half. Notch and grade the seam allowance around the curve. Press the seams open, then turn each half-circle right side out. Place the seams on edge and press flat.

figure 3

4 Mark the exact center of the long front edge of the canopy panel. Place a scallop on each side of the mark and pin in place, right sides facing, and scallop edges together. Pin the scallops along the front edge, allowing room for a ¹/₂" seam allowance at each end of the panel. Baste the scallops to the panel.

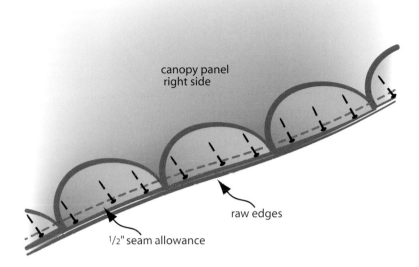

canopy panel right side

raw edges

¹/₂" seam allowance

figure 4

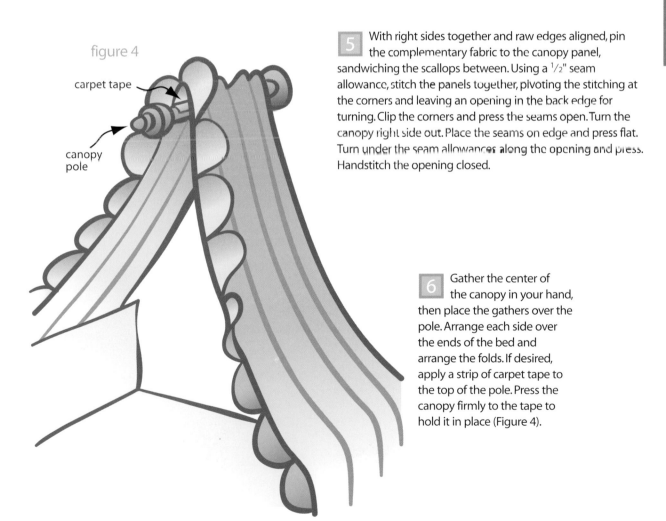

carpet tape

canopy pole

5 With right sides together and raw edges aligned, pin the complementary fabric to the canopy panel, sandwiching the scallops between. Using a ¹/₂" seam allowance, stitch the panels together, pivoting the stitching at the corners and leaving an opening in the back edge for turning. Clip the corners and press the seams open. Turn the canopy right side out. Place the seams on edge and press flat. Turn under the seam allowances along the opening and press. Handstitch the opening closed.

6 Gather the center of the canopy in your hand, then place the gathers over the pole. Arrange each side over the ends of the bed and arrange the folds. If desired, apply a strip of carpet tape to the top of the pole. Press the canopy firmly to the tape to hold it in place (Figure 4).

decorating projects • 141

materials

8"- to 10"-diameter wood
  plaque with routed edges
³/₄" galvanized floor flange
³/₄×12" galvanized nipple
  (steel pipe with threaded
  ends)
³/₄"-diameter wood dowel,
  20" long
Finial with dowel screw or
  hanger bolt
10 (³/₄") wood screws
8 (1¹/₂") wood screws
Wall anchors

tools

Screwdriver
Electric drill and drill bits
Paint

skill level: beginner
time required: ³/₄ day

Look for a mounting pole at fabric centers, or substitute a swing-arm drapery rod for the pole and finial. Shop for a vintage swing-arm drapery rod at antiques stores or flea markets, or look for a new one at specialty stores that carry a wide selection of drapery hardware. To assemble a pole similar to the one shown on page 138, use materials from a home improvement center.

1 Place the flange on the center front of the wood plaque (Figure 1). Mark screw holes on the plaque and drill a pilot hole at each mark. Attach the flange with ³/₄" wood screws. Mark four Xs on the plaque for attachment to the wall.

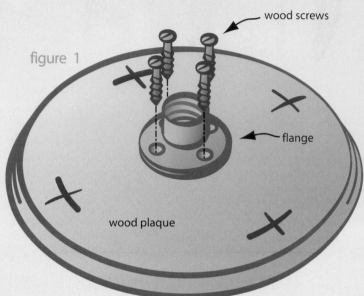

figure 1

wood screws

flange

wood plaque

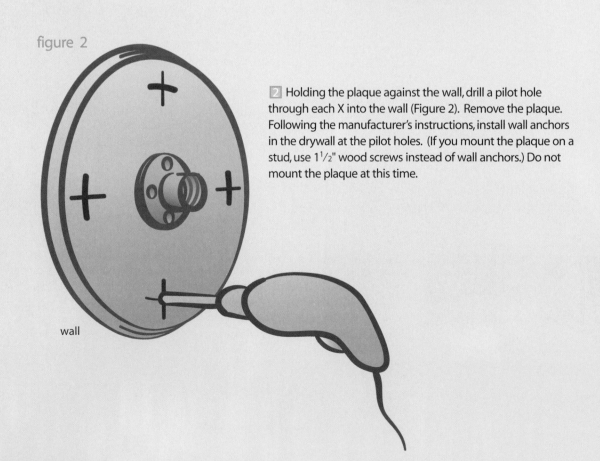

figure 2

2 Holding the plaque against the wall, drill a pilot hole through each X into the wall (Figure 2). Remove the plaque. Following the manufacturer's instructions, install wall anchors in the drywall at the pilot holes. (If you mount the plaque on a stud, use 1¹/₂" wood screws instead of wall anchors.) Do not mount the plaque at this time.

wall

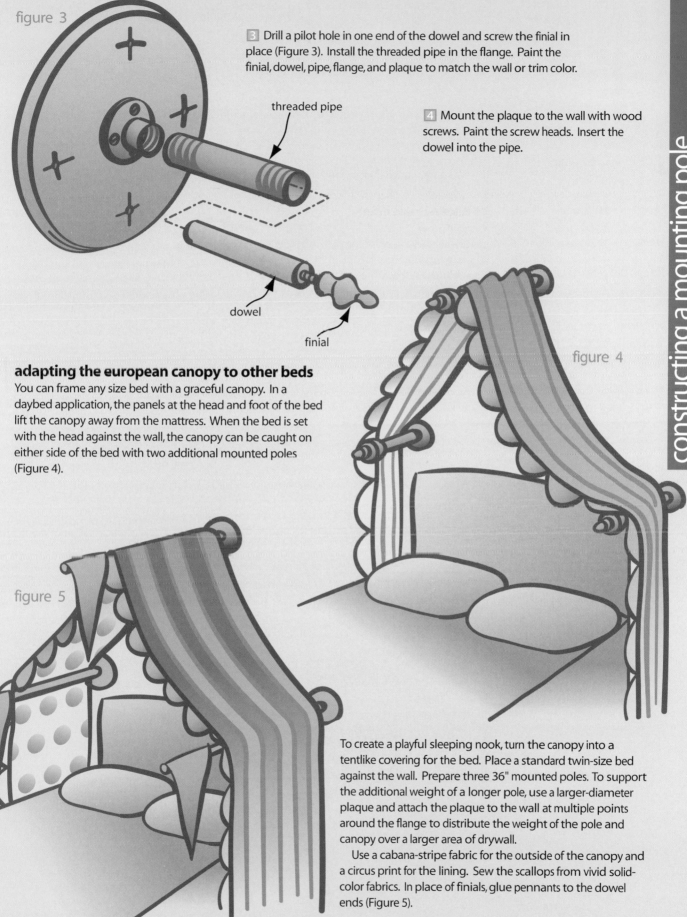

figure 3

3 Drill a pilot hole in one end of the dowel and screw the finial in place (Figure 3). Install the threaded pipe in the flange. Paint the finial, dowel, pipe, flange, and plaque to match the wall or trim color.

threaded pipe

4 Mount the plaque to the wall with wood screws. Paint the screw heads. Insert the dowel into the pipe.

dowel

finial

figure 4

adapting the european canopy to other beds

You can frame any size bed with a graceful canopy. In a daybed application, the panels at the head and foot of the bed lift the canopy away from the mattress. When the bed is set with the head against the wall, the canopy can be caught on either side of the bed with two additional mounted poles (Figure 4).

figure 5

To create a playful sleeping nook, turn the canopy into a tentlike covering for the bed. Place a standard twin-size bed against the wall. Prepare three 36" mounted poles. To support the additional weight of a longer pole, use a larger-diameter plaque and attach the plaque to the wall at multiple points around the flange to distribute the weight of the pole and canopy over a larger area of drywall.

Use a cabana-stripe fabric for the outside of the canopy and a circus print for the lining. Sew the scallops from vivid solid-color fabrics. In place of finials, glue pennants to the dowel ends (Figure 5).

materials

5³/₄ yards 54"-wide
  decorator fabric*
5³/₄ yards 54"-wide
  lining fabric*
2¹/₂ yards 54"-wide backing
  fabric (if making a quilted
  bedspread)*
Cotton batting or low-loft
  polyester batting (if making
  a quilted bedspread)*
Dinner plate
6¹/₂ yards of cording

sewing tools

Sewing machine
Iron and ironing board
Vanishing fabric marker
Pins
Needle and thread
Scissors
Tape measure
Liquid ravel preventer
Zipper foot

skill level: intermediate
time required: 2 days
*Yardage and instructions are
  for a twin-size daybed.

1 For an unquilted bedspread, cut a 39×76" top panel from decorator fabric and a matching panel from lining fabric. For a quilted bedspread, cut the top, batting, and backing to measure 48×85" and cut a lining 39×76". Sandwich the batting between the backing and the top. Pin, then loosely hand-baste, the layers together. Machine- or hand-quilt through all layers in the desired pattern (see page 148). Trim the quilted panel to 39×76".

2 For the length of the front scalloped valance panel, measure the depth of the mattress and add 4". Cut one 63" band and one 72" band to this measurement from decorator fabric. Cut matching bands from lining fabric. Place the front valance bands together with right sides facing, aligning the long raw edges and one short edge. Stitch the bands together along the short edge using a ¹/₂" seam allowance. Press the seam open. Repeat for the lining bands.

3 For the length of the back and side valances, measure the depth of the mattress and add 2". Cut two 47¹/₂" side bands and one 76" back band to this measurement from decorator fabric. Cut matching bands from lining fabric. With right sides together and raw edges aligned, pin a lining to one side valance. Stitch the short ends together using a ¹/₂" seam allowance. Press the seams open. Place the seams on edge and pin the seam allowances to face the center of the panel. Stitch across the bottom edge. Press the seam open as far as possible into the corners. Turn the panel right side out. Place the seam on edge and press flat. Repeat for the remaining side and back valances.

4 With right sides together and raw edges aligned, pin the front valance to the front valance lining. Using a ¹/₂" seam allowance, baste the panels together on the short edges and the bottom edge. To prepare the panel for pleats, press under 4¹/₂" on each short edge. Measure and mark 17 intervals, each 8¹/₂", across the width of the fabric (Figure 1). Mark the intervals with pins at the top and bottom of the panel. If necessary, adjust the width of the intervals to fit 17 sections into the available width. With the vanishing fabric marker, draw lines at each segment from the top to the bottom of the panel. Open out the folded edges.

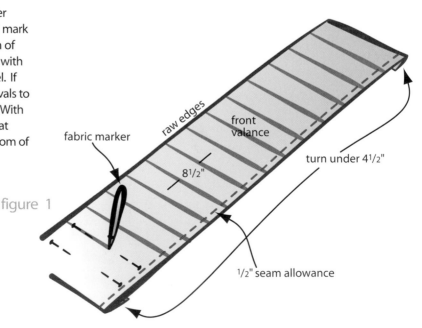

figure 1

fabric marker

raw edges

front valance

8¹/₂"

turn under 4¹/₂"

¹/₂" seam allowance

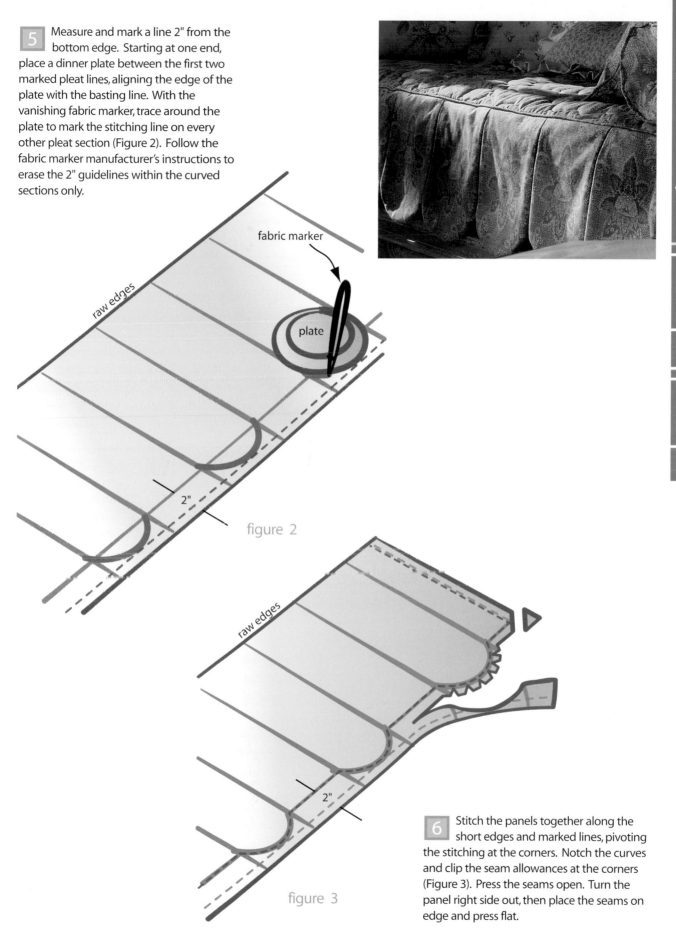

5 Measure and mark a line 2" from the bottom edge. Starting at one end, place a dinner plate between the first two marked pleat lines, aligning the edge of the plate with the basting line. With the vanishing fabric marker, trace around the plate to mark the stitching line on every other pleat section (Figure 2). Follow the fabric marker manufacturer's instructions to erase the 2" guidelines within the curved sections only.

fabric marker

raw edges

plate

2"

figure 2

raw edges

2"

figure 3

6 Stitch the panels together along the short edges and marked lines, pivoting the stitching at the corners. Notch the curves and clip the seam allowances at the corners (Figure 3). Press the seams open. Turn the panel right side out, then place the seams on edge and press flat.

valanced bedspread continued

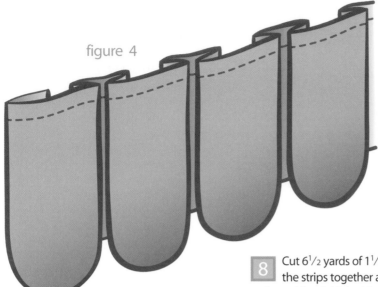

figure 4

7 Working with one pair of scallops at a time, bring the scallops together to meet at the center of the intervening pleat (Figure 4). Pin the pleats in place, then baste across the top of the valance panel, using a $1/2$" seam allowance.

8 Cut $6^1/2$ yards of $1^1/2$"-wide bias strips from the remaining fabric. Stitch the strips together at the short ends to make a continuous length. To make welting, fold the bias strip with wrong sides facing around the cording, matching the long raw edges. Using the zipper foot, baste close to the cording.

9 Pin the welting to the right side of the top panel (from Step 1), aligning the raw edges and beginning at the center on one short side. Clip the welting seam allowance at the corners. Where the welting ends meet, overlap them 1" and cut the welting. To make a neat joining, remove a few stitches from the welting fabric cover at each end. Fold back the fabric, cut the cord ends to meet, and refold the fabric over the cording, turning under the raw edges. Using the zipper foot, baste the welting to the front panel, pivoting the stitching at the corners.

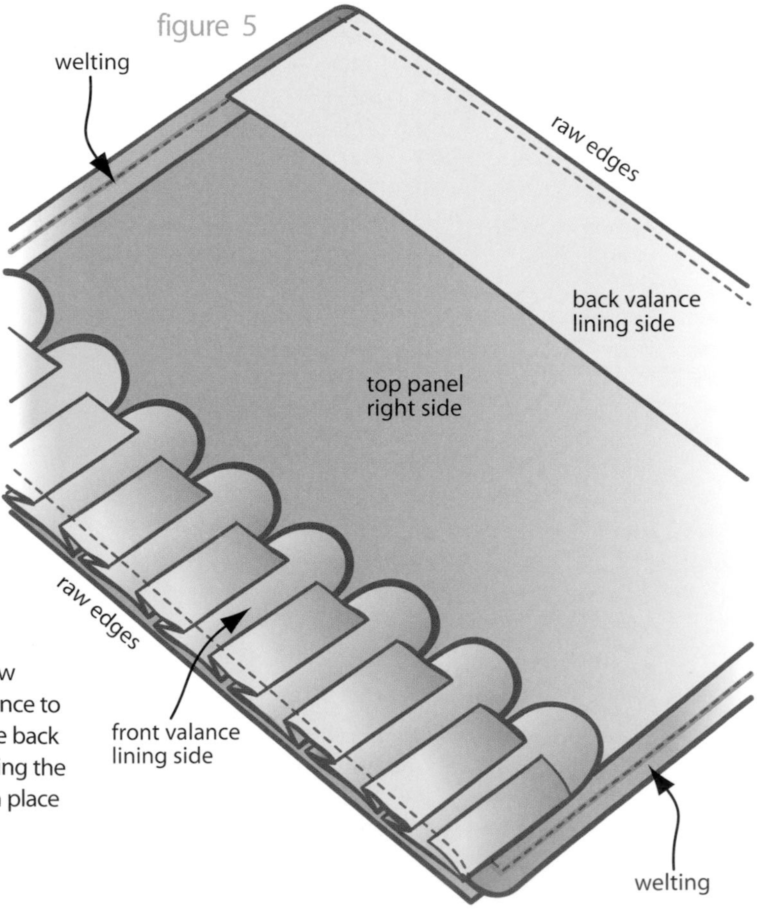

10 With right sides together and raw edges aligned, pin the front valance to one long edge of the top panel; pin the back valance to the opposite long edge. Using the zipper foot, baste the valance panels in place (Figure 5).

figure 5

welting

raw edges

back valance lining side

top panel right side

raw edges

front valance lining side

welting

valanced bedspread how to

11 With right sides together and raw edges aligned, pin one side valance panel to each side of the top panel, wrapping the excess side valance around the front corners (Figure 6). Clip the seam allowance on each side valance at the front corner. Using the zipper foot, baste each side valance panel to the top panel, avoiding the scallops in the side seam.

figure 6

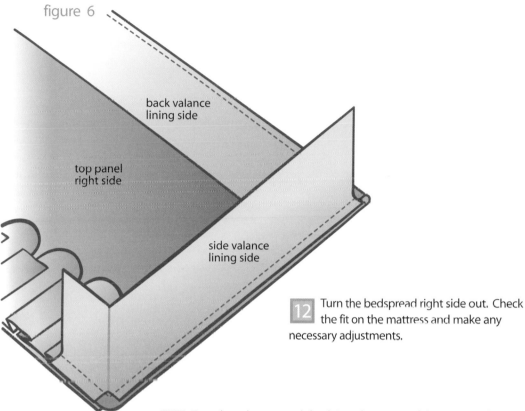

back valance
lining side

top panel
right side

side valance
lining side

12 Turn the bedspread right side out. Check the fit on the mattress and make any necessary adjustments.

13 Turn the valance panels back into the center of the top panel, smoothing them as flat as possible. Place the lining, facedown, over the top panel, aligning raw edges. Pin in place. Using the zipper foot, stitch the lining to the top panel, pivoting the stitching at the corners and leaving an opening at the side for turning. Press the seam open. Grade the seam allowances. Turn the bedspread right side out through the opening. Press all seams, turning under the seam allowance along the opening at the same time. Hand-stitch the opening closed.

MAKING WELTING FROM BIAS STRIPS

Cut bias strips as directed in each individual project. With right sides facing, stitch the strips together at the short ends to make a continuous length. To keep seams smooth and to minimize bulk, place the bias strips at a 90-degree angle and, with right sides together, stitch with the straight grain. Press seams open and trim. To make welting, fold the bias strips around the cording with wrong sides facing and matching the long raw edges. Using a zipper foot and a long continuous stitch length, baste close to the cording.

materials

Top panel
Cotton batting or low-loft
  polyester batting
Backing panel
1"-long nickel-plated
  safety pins

sewing tools

Sewing machine
Monofilament polyester
  or nylon machine-
  quilting thread
Sewing thread
Vanishing fabric marker
Walking foot
Bulldog clips or clothespins

skill level: varies with
  quilting design
time required: varies
  with quilting design

Add interest to the top panel of the valanced bedspread with quilting. If you are experienced with machine quilting, incorporate curves into the panel design with free-motion quilting. If you are a beginner, start with straight-line patterns, such as a grid of diamonds or squares. Machine quilting will be more successful if you use a walking foot (or even-feed foot), a specially designed sewing machine attachment. (Check with quilting shops and fabric stores for this attachment, or contact the manufacturer of your sewing machine.) This foot moves all fabric layers under the needle at the same rate. In straight-line quilting, the walking foot reduces puckers and wrinkles.

1 Draw a quilting pattern on the top panel with the vanishing fabric marker. Layer the backing, batting, and top panel with raw edges aligned (Figure 1). Begin at the center of the panel and work toward the outside edges, using safety pins to hold the layers together and placing the pins in a grid and 4" to 6" apart.

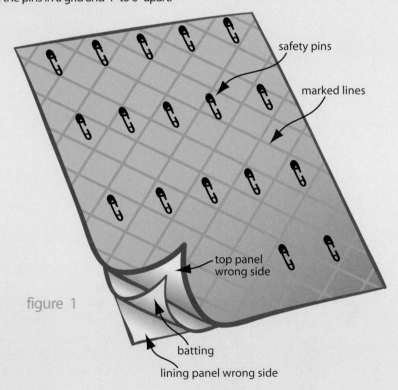

safety pins

marked lines

top panel
wrong side

figure 1

batting

lining panel wrong side

2 With the walking foot attached to the sewing machine, thread the needle with quilting thread. Wind the bobbin with regular sewing thread. Lengthen the stitch length to six to eight stitches per inch. Practice quilting on test fabrics first to become comfortable with the walking foot and to test your pattern design.

3 Roll each short end of the sandwiched unit toward the center and secure with a pair of clips or clothespins (Figure 2). *Note: Because the quilting pattern shown in Figure 2 is a diagonal design, the panel is rolled from opposing corners.* Begin quilting at the center of the panel. As you work, roll fabric to the left of the needle and unroll fabric on the right. Remove the safety pins as you quilt.

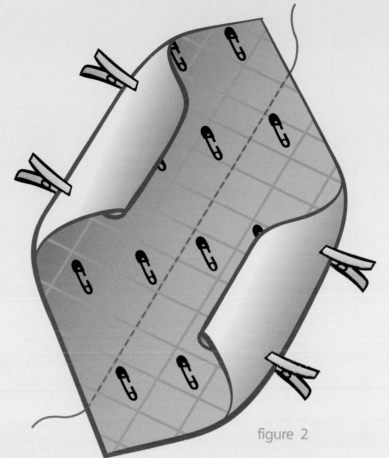

figure 2

4 To secure the thread at the beginning of each line of stitching, shorten the stitch length as much as possible. Make several tiny stitches. Reset the stitch length at six to eight stitches per inch. Anchor threads at the end of the stitching line in the same way (Figure 3)

figure 3

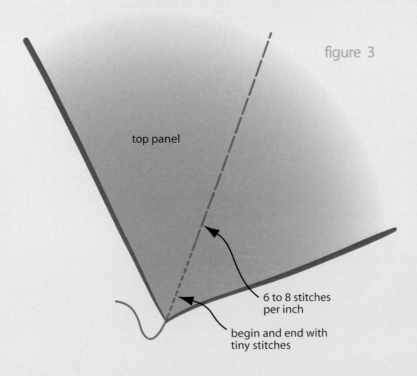

top panel

6 to 8 stitches per inch

begin and end with tiny stitches

5 Reroll the panel as described in Step 3, then turn the panel to stitch the opposite end. For quilting in a lengthwise direction, roll the quilt from the long edges and secure each roll with at least two clips or clothespins. When you are finished quilting, trim the thread ends and trim the edges of the top panel to the required size.

roller blind

1 This blind mounts inside the window frame. Measure the height and width of the window inside the frame. To determine yardage for one blind, add 2" to the width and 10" to the length. For Roman blind cord yardage, multiply 7 times the measured height of the window. The 1×2 board (the mounting board) and the dowel (to weight the lower edge of the blind) must equal the window width.

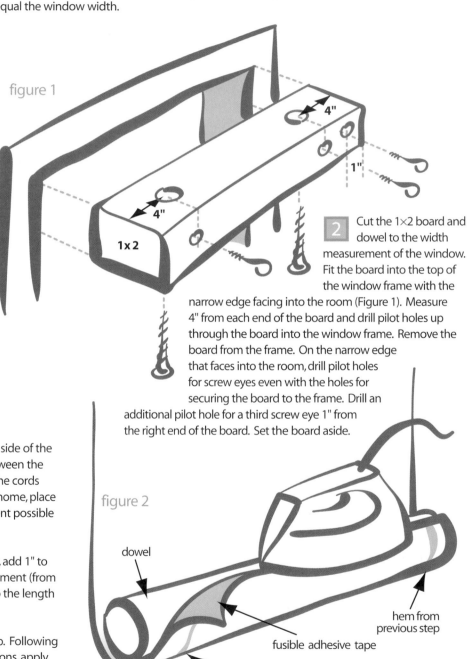

figure 1

1 x 2

2 Cut the 1×2 board and dowel to the width measurement of the window. Fit the board into the top of the window frame with the narrow edge facing into the room (Figure 1). Measure 4" from each end of the board and drill pilot holes up through the board into the window frame. Remove the board from the frame. On the narrow edge that faces into the room, drill pilot holes for screw eyes even with the holes for securing the board to the frame. Drill an additional pilot hole for a third screw eye 1" from the right end of the board. Set the board aside.

3 Install the cleat on the right side of the window frame midway between the top and bottom. The cleat holds the cords taut (if you have small children at home, place the cleat closer to the top to prevent possible entanglement with the cords).

4 For the cut size of the fabric, add 1" to the window width measurement (from Step 1) for the side hems and 8" to the length measurement; cut the fabric.

5 Lay the fabric wrong side up. Following the manufacturer's instructions, apply the fusible adhesive tape along each side edge of the fabric. Remove the paper backing. Fold each edge by the width of the fusible tape to the wrong side and finger-press. Follow the manufacturer's instructions to fuse the hems in place. Apply one strip of fusible adhesive tape to the top edge of the fabric, but do not remove the paper backing.

figure 2

dowel

hem from
previous step

fusible adhesive tape

hem from
previous step

6 Lay the fabric right side up. Apply two strips of fusible adhesive tape side-by-side to the bottom edge of the fabric. Remove the paper backing. Center the dowel on the edge of the fabric over the fusible surface. Begin rolling the dowel inside the lower edge of the fabric. Fuse the fabric to the dowel as you roll (Figure 2).

7 Remove the paper backing from the fusible adhesive tape at the top edge of the fabric. Center the narrow edge of the board with the pilot holes on the fusible surface. Fuse the fabric to the board. Wrap the fabric smoothly around the board, overlapping the fused edge (Figure 3). Punch a small hole through the fabric into each pilot hole.

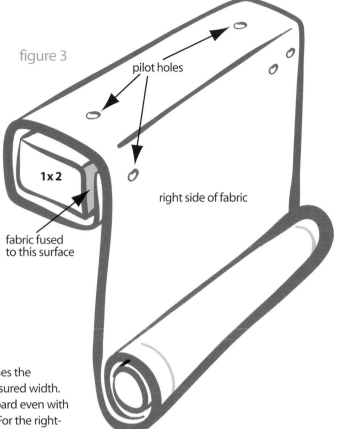

figure 3

pilot holes

1 x 2

right side of fabric

fabric fused
to this surface

8 For the left-hand cord, cut a length 3 times the measured window length plus the measured width. Staple one end of the cord to the top of the board even with the pilot hole for the left screw eye (Figure 4). For the right-hand cord, use the remaining length and staple one end to the top of the board even with the pilot hole that is 4" from the right end of the board.

9 Install the board in the top of the window frame with wood screws. Install screw eyes in the front. Take each cord down the back of the blind, under the dowel at the bottom edge to the front of the blind and through the screw eye at the top. Thread both cords through the extreme right screw eye (Figure 4). Begin rolling the blind from the dowel edge. Pull the cord snugly along the blind. Trim the cord ends even. To raise the blind, gently pull the cords together, causing the fabric to continue rolling around the dowel. Secure the cords to the cleat with a figure-eight motion.

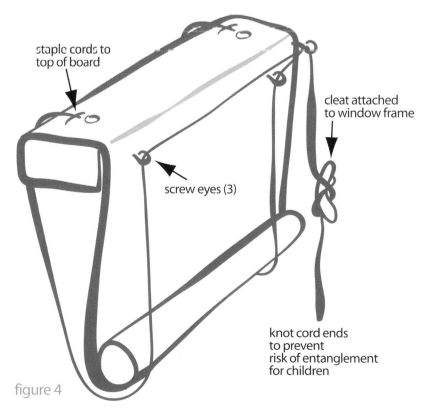

staple cords to
top of board

cleat attached
to window frame

screw eyes (3)

knot cord ends
to prevent
risk of entanglement
for children

figure 4

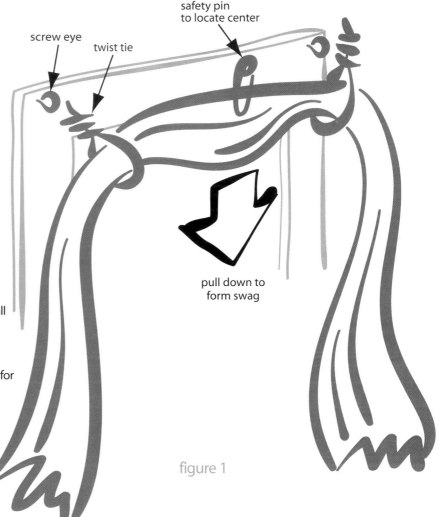

materials

54"-wide decorator fabric*
$\frac{7}{8}$"-wide paper-backed
   fusible adhesive tape*
Covered wire twist ties (for
   kitchen or trash bags)
2 screw eyes

tools

Electric drill and drill bits

sewing tools

Iron and ironing board
Pressing cloth
Scissors
Tape measure
Large safety pins
Sewing machine

skill level: beginner
time required: $\frac{1}{2}$ day

*Purchase materials after
taking measurements.

knotted swag

1 Mount this swag with screw hooks directly into the window frame. One continuous length of fabric spans the top of the window, knots at each corner, and falls to the floor; twist ties hold the knots. Measure the height from the top of the window frame to the floor and the window width. For the swag, you need a length of 54"-wide fabric two times the height plus the width plus an additional yard for the knots and puddles.

safety pin
to locate center

screw eye

twist tie

pull down to
form swag

figure 1

2 Drill pilot holes in the window molding at each top corner. Install one screw eye in each hole (Figure 1).

3 Trim the selvage edges from the fabric. Test a small scrap of fabric for use with fusible adhesive. If the fabric is compatible, fuse the hems in place. Lay the fabric wrong side up. Following the manufacturer's instructions, apply fusible adhesive tape to the long edges of the fabric. Remove the paper backing. Fold each edge to the wrong side by the width of the fusible surface and finger-press. Fuse the hems in place. Repeat to fuse the hems on each short edge of the fabric. If the fabric cannot be fused, machine stitch $\frac{1}{2}$" from each raw edge of the fabric. Turn the raw edge to the wrong side along the stitches. Finger-press. Turn again to make a double hem and press with an iron. Machine stitch through all layers close to the first line of stitches.

4 Mark the center of one long edge of the fabric with a large safety pin. Measure one-half the window width on each side of the center mark. Use additional pins to mark these as corners. Holding one marked corner in your hand, loosely fold the width of the fabric back and forth in accordion pleats. Gather the pleats with a twist tie. Repeat at the opposite marked corner. Remove the pins at the corners, but leave the center pin for reference.

5 Place the fabric at the window by hanging the twist ties on the screw eyes. Gently pull the top edge of the fabric outward to make the top of the drape taut. Redress the pleats along the center section as needed. Gently pull down the lower edge of the fabric to make the swag.

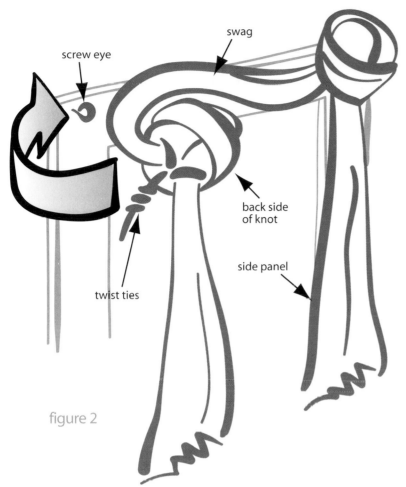

figure 2

6 Remove the fabric from the window. Make a knot (see box below) beyond each twist tie. Both the swag center and side panel will appear to come from the back of the knot.

7 Return the swag to the window to check for fit. Adjust each knot as needed. Gather the fabric for each side panel into a twist tie, hiding the tie behind the knot. To secure the knot, twist the tie with the side panel tie; secure the ties to the screw eyes (Figure 2).

TECHNIQUES MADE EASY

secrets of a great knot Tying a great decorative knot is easy when you take it step by step.

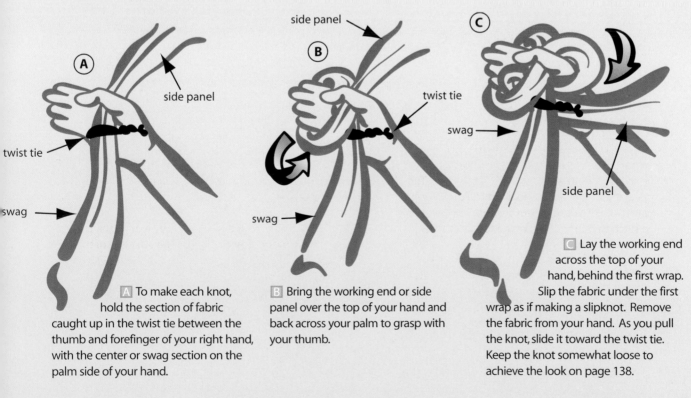

A To make each knot, hold the section of fabric caught up in the twist tie between the thumb and forefinger of your right hand, with the center or swag section on the palm side of your hand.

B Bring the working end or side panel over the top of your hand and back across your palm to grasp with your thumb.

C Lay the working end across the top of your hand, behind the first wrap. Slip the fabric under the first wrap as if making a slipknot. Remove the fabric from your hand. As you pull the knot, slide it toward the twist tie. Keep the knot somewhat loose to achieve the look on page 138.

materials

9×24" upholstery foam
    bolster
High-loft polyester
    upholstery batting
3/4 yard 54"-wide lining fabric
1 3/4 yards 54"-wide
    decorator fabric
6/32" filler cord
Zipper
2 (2") buttons to cover

tools

Electric knife

sewing tools

Sewing machine
Iron and ironing board
Vanishing fabric marker
Pins
Needle and thread
Scissors
Tape measure
Liquid ravel preventer
Zipper foot

skill level: advanced
time required: 8 hours

bolster pillow

1 Cut four 9"-diameter circles and one 25×29" panel from batting. Cut one 25×29" panel from lining.

2 Cut one 25×32" center panel and two 10"-diameter circles for the end panels from fabric. Cut 1 1/2 yards of 1 1/2"-wide bias strips for the welting.

3 To make the welting, fold the bias strip around the filler cord, matching long raw fabric edges. Using the zipper foot and a long stitch length, baste close to the cord, encasing it in the fabric. Pin the welting to the right side of each end panel. With raw edges aligned, clip the seam allowance of the welting to ease it around each circle (Figure 1). Where the welting ends meet, overlap the ends 1". Cut the welting. Remove the stitching from the fabric cover on each end. Unfold the fabric and cut the ends of the cord to meet. Refold one end of the cover over the cord. On the opposite end, turn under the cover 1/2" and refold the fabric around the cord, concealing the raw ends of the fabric. Using the zipper foot and long stitch length, baste the welting to each end panel. Set the end panels aside.

cord

right side
end panel

welting
folded edge

align raw edges

figure 1

4 On the right side of the center panel, place the zipper tab face down, centered, on one 25"-long edge. Align the tape edge of the zipper with the raw edge of the panel. Using the zipper foot, stitch the zipper tape to the fabric. With right sides together and raw edges aligned at the zipper end of the panel, place the lining on the center panel. Using the zipper foot, stitch the lining to the panel, catching the zipper tape in the seam. Press the seam. Turn right side out, placing the zipper on edge. Press flat.

5 Lay the center panel wrong side up. Lift the lining. With raw edges aligned, layer the batting on the wrong side of the panel. Pin the batting to the panel from the right side of the panel. Smooth the lining over the layers (Figure 2).

right side
lining

batting

wrong side
fabric center panel

back side zipper

figure 2

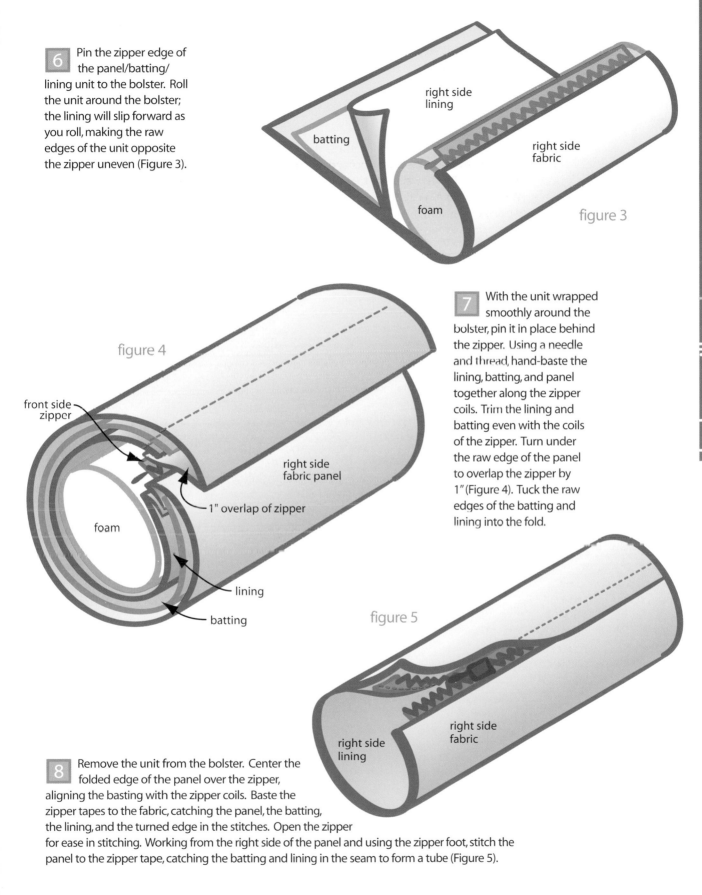

6 Pin the zipper edge of the panel/batting/lining unit to the bolster. Roll the unit around the bolster; the lining will slip forward as you roll, making the raw edges of the unit opposite the zipper uneven (Figure 3).

right side lining

batting

right side fabric

foam

figure 3

figure 4

front side zipper

1" overlap of zipper

foam

right side fabric panel

lining

batting

7 With the unit wrapped smoothly around the bolster, pin it in place behind the zipper. Using a needle and thread, hand-baste the lining, batting, and panel together along the zipper coils. Trim the lining and batting even with the coils of the zipper. Turn under the raw edge of the panel to overlap the zipper by 1" (Figure 4). Tuck the raw edges of the batting and lining into the fold.

figure 5

right side lining

right side fabric

8 Remove the unit from the bolster. Center the folded edge of the panel over the zipper, aligning the basting with the zipper coils. Baste the zipper tapes to the fabric, catching the panel, the batting, the lining, and the turned edge in the stitches. Open the zipper for ease in stitching. Working from the right side of the panel and using the zipper foot, stitch the panel to the zipper tape, catching the batting and lining in the seam to form a tube (Figure 5).

bolster pillow how to

bolster pillow continued

9 Adjust the pressure foot to a lower weight. Using a long stitch length and working with the panel on the top side of the fabric layer, baste $1/2$" from the raw edges on each end of the tube in a continuous line around each end. Turn back the panel and lining. Trim the batting from each seam allowance. Clip the seam allowances of the lining and batting.

10 Open the zipper. With right sides together and raw edges aligned, align the basting in the end panel with the basting in the end of the tube. Pin one end panel to each end of the tube (Figure 6). Return the pressure foot weight to the usual setting. Using the zipper foot and long stitch length, baste the end panels to the tube following the basting lines. Turn the seam right side out to check for puckers in either piece of fabric. Remove the stitches and adjust the seams, if necessary. Using a normal stitch length, restitch each end along the basting. Grade the seam allowances. Press. Turn right side out. Press the seams.

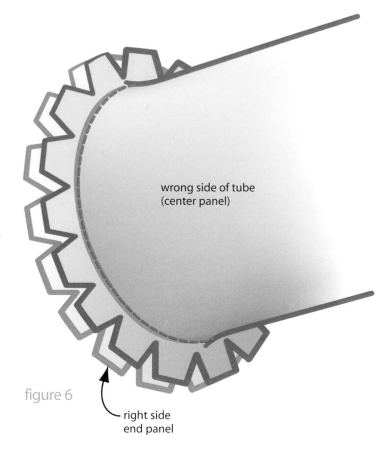

wrong side of tube (center panel)

figure 6

right side end panel

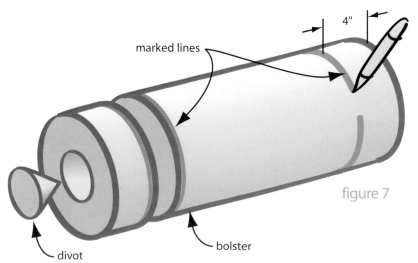

marked lines

divot

bolster

4"

figure 7

11 On the bolster, measure 4" from each end. Using a permanent marker, mark a line around the bolster. Using an electric knife and following the line, cut the ends off the bolster. (The bolster will be reassembled later, and the end pieces will be used to make button-tufted ends.) On each end piece, mark the center. Using an electric knife, cut a cone-shaped divot from the foam at the center mark (Figure 7).

12 On each end piece of the bolster, layer two batting circles. Insert one batting/foam unit into each end of the bolster cover. Following the manufacturer's instructions, cover the two buttons with fabric. Using a tufting needle and doubled buttonhole thread, stitch one button to the center of each end of the bolster cover. Pass the needle through the batting and slice of bolster foam, pulling the button deep into the padding. Use a small piece of fabric folded into quarters to anchor the stitches on the back side of the bolster slice (Figure 8). Knot the thread ends on the back of the bolster slice.

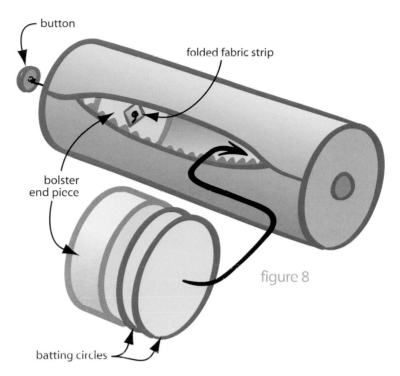

button

folded fabric strip

bolster end piece

batting circles

figure 8

13 Insert the center section of the bolster foam into the cover through the zipper. Align the bolster center with the bolster end slices. Close the zipper.

BOLSTER FORMS

■ Solid foam bolsters are sold through upholstery supply wholesalers. Call on these businesses for the supplies you might need to sew for your home; they often deal directly with individuals.

■ If you are unable to locate a source for a solid bolster, you can create a suitable foam bolster with supplies found at local fabric stores. Foam is generally available in 24" widths. To make a 9×24" bolster, purchase 4 yards of ¹/₂"-thick foam. Beginning at one short edge, roll the foam tightly, keeping the side edges even. Pin the edge of the foam to the roll. Measure the diameter. Reroll, if necessary, to make the bolster smaller or larger. Using a tufting needle or other large needle, make large stitches over the edge into the roll to secure the rolled shape of the bolster (Figure 1).

■ To make the deep-button cushion with this homemade bolster, purchase another yard of ¹/₂"-thick foam and cut two 9"-diameter circles for the end slices.

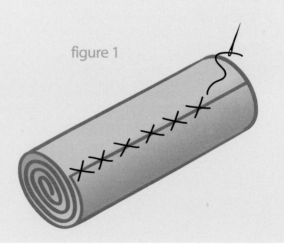

figure 1

Stitching your own pillow coverings lets you choose textures, colors, and patterns that underscore the existing color palette and style in a room. From bold and contemporary to frilly and romantic, pillows define your decorating style.

pillow collection

Pile your bed high with custom-made pillows to create a designer look and a cocoon of comfort. Stacked from back to front on this king-size bed are three standard pillows with gussets, two king-size pillows with flange borders, two 16-inch-square pillows with welt edges (see page 48 for instructions for 18-inch versions), and one 6×16-inch neckroll.

The variety of shapes and sizes underlines a longing for comfort. Use the neckroll for an arm rest, prop a book on an accent pillow, or slip a firm gusset-style cushion behind your back for reading in bed. Suddenly, this comfortable collection becomes a necessity.

The flange-bordered king-size shams have a French-back closure rather than a zipper. This easy-to-construct backing involves two pieces of overlapping fabric—no zippers, buttons, or snaps—and works well on square or rectangular pillows.

gusset pillow

1 To determine the best placement of the fabric design, drape the fabric over the pillow before you cut. Place stripes or plaids symmetrically on each panel and center prominent patterns. For standard-size pillows, cut two 21×27" panels. For queen-size pillows, cut two 21×31" panels. For king-size pillows, cut two 21×37" panels.

2 Cut 6¹/₂ yards of 1¹/₂"-wide bias strips for welting. Stitch the strips together at the short ends to make a continuous length. Fold the bias strip around the cording with wrong sides facing and matching the long raw edges. Using the zipper foot, baste close to the cording to encase it in fabric.

3 From complementary fabric, cut three gusset and two zipper gusset panels. For standard size pillows, cut three 3×27" and two 3×21" panels. For queen-size pillows, cut three 3×31" and two 3×21" panels. For king-size pillows, cut three 3×37" and two 3×21" panels.

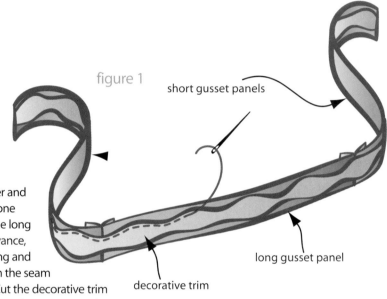

figure 1

short gusset panels

long gusset panel

decorative trim

4 With right sides together and raw edges aligned, pin one short gusset to each end of one long gusset. Using a ¹/₂" seam allowance, stitch the ends together, starting and stopping the stitching ¹/₂" from the seam ends. Press the seams open. Cut the decorative trim to fit the pieced gusset. Apply ravel preventer to the cut ends of the trim. Let dry. Center and hand-stitch the trim on the pieced gusset, taking small, even stitches for a neat application (Figure 1).

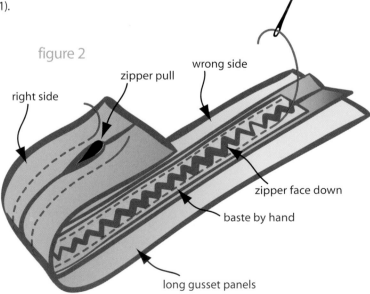

figure 2

right side

zipper pull

wrong side

zipper face down

baste by hand

long gusset panels

5 With right sides facing, place the remaining two long gussets together. Using a 1" seam allowance, baste the gussets together along one long edge. Press the seam open. Center the zipper facedown over the wrong side of the basted seam (Figure 2). Hand-stitch the zipper tapes to the fabric. Turn to the right side and use the zipper foot to stitch the zipper in place, following the manufacturer's instructions for a centered zipper installation. Remove the basting stitches. Trim the strip to 3" wide with the zipper at the center.

6 With right sides together and short edges aligned, pin the decorated gusset to the zippered gusset to make a loop. Using a ½" seam allowance, stitch the ends together, starting and stopping the stitching ½" from each end of the seams.

7 Pin the welting to the right side of the front panel, aligning the raw edges and beginning at the center bottom edge of the panel. Clip the seam allowance at the corners. Where the welting ends meet, overlap the ends 1". Cut the welting and remove the stitching from the fabric cover on each end. Unfold the fabric and cut the cording ends to meet. Refold one end of the cover over the cording. Turn under ½" on the remaining end and refold the fabric around the cording, concealing the raw end of the casing. Using the zipper foot, baste the welting to the front panel, pivoting the stitching at the corners. Baste the welting to the back panel in the same manner.

8 With right sides together and raw edges aligned, pin the gusset to the front panel, placing the gusset seams at the panel corners (Figure 3). Insert the pins on the wrong side of the gusset to sew the seam from that side of the fabric. Using the zipper foot, baste the gusset to the front panel, pivoting the stitching at the corners.

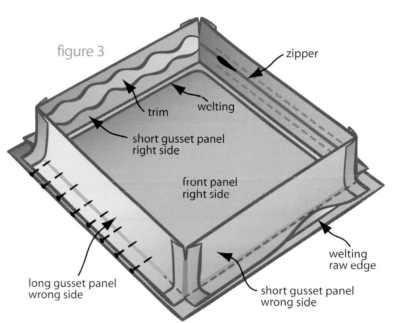

figure 3

zipper
trim
welting
short gusset panel right side
front panel right side
welting raw edge
long gusset panel wrong side
short gusset panel wrong side

9 Open the zipper. With right sides together and raw edges aligned, pin the gusset to the back panel, placing the gusset seams at the panel corners (Figure 4). Insert the pins on the wrong side of the back panel and sew the seam from that side. (This ensures that both sides of the gusset will be stitched in the same direction, minimizing puckering on the finished seam.) Using the zipper foot, baste the gusset to the back panel, pivoting the stitching at the corners.

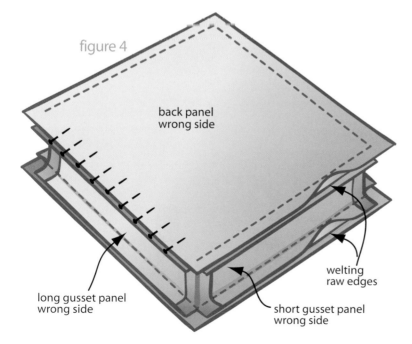

figure 4

back panel wrong side

long gusset panel wrong side
short gusset panel wrong side
welting raw edges

10 Turn the cover right side out. The seams should be smooth and unpuckered. If necessary, remove stitches and rebaste to make each seam smooth. Using a regular stitch length, sew the gusset to the front panel along the basting lines, working with the wrong side of the front panel faceup. Repeat to stitch the gusset to the back panel. Finish the seam allowances. Press the seams.

11 Turn the cover right side out and insert the cushion through the opening. Adjust the cushion to match the top and bottom corners at the welting.

materials

Standard, queen, king, or
 European square bed pillow
54"-wide decorator fabric
3¼ yards of cording with lip

sewing tools

Sewing machine
Iron and ironing board
Vanishing fabric marker
Ruler
Pins
Needle and thread
Scissors
Tape measure
Liquid ravel preventer
Zipper foot

skill level: intermediate
time required: ½ day

fabric chart

Estimates are for solid fabrics. Purchase additional yardage to match pattern repeats.

	Standard	Queen	King	European Square
Yards	2¼	2½	2½	2¼

1 Center any prominent fabric motif on the front panel and place geometric designs symmetrically. Cut panels as follows.

Standard bed pillows: Cut one 22×28" front panel, two 22×20" back panels, four 4×29" flange strips, and four 4×35" flange strips.

Queen bed pillows: Cut one 22×32" front panel, two 22×22" back panels, four 4×29" flange strips, and four 4×39" flange strips.

King bed pillows: Cut one 22×38" front panel, two 22×25" back panels, four 4×29" flange strips, and four 4×45" flange strips.

European square pillows: Cut one 28"-square front panel, two 22×20" back panels, and eight 4×35" flange strips.

2 Working on the right side of the front panel, pin the lip of the cording to the fabric edges, beginning at the center of one edge. Clip the cording lip at the corners and around any curves. Where the cording ends meet, join the ends. Apply liquid ravel preventer to the cut edges. Let dry. Using the zipper foot, baste the cording to the front panel.

3 To make the flange border, lay out two short and two long flange strips to fit the front panel, aligning raw edges in the corners (Figure 1). Place a ruler from the outer corner to the inner corner. Use the vanishing fabric marker to mark a stitching line along the ruler. Mark the upper, then lower, strip. Repeat for the remaining flange strips.

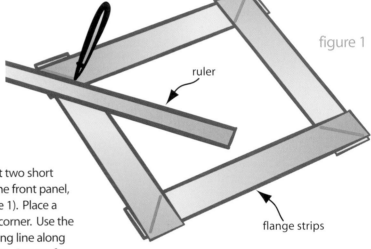

figure 1

ruler

flange strips

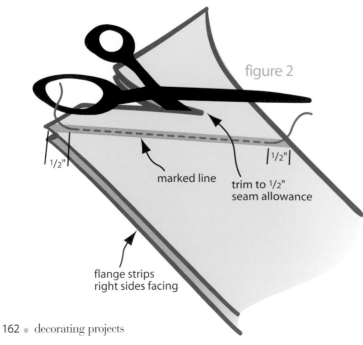

figure 2

½"

marked line

trim to ½"
seam allowance

½"

flange strips
right sides facing

4 With right sides facing and raw edges aligned, match the marked lines on the flange strips at each corner. Beginning ½" from the inner corner, stitch on the marked line, stopping ½" from the end of the marked line (Figure 2). Trim away the corner fabric ½" from the seam line. Press the seam open. Make front and back flanges.

5 With right sides together and raw edges aligned, pin the front and back flanges together along the outer edges. Using a ½" seam allowance, stitch the outer edges, pivoting the stitching at the corners. Clip the corners and grade the seam allowance. Press the seams open. Turn the flange right side out with the seams on edge and press flat.

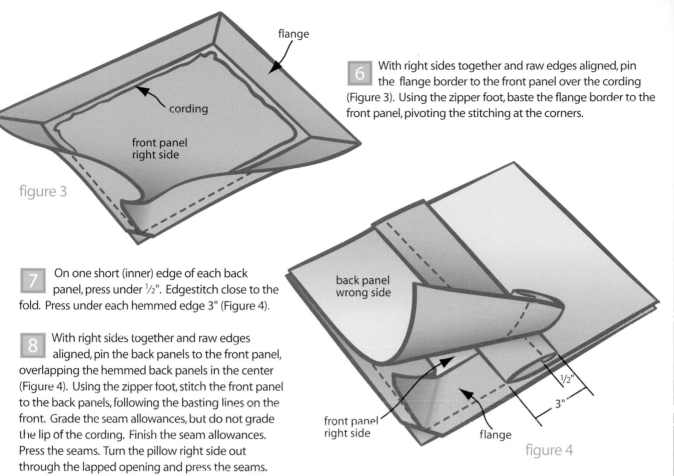

flange

cording

front panel
right side

figure 3

6 With right sides together and raw edges aligned, pin the flange border to the front panel over the cording (Figure 3). Using the zipper foot, baste the flange border to the front panel, pivoting the stitching at the corners.

back panel
wrong side

front panel
right side

flange

1/2"

3"

figure 4

7 On one short (inner) edge of each back panel, press under 1/2". Edgestitch close to the fold. Press under each hemmed edge 3" (Figure 4).

8 With right sides together and raw edges aligned, pin the back panels to the front panel, overlapping the hemmed back panels in the center (Figure 4). Using the zipper foot, stitch the front panel to the back panels, following the basting lines on the front. Grade the seam allowances, but do not grade the lip of the cording. Finish the seam allowances. Press the seams. Turn the pillow right side out through the lapped opening and press the seams. Insert the bed pillow.

MORE GOOD IDEAS
shaped borders

For a variation on the mitered flange border, make a scalloped edge.

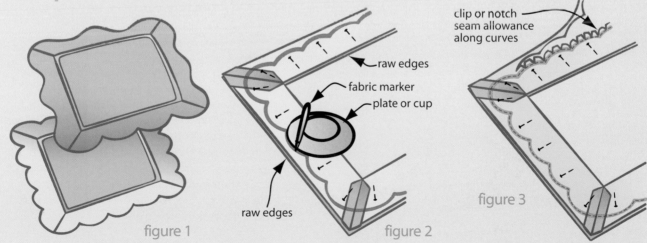

raw edges

fabric marker

plate or cup

raw edges

figure 1

figure 2

clip or notch
seam allowance
along curves

figure 3

1 Cut the front and back panels and the flange strips. Sew the mitered corner seams of the strips as directed in Step 4 on page 162 (Figure 1).

2 With right sides together and raw edges aligned, pin the flange borders together. Using a vanishing fabric marker, draw curves along the outer edge of the flange using the lip of a cup or the rim of a dessert plate for a template to center the scallop design (Figure 2). Leave at least 1/4" for a seam allowance all along the outer raw edges.

3 Stitch the front and back flange borders together along the marked line, pivoting the stitching at the sharp turns between the scallops. Grade the seam allowance. Clip or notch the seam allowance along the curves (Figure 3). Press the seam. Turn right side out, placing the seams on edge, and press flat.

4 With right sides together and raw edges aligned, stitch the flange border to the front panel. Complete the pillow as directed.

neckroll pillow

1 Cut one 17×21" center panel and two 7"-diameter circles for the end pieces from fabric. On each end piece, staystitch ½" from the edge to stabilize the shapes.

2 With right sides together and raw edges aligned, match the 17" edges of the center panel. Mark the center third of the seam for the opening (Figure 1). Using a ½" seam allowance, stitch each end of the seam from the opening to the ends, forming a tube. Press the seam open. Turn right side out.

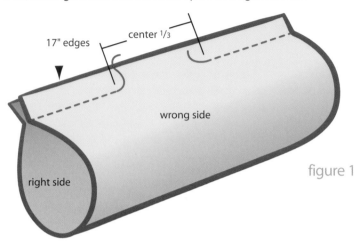

17" edges   center ⅓

wrong side

right side

figure 1

3 At each end of the tube, pin cording to the right side of the fabric, aligning the edge of the cording lip with the raw edges of the fabric. Where the cording ends meet, blend the ends. Apply liquid ravel preventer to the cut edges. Let dry. Using the zipper foot, baste the cording to the tube.

4 With the wrong side of the tube facing out, slip the pillow form into the tube. With right sides facing, pin one end panel to one end of the tube. Align the staystitching line in the end panel with the basting line for the cording on the tube (Figure 2). Hand-baste the end panel to the tube along the stitching line. Do not catch the pillow form in the stitches. Baste the opposite end panel to the opposite end of the tube in the same manner.

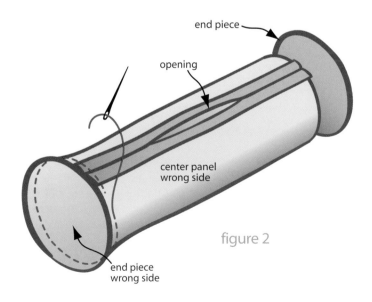

end piece

opening

center panel
wrong side

end piece
wrong side

figure 2

5 Remove the pillow form through the opening in the tube seam. Using the zipper foot, machine-baste the end panels to the tube along the line of hand-basted stitches. Turn right side out through the opening in the tube and check the seams to make sure they're straight and not puckered. If necessary, remove stitches and rebaste.

6 Turn the pillow cover wrong side out. Restitch each end panel to the tube; remove any visible basting stitches. Notch the seam allowances of the end panels and press the seam, turning the tube seam allowance and the cording lip toward the tube (Figure 3).

7 Turn the pillow cover right side out through the opening. Insert the pillow form. Turn the seam allowances at the opening to the inside and hand-stitch the opening closed.

figure 3

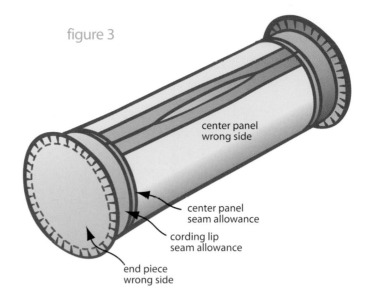

center panel
wrong side

center panel
seam allowance

cording lip
seam allowance

end piece
wrong side

CHOOSING THE RIGHT
FILLER CORD FOR WELTING AND TRIM

Size	Diameter	Type	Best Use
#00	$^{4}/_{32}$"	Tiny	Use with fine, lightweight fabrics.
#0	$^{5}/_{32}$"	Tailored	Use with most projects, all fabrics except heavyweight tapestries or upholstery fabrics; gives a formal or defined edge; neatly eases around corners and curves.
#1	$^{6}/_{32}$"	Tailored	Slightly larger than #0 filler cord; interchangeable on decorating projects.
#2	$^{8}/_{32}$"	Casual	Larger cord creates thicker welting; appearance on finished item will be more casual because this size welting does not make crisp corners.
#4	$^{12}/_{32}$"	Large	Use for novelty effects where you want the welting to be a feature in the finished project; finished welting has a bulky appearance.
#6	$^{22}/_{32}$"	Fat	Smaller of the two cords called "fat cord"; use as a decorative trim on tableskirts; use where exaggerated look of welting is desired.
#8	1"	Fat	Larger of the two cords called "fat cord"; use where tube-like welting is desired finished look.

MORE GOOD IDEAS

scents of pleasure
Roll a soothing sachet of lavender or chamomile into a neckroll to bring fragrance to the bed. As you move or touch the pillow, the fresh scent will be released.

1 Cut two pieces of lightweight cotton 1" smaller all around than the panel section of the neckroll. With wrong sides facing, zigzag-stitch along three sides. Stitch three lines through the center of the piece, forming four channels that remain open on one edge.

2 Spoon a tablespoon of potpourri, lavender buds, or chamomile leaves into each channel, shaking it toward the closed end. Zigzag across the channels to hold the potpourri in place. Repeat to fill more potpourri pockets, stopping at least 1" from the end of the fabric.

3 Wrap the quilted sachet around the neckroll form before slipping the pillow into the cover. Renew the fragrance by squeezing the pillow to crush the leaves or buds. When the fragrance weakens, make a replacement sachet.

special rooms

Let your personal style shine

in any space. Transform often-forgotten areas, such as outdoor living areas—and even bathrooms and entryways—into natural extensions of your indoor decorating sensibilities.

See page 192 for slipcover instructions.

Add a bit of kick to a rustic chair with a flirty pleated skirt. Knife pleats are the perfect option for a hard-edged outdoor chair— the crisp folds complement the rigid materials of the chair, and the fullness adds softness and fun.

knife-pleated chair skirt

Outdoor chairs, no matter how they are constructed, are generally rigid and fairly straight-lined. To soften them physically and visually, sew a skirted cushion. Slight padding invites you to relax, and bias-cut knife pleats break the straight lines and add a bit of swing and action to the chair. Choose a picnic-style fabric to keep the look outdoorsy, whether the chair lives indoors or outside in a sheltered area.

OUTDOOR FABRICS

Use acrylic outdoor fabrics to dress up your fresh-air living spaces. These fabrics are sun- and moisture-resistant, but they look and feel like woven cotton. The variety of fabric colors and patterns available means you can expect more than awning stripes.

■ For weatherproof outdoor cushions, ask for materials used in marine upholstery. Instead of cotton cord for the welting, select narrow plastic tubing. Use polyester thread and choose thin mildew-resistant cushions. Look for these special materials at sewing centers or upholstery supply stores.

■ If you use indoor fabrics for deck and patio furniture, create a safe and convenient place to store them when they are not being used. Pile pillows in a basket just inside the kitchen door. Or, for out-of-the-way storage that protects fabrics from dust, moisture, and dirt, store chair cushions or tablecloths in a lidded plastic storage container in the garage.

■ Treat indoor fabrics with spray-on water repellent to protect them from inevitable moisture, as well as dirt and stains.

materials

Paper
1"-thick foam*
1/8"- to 1/4"-loft bonded
  polyester batting*
54"-wide contrasting fabric
  for welting*
1/4" plastic tubing*
54"-wide decorator fabric*

sewing tools

Sewing machine
Zipper foot
Needle and thread
Vanishing fabric marker
Scissors
Tape measure
Iron and ironing board

skill level: beginner
time required: 1/2 day
*Purchase materials after
taking measurements.

1 Place the paper on the chair seat and mark the seat edges. Cut along the marked lines to make a pattern. Refit the pattern on the chair, adjusting as necessary. Crease the paper pattern in half from center front to center back (Figure 1).

2 Using the pattern, cut one cushion from foam. Wrap the cushion in batting, pinning and trimming the batting to cover the foam smoothly. Using a needle and thread, loosely hand-stitch the batting edges together around the foam cushion. Remove the pins and set the cushion aside.

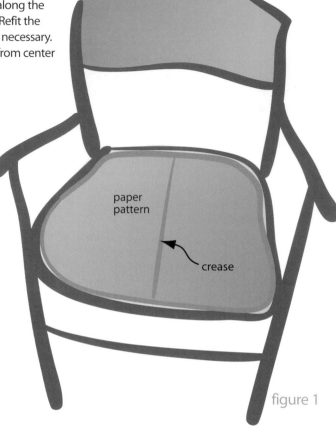

figure 1

3 Cut enough 1 1/2" bias strips from contrasting fabric to equal the circumference of the pattern plus 6". Handle the bias strips carefully to avoid stretching them. Stitch the strips together at the narrow ends to make a continuous length. Fold the strip around the plastic tubing, matching raw edges. Using the zipper foot and a long stitch length, baste close to the tubing to encase it in fabric.

4 To cut the top seat panel, place the pattern on the right side of the fabric, centering any fabric design and aligning the pattern crease with the straight grain of the fabric. Mark a 1" allowance around the pattern edge. Cut out the top panel along the marked line. Reposition the pattern to cut out the bottom panel in the same manner.

figure 2

5 Pin the welting to the right side of the top panel, beginning along the center of one side and aligning raw edges. Clip the seam allowance of the welting at the corners and around the curves. Where the ends of the welting meet, overlap the ends 1"; cut the welting. Remove the stitching from the fabric casing on both ends. Unfold the fabric and cut the tube ends to meet. Refold one end of the casing over the tube. On the remaining end, turn under the casing 1/2" and refold the fabric around the tube, concealing the raw ends of the fabric casing (Figure 2). Using the zipper foot and a long stitch length, baste the welting to the top panel.

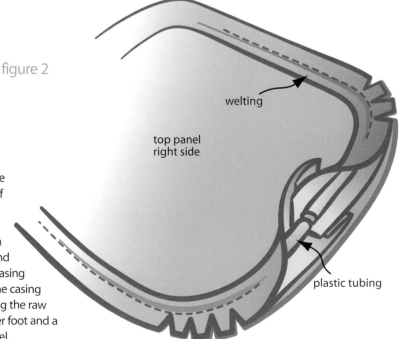

6 Measure around the edge of the top panel. Multiply that measurement by 4 for the length of fabric for the pleated ruffle. Cut enough 7"-wide bias strips to equal this length. Cut bias strips individually, matching the fabric pattern across the narrow fabric ends and adding 1/2" seam allowances to each end of every strip. Handle the strips carefully to avoid stretching or distortion.

7 Using 1/2" seam allowances, stitch the bias strips together at the narrow ends to make a continuous loop. Press the seams. Fold and press the loop in half lengthwise, wrong sides together. Along the long raw edge, measure and mark 1/2" followed by 1 1/2" consecutively. To make a knife pleat, match a 1 1/2" mark to an adjacent 1/2" mark; pin the pleat in place. The pleats will be 3/4" deep with a 1/2" space between each pleat (Figure 3).

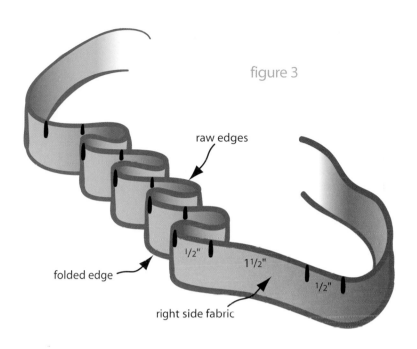

figure 3

raw edges

folded edge

1/2"

1 1/2"

1/2"

right side fabric

8 With right sides together and raw edges aligned, fit the pleats to the top panel over the welting. If necessary, make deeper or shallower pleats at the top panel corners to fit; small adjustments of up to 1/2" will not be apparent in the finished cushion. Using the zipper foot, baste the pleated skirt to the top, catching the welting in the stitches. Press the seam.

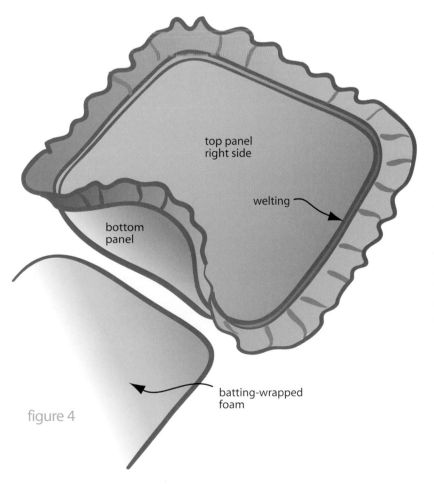

top panel right side

welting

bottom panel

batting-wrapped foam

figure 4

9 With right sides together, stitch the top panel to the bottom panel along previous basting lines, catching the welting and pleated skirt in the stitches. Pivot the stitching at the corners and leave an opening large enough for turning and inserting the cushion. Press the seam. Turn the cover right side out. Insert the cushion in the cover through the opening (Figure 4). Hand-stitch the opening closed.

For a tailored edging that gives a plain pillow impact, add a flange. The flange design is simply an extended knife-edge pillow with a pocket at the center to hold the pillow form. The contrast between the flat flange and the plump pillow makes the cushion look generous and comfortable.

flange pillow

The extended frame around a flange pillow enhances its decorative impact in the room by creating a larger splash of color and pattern. The flat border is usually 2 to 4 inches wide, but you may want to make the flange larger or smaller, depending on the size of the pillow and the fabric motif. A small accent pillow made from a tiny print, for example, could be framed with an oversize flange to give it more importance, or with a narrow one to emphasize its petite dimensions.

Take cues from your fabric for the width of the flange. Use checks and plaids as units to determine the width of the border. If you're working with a floral design, consider the best frame for the largest blossom or bouquet in the fabric. The instructions on the pages that follow are for a pillow that measures 30 inches square overall, with a 3-inch-wide flange surrounding a 24-inch square pillow form.

See page 48 for basic pillow instructions.

flange pillow

1 Cut two 31" squares from decorator fabric for the front and back panels. Center geometric and floral motifs on the squares to achieve a balanced or symmetrical placement.

2 Cut 4 yards of 1½"-wide bias strips from contrasting fabric. Stitch the strips together at the short ends to make a continuous length. To make welting, fold the bias strip around the cord, with wrong sides together and long raw edges matching. Using the zipper foot and a long stitch length, baste close to the cord, encasing the cord in the fabric.

3 With raw edges aligned and beginning at the center of the bottom edge of the panel, pin the welting to the right side of the front panel. Clip the seam allowance of the welting at the corners. Where the welting ends meet, overlap the ends 1". Remove the stitching from the fabric cover on each end. Unfold the fabric and cut the ends of the cord to meet. Refold one end of the cover over the cord. On the remaining end, turn the cover under ½" and refold the fabric around the cord. Using the zipper foot and a long stitch length, baste the welting to the front panel (Figure 1).

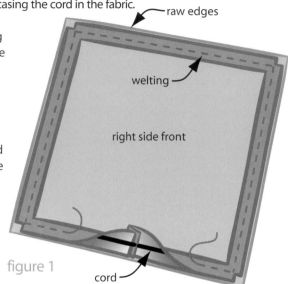

raw edges
welting
right side front
cord

figure 1

4 With right sides together and raw edges aligned, stitch the front panel to the back panel, using the zipper foot and following the basting line on the front panel. Stitch all corners, pivoting the stitching at the corners and leaving a long opening in the bottom edge for turning. Clip the corners and grade the seam allowances. Press the seam, then turn right side out. Place the seam on edge. Press flat.

5 Measure and mark a line 2" from each edge of the pillow (Figure 2). Pin the layers together along the line. Topstitch on the line, stitching all corners and pivoting the stitching at the corners. Leave an opening in the bottom (aligned with the opening in the outer bottom edge) to insert the pillow form.

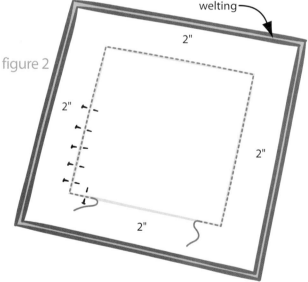

welting
figure 2
2"
2"
2"
2"

6 Insert the pillow form into the cover. Shake the pillow away from the bottom edge and openings. Pin the front and back layers together along the marked line at the bottom of the pillow form. Topstitch along the line (Figure 3), having a helper support the pillow as you topstitch this edge of the pocket closed. If you are working alone, stack books beside the sewing machine to support the pillow. Hand-stitch the opening at the welt edge closed. Fluff the pillow to distribute the filling in the center pocket.

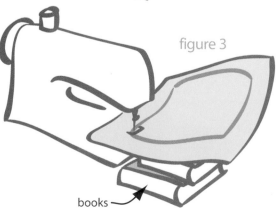

figure 3
books

low-sew option

Instead of basting a pocket at the center of the pillow cover, use buttons to outline the pillow form. Mark points for 16 buttons surrounding the center. Stitch the buttons to the cover through the top and back panels. For a fully finished look, tack a second group of 16 buttons over the threads on the back panel.

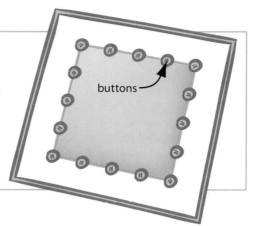

buttons

creating a shaped flange

Exercise your creativity with custom-shaped edges that lend a look unique to your home. Outline a wavy edge with welting for emphasis and definition (Figure 1).

1 Determine the finished size of the pillow at its widest and highest point and add 1" to the side-to-side and to the top-to-bottom measurements. From fabric, cut the front and back panels to this size. Set the back panel aside.

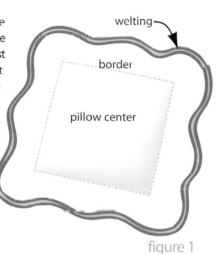

welting

border

pillow center

figure 1

2 On the right side of the top panel, measure and mark lines ¹/₂" from each raw edge. Measure the finished width of the flange from this line toward the panel center. Mark a stitching line to indicate the pillow center.

3 Make a paper pattern of the shape for the pillow edge. Place this pattern along each edge and

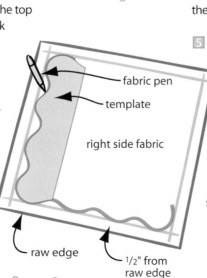

fabric pen

template

right side fabric

raw edge

¹/₂" from raw edge

figure 2

trace the stitching line (Figure 2). Do not allow the stitching line to intrude on the ¹/₂" allowance at the raw edges.

4 Pin and baste welting to the right side of the top panel, basting along the marked stitching line of the shaped edge on the top panel (Figure 3). Clip the seam allowance of the welting to ease the welting around the curves. Finish the ends of the welting, as described in Step 3. Trim the top panel to meet the raw edges of the welting.

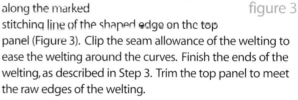

marked line

right side

raw edge

figure 3

5 With right sides together, center the top panel on the bottom panel. Pin the layers together along the basting line for the welting, then stitch the panels together along the basting line. Stitch around all corners, leaving a long opening in one edge for turning. Trim the bottom panel even with the seam allowance of the top panel. Trim the edges even. Clip the curves and turn the cover right side out. Place the welting-trimmed seam on edge and press flat. Finish the center pocket in the pillow as for the cover with straight edges (see Steps 4 and 5, page 174).

flange pillow how to

Unconventional furniture has distinctive appeal but may be hard-edged and uncomfortable without cushions. Vintage benches, settees, and church pews benefit physically and visually from cushions and pillows. A thin box cushion and matching pillows are a practical choice to add comfort while showcasing the lines of the piece.

settee cushion

T ake care when adding upholstery to antiques with admirable lines. The new cushion should enhance rather than detract from the architecture of the piece. The stripes on the top, bottom, and underside of the cushion shown at left form a pleasing continuous line. For an easy care cushion and a smoother, tighter fitting cover, encase the foam and batting in muslin before inserting them into the zippered decorative cover.

See page 48 for pillow instructions.

CHOOSING A BATTING

All of the materials used in your project affect the appearance and comfort of the finished piece. High-density foam wrapped in polyester batting, for example, will feel different than foam covered with cotton batting.

polyester batting is sold in most sewing centers in a variety of densities. For the springiest cushion, choose extra-loft batting or high-density upholsterer's batting. A cushion wrapped in these materials will return to its original shape. Polyester batting keeps a cushion crisp and well defined.

cotton batting or padding may be difficult to find in fabric stores, where you're more likely to find lightweight cotton quilt batts, which can be layered to create thicker pads. For generously plush cotton batting, go to upholsterer's supply outlets. This loosely matted padding fits around the foam before both are encased in a muslin sleeve. Cotton padding successfully re-creates an antique look and will have more heft. With heavy use, such cushions will become compressed over time.

materials

2"-thick high-density
  upholstery foam*
45"-wide 1"-loft (8 oz.)
  bonded polyester batting or
  multiple layers of $^1/8$"-
  to $^1/4$"-loft bonded
  cotton batting*
45"-wide muslin*
54"-wide decorator fabric*
$^6/32$" filler cord*
Zipper (8" longer than back
  edge of seat cushion)*

sewing tools

Sewing machine
Needle and thread
Pins
Tape measure
Scissors
Iron and ironing board
Zipper foot

skill level: intermediate
time required: 2 days
*Purchase materials after
taking measurements.

figure 1

1 Measure the bench seat from side to side and front to back (Figure 1). If the back edge of the seat is narrower than the front edge, measure both edges. Cut the foam to the measured size and check the fit on the bench; the cushion should lie flat without bunching at the sides or back. Wrap the foam in batting, pinning and trimming the batting to cover the foam smoothly. Loosely hand-stitch the batting edges together. Remove the pins.

2 To make a muslin sleeve for the batting-wrapped cushion, measure the girth of the cushion and add 2". Measure the length of the cushion from side to side, including the depth of the batting-wrapped foam at each end, and add 2". Cut a piece this size from a single length of extra-wide muslin. If you must seam fabric for the required width, place the seam on a corner of the cushion.

3 Wrap the muslin around the cushion, folding the long edges under to meet at one corner (Figure 2). Hand-stitch with tiny stitches to secure the folded edges. Wrap each end of the muslin as if wrapping a package, minimizing the fabric bulk as much as possible. Hand-stitch with tiny stitches to secure the folded edges.

figure 2

muslin

turn under
raw edges

batting-wrapped
foam

4 To cut the top and bottom fabric panels, measure the cushion top from side to side and front to back. Add 1" to each measurement. To determine the best pattern placement, drape the fabric over the cushion before you cut. Place stripes or plaids symmetrically and center floral motifs or other prominent patterns; take special care when placing directional patterns and motifs. Cut two identical pieces to this size for the top and bottom panels.

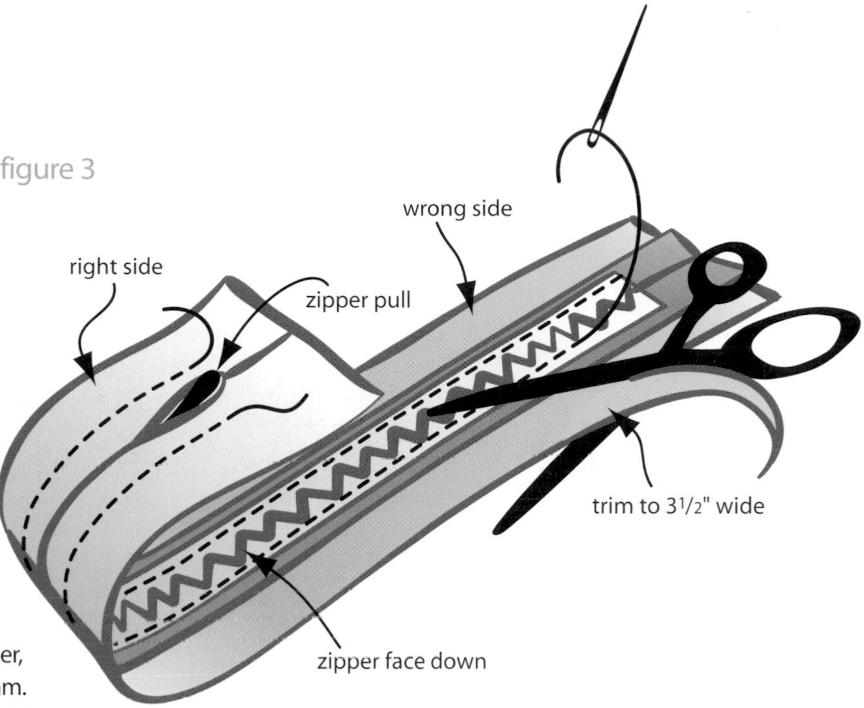

figure 3

right side

wrong side

zipper pull

trim to 3¹/₂" wide

zipper face down

5 For the zippered back gusset, measure the back edge of the cushion length and add 9". Cut two 4"-wide strips from fabric to this length, matching the pattern across the long edges. With right sides together and long raw edges aligned, use a ³/₄" seam allowance to baste the strips together along one long edge. Press the seams open. On the wrong side, center the zipper, tab side down, over the basted seam. Hand-baste the zipper tapes to the fabric (Figure 3). Turn the gusset to the right side. Using the zipper foot, stitch the zipper in place following the manufacturer's instructions for centered zipper installation. Remove the basting stitches. Trim the strip to 3¹/₂" wide with the zipper at the center.

6 To make straight-match welting, cut 1¹/₂"-wide strips across the width of the fabric (rather than on the bias). Cut enough strips to equal twice the seat cushion circumference plus 36". Stitch the strips together at the narrow ends to make a continuous length. Press the seams. To make welting, fold the strip around the filler cord, matching long raw edges. Using the zipper foot and a long stitch length, baste close to the cord to encase it in the fabric.

7 Pin the welting to the right side of the top panel, beginning near the center back and aligning the raw edges. Match the welting pattern with the pattern along the edge of the front panel, repositioning the welting as necessary. (*Note: Because the cushion has a zippered gusset, it will have definite front and back edges.*) Clip the welting seam allowance at the corners. Overlap the welting 1" and cut the ends. Remove the stitching from the casing, unfold the fabric, and cut the cords to meet. Refold one casing over the cord. Turn under ¹/₂" of the opposite end and refold it around the cord to conceal the raw edge. Using the zipper foot and a long stitch length, baste the welting to the top panel, pivoting at the corners (Figure 4). Baste the welting to the bottom panel in the same manner.

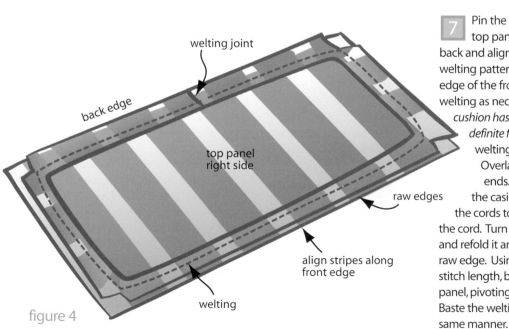

welting joint

back edge

top panel right side

raw edges

align stripes along front edge

welting

figure 4

settee cushion how to

8 With right sides together and raw edges aligned, center the zippered gusset on the back edge of the top panel. Insert the pins on the wrong side of the top panel to sew the seam from that side of the fabric. Using the zipper foot and a long stitch length, baste the zippered gusset to the long back edge, starting and stopping the seam $1/2$" from the corners (do not sew around the corners). Remove each pin as the needle approaches. Clip the seam allowance of the zippered gusset to each corner (Figure 5).

9 For the front gusset, measure the front long edge from side to side. Measure the side edge from front to back and double the measurement. Add the two measurements and cut one $3^1/2$"-wide strip to this length, matching the pattern to the top panel.

10 With right sides together and raw edges aligned, center the front gusset on the front edge of the top panel. Match the pattern in the gusset to the pattern in the top panel and welting. Insert the pins on the wrong side of the top panel to sew the seam from that side of the fabric. Using the zipper foot and a long stitch length, baste the front gusset to the long front edge, starting and stopping the seam $1/2$" from the corners. Remove each pin as the needle approaches. Clip the seam allowance of the front gusset to each corner.

11 With right sides together and raw edges aligned, pin one end of the back gusset (near the zipper stop) and the front gusset to one side edge of the top panel. Bring the narrow gusset ends together, right sides facing, to determine the seam line. Stitch the back gusset and front gusset together at the zipper stop (Figure 5). (Seam allowance depths will differ on the front and back gussets.) Trim the gusset seam allowance and press the seam toward the front section.

12 Repin the gusset to the top panel, inserting the pins on the wrong side of the top panel to sew the seam from that side. Using the zipper foot and a long stitch length, baste the gusset to the side edge of the top panel, stitching around the corners and removing the pins. Pivot the stitching at the corners.

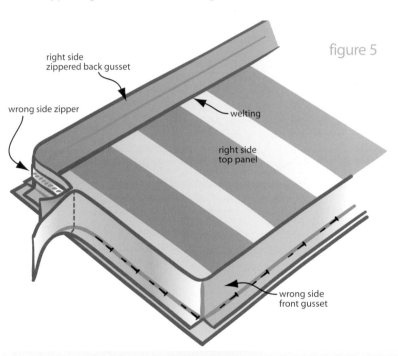

figure 5

right side zippered back gusset

wrong side zipper

welting

right side top panel

wrong side front gusset

JOINING FABRIC WIDTHS

Use one of these options to join fabric widths for benches that are wider than standard 54"-wide decorator fabric:

1. To straight-match fabric, seam together fabric widths to match the pattern repeat. With a stripe or plaid fabric, place the seam at the edge or in the center of one lengthwise stripe or plaid component. The seams in the tone-on-tone stripe of the bench cushion shown on page 176 are well concealed. For floral or all-over designs, you may need to purchase additional yardage to accommodate the repeat. Look at the selvage markings to find the manufacturer's repeat symbol (see page 117). Add at least twice the length of the repeats to the yardage, one each for the top and bottom panels, to seam together fabrics for a straight match.

2. Take a cue from cottage style and combine fabrics to create the required width. The objective is to choose fabrics in different scales. A large floral design, for example, could make up three-fourths of the width, and each end (one-eighth of the full width) could be a complementary small scale design. Repeat the complementary fabric in the gusset to strengthen its decorative impact and accent the combination with welting in the seam lines.

13 With right sides together and raw edges aligned, pin the gusset back section to the remaining side edge of the top panel, pinning to within 4" of the zipper pull. Pin the gusset front section to the top panel, holding back the loose end of the back section and adjusting the length of the front section to conceal the zipper pull. Fold the narrow end of the gusset front section to create a 1" pleat (Figure 6). Match the front and back narrow ends to make a seam line. Trim the excess seam allowance. Stitch the back and front gussets together at the top of the zipper. Press the seam toward the front gusset. Keeping the pleat in place, repin the gusset to the top panel, inserting the pins on the wrong side of the top panel to sew the seam from that side. Using the zipper foot and a long stitch length, baste the gusset to the side edge of the top panel, pivoting the stitching at the corners and removing each pin as the needle approaches.

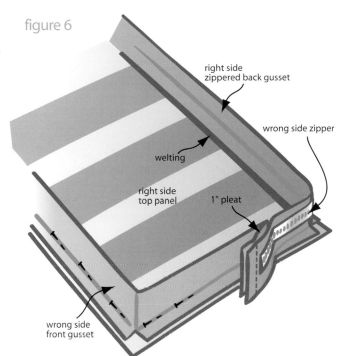

figure 6

right side zippered back gusset

wrong side zipper

welting

right side top panel

1" pleat

wrong side front gusset

wrong side top panel

stitching direction

stitching direction

wrong side back gusset

seam

wrong side front gusset

figure 7

14 Open the zipper. With right sides facing and raw edges aligned, pin the remaining raw edges of the gusset to the bottom panel. Keep the pleat in place. Insert the pins on the wrong side of the gusset to sew the seam from that side of the fabric. Stitch both sides of the gusset in the same direction to ensure smooth seams (Figure 7). Clip the gusset seam allowance at the corners. Using the zipper foot and a long stitch length, baste the gusset to the bottom panel, removing pins and pivoting the stitching at the corners. Turn right side out through the zipper.

15 Look at the right side of each seam to check for puckers or unwanted pleats in the gusset; if necessary, remove stitches and restitch for a smooth seam. Set the stitch length at the normal setting. Turn the cushion cover wrong side out and sew the gusset to the top panel along the basting lines, working with the wrong side of the top panel up. Sew the gusset to the bottom panel along the basting lines, working with the wrong side of the gusset up. Press the seams and turn right side out. Insert the cushion through the zippered opening. Close the zipper and conceal the tab in the pleat (Figure 8).

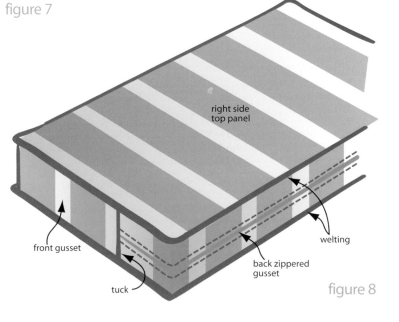

right side top panel

welting

back zippered gusset

front gusset

tuck

figure 8

Making your own cornice lets you be creative and design a window topper that's suited to your room. Keep in mind the type of shade or curtain it will be combined with. Here, the scalloped edge of the cornice repeats harmoniously in the softly gathered edge of the shade.

hard cornice and soft shade

Large windows flood rooms with light. In a bathroom, however, large windows raise questions of privacy. One beautiful solution is to team a cornice box with a soft shade for light control; the balloon-like shade can be lifted or lowered as needed. Constructed similar to a Roman shade, this treatment gathers loosely along two columns of rings. The result is a loosely draped pouf with a soft, unstructured look.

To keep the window treatment uncluttered, cover the cornice box with the same paper as the surrounding walls. In this room, the pale colors and simple design help expand the space. The shade mounts inside the top of the box, which conceals the the shade mechanics. The box mounts on the wall on a 2×4 pine board.

materials

³⁄₈" plywood*
2×4 pine board*
12 (1") No. 6 wood screws
3 (1¹⁄₄") No. 8 wood screws
3 (3") No. 8 wood screws
5 (2") No. 8 wood screws
Wallpaper
Clear-drying fabric glue
Bobble fringe trim
54"-wide decorator fabric*
54"-wide lining fabric*
1×2 pine board*
Shade-and-blind tape or
    plastic O-rings
Shade-and-blind cord
4 curtain weights
Cleat with fasteners
3 screw eyes

tools

Electric drill and drill bits
Jig saw
Screwdrivers
Wallpaper hanging tools
    (knife, brush, and water tray)

sewing tools

Sewing machine
Iron and ironing board
Vanishing fabric marker
Pins
Needle and thread
Scissors
Tape measure
Liquid ravel preventer

skill level: advanced
time required: 2 days
*Purchase materials after
taking measurements.

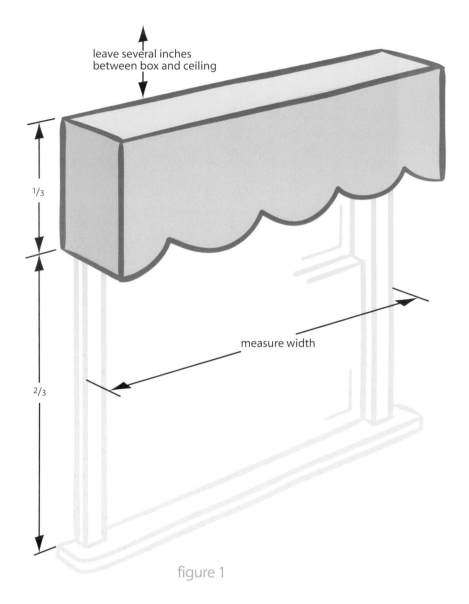

leave several inches
between box and ceiling

1/3

2/3

measure width

figure 1

1   The cornice box attaches to a mounting board above the window (see page 107 for more information). To determine the measurements of the box, measure the width of the window frame and determine the placement for the cornice top, allowing several inches between the box and the ceiling. Measure from that point to the windowsill and divide by 3 for the finished height of the box (Figure 1).

2   Cut the following pieces from plywood: the cornice front (window width plus 5" by the height of the box), the cornice top (window width plus 5" by 5" wide), and two cornice sides (5" by the height of the box less ³⁄₈"). For the lower edge of the cornice front, trace the edge of a dinner plate to draw a scalloped edge. Using a jig saw, cut along the marked line.

3   Place the cornice top on the edge of each side piece, making sure the corners are flush and square. Drill pilot holes through the top into the sides and attach with 1" screws. Place the cornice front on the front edge of the sides and top, aligning the edges. Drill pilot holes through the front into the sides and top and attach with 1" screws. Paint the inside of the box and all edges in a color to match the wallpaper background. Cut a 2×4 board to equal the window width less 1". Paint it to match the wallpaper.

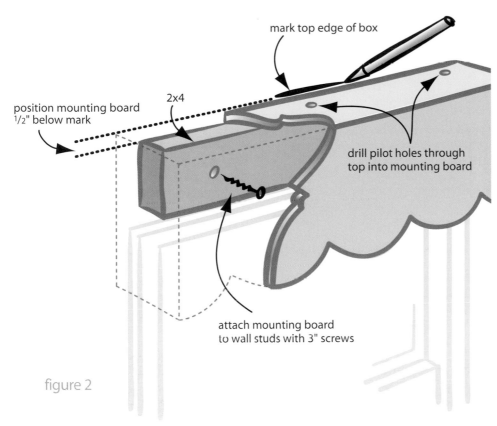

mark top edge of box

position mounting board
1/2" below mark

2x4

drill pilot holes through
top into mounting board

attach mounting board
to wall studs with 3" screws

figure 2

4 Hold the cornice board above the window for placement. Lightly mark the top edge on the wall. Center the 2×4 board over the window 1/2" below the mark, with the wide side of the board against the wall. Drill pilot holes through the 2×4 board into the wall at the wall studs and install the mounting board with 3" screws. Center the cornice box on the mounting board, making sure the box is flush with the wall. Drill several pilot holes through the top of the box into the mounting board (Figure 2). Remove the box.

5 Plan the wallpaper layout on the box. Arrange lengths of wallpaper to cover the box, wrapping the paper from the bottom front edge, up and across the top to the back edge in one continuous piece (Figure 3). Do not cut the wallpaper to match the shaped lower edge of the box at this time. Match the pattern at the corners. Following the manufacturer's instructions, apply the paper to the box. Let dry.

6 Trim the lower edge of the paper along the shaped edge of the box. Punch small holes through the paper at the pilot holes on the box top. Glue the braided edge of the bobble trim to the shaped edge, covering the raw edge of the wallpaper.

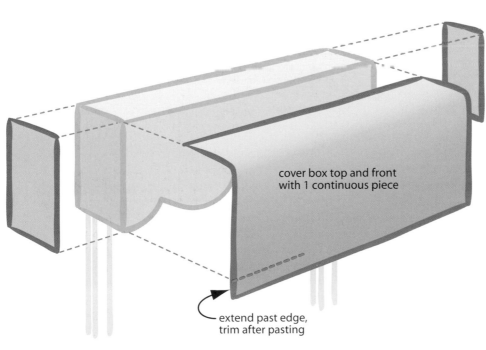

cover box top and front
with 1 continuous piece

extend past edge,
trim after pasting

figure 3

7 Cut the 1×2 board to equal the measured window width. Center the board in the top of the cornice box with the wide edge against the box top (Figure 4). Allow 2" at the back edge of the box. Measure 4" from each end of the 1×2 board. Drill pilot holes through the board into the box top, then remove the board from the cornice box. Divide the length of the board into four equal sections. Mark one point at the first and third dividers for screw eyes and drill one shallow pilot hole at each mark. Drill an additional pilot hole for a third screw eye 1" from the right end of the board. Set the board aside.

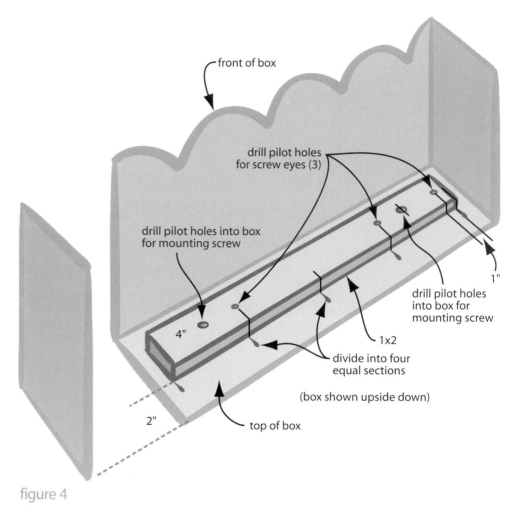

front of box

drill pilot holes for screw eyes (3)

drill pilot holes into box for mounting screw

drill pilot holes into box for mounting screw

1"

4"

1×2

divide into four equal sections

(box shown upside down)

2"

top of box

figure 4

8 Place the cleat on the right side of the window frame about midway between the top and bottom to hold the cords taut. (If you have small children in your home, place the cleat closer to the top of the frame, lowering the risk of possible entanglement.) Drill pilot holes in the frame. Mount the cleat with fasteners according to the manufacturer's instructions.

9 Measure the window length from the top of the 2×4 cornice mounting board to the windowsill and add 5". Measure the window frame from side to side and add 3". Trim the selvages from the fabric. Cut one front panel from fabric to this size. If necessary, stitch together fabric pieces to make one front panel the required size, starting each cut at the same point in the fabric repeat.

10 For the lining panel, measure the window length from the top of the 2×4 mounting board to the windowsill and add 3". Measure the window frame from side to side. Trim the selvages from the lining. Cut one front panel from lining to this size. If necessary, stitch together fabric pieces to make one front panel the required size.

11 Lay the front panel right side up. Place the top edge of the lining 3" from the top edge of the front panel. Smooth the lining along the length of the panel; the lower edges will not align. Slide the lining to one side edge. Pin the edges together. Using a $1/2$" seam allowance, stitch the front and lining together on the pinned edge. Slide the lining to the opposite side edge of the front. Stitch the front and lining together in the same manner. Press the seams open.

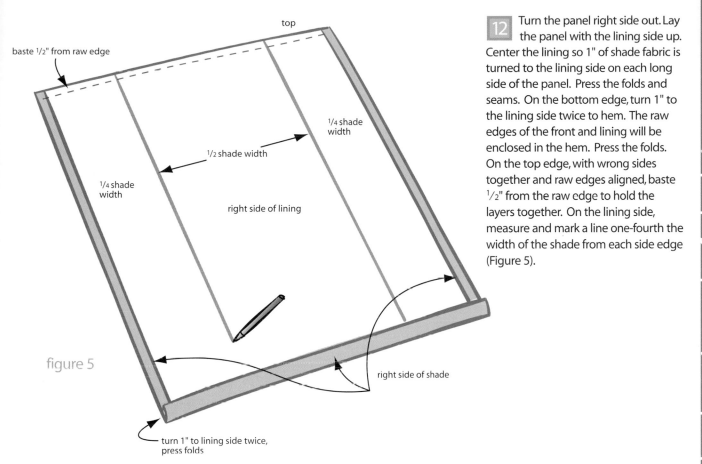

baste 1/2" from raw edge

top

1/4 shade width

1/2 shade width

1/4 shade width

right side of lining

right side of shade

figure 5

turn 1" to lining side twice, press folds

12 Turn the panel right side out. Lay the panel with the lining side up. Center the lining so 1" of shade fabric is turned to the lining side on each long side of the panel. Press the folds and seams. On the bottom edge, turn 1" to the lining side twice to hem. The raw edges of the front and lining will be enclosed in the hem. Press the folds. On the top edge, with wrong sides together and raw edges aligned, baste 1/2" from the raw edge to hold the layers together. On the lining side, measure and mark a line one-fourth the width of the shade from each side edge (Figure 5).

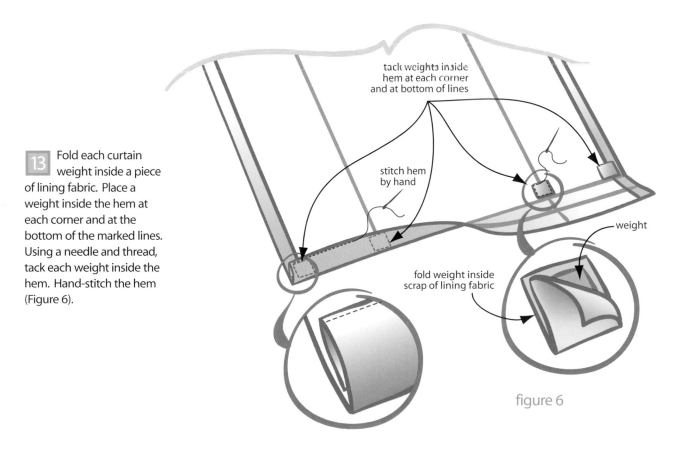

tack weights inside hem at each corner and at bottom of lines

stitch hem by hand

weight

fold weight inside scrap of lining fabric

13 Fold each curtain weight inside a piece of lining fabric. Place a weight inside the hem at each corner and at the bottom of the marked lines. Using a needle and thread, tack each weight inside the hem. Hand-stitch the hem (Figure 6).

figure 6

decorating projects • 187

hard cornice and soft shade continued

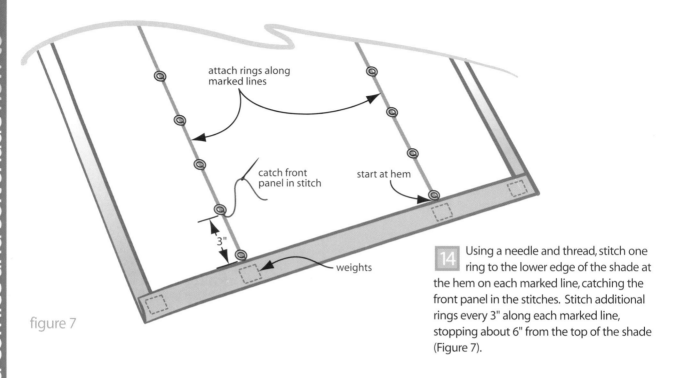

attach rings along marked lines

catch front panel in stitch

start at hem

3"

weights

figure 7

14 Using a needle and thread, stitch one ring to the lower edge of the shade at the hem on each marked line, catching the front panel in the stitches. Stitch additional rings every 3" along each marked line, stopping about 6" from the top of the shade (Figure 7).

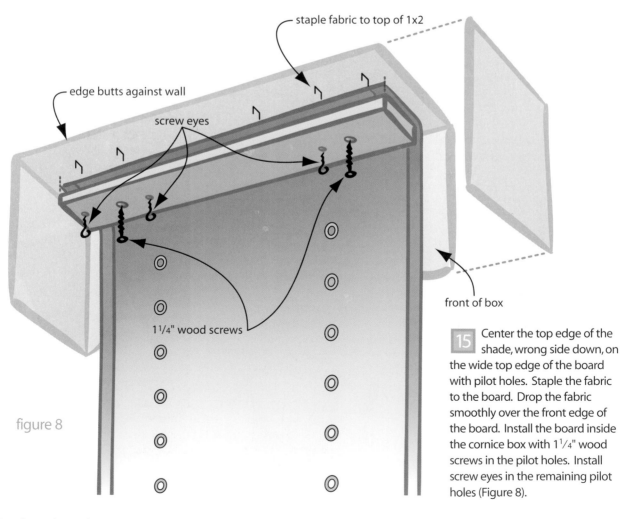

staple fabric to top of 1x2

edge butts against wall

screw eyes

1 1/4" wood screws

front of box

figure 8

15 Center the top edge of the shade, wrong side down, on the wide top edge of the board with pilot holes. Staple the fabric to the board. Drop the fabric smoothly over the front edge of the board. Install the board inside the cornice box with 1 1/4" wood screws in the pilot holes. Install screw eyes in the remaining pilot holes (Figure 8).

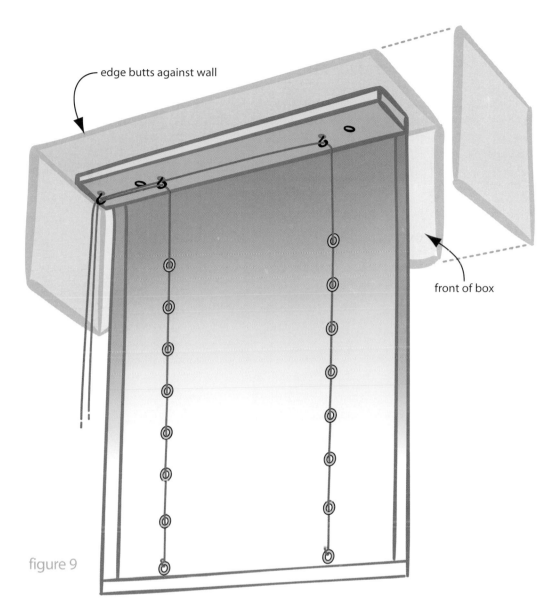

edge butts against wall

front of box

figure 9

16 Working from the back of the shade, as shown in Figure 9, cut a length two times the measured shade length plus the measured width for the right-hand cord. Tie one end of the cord to the lowest ring on the right side of the shade. Tie one end of the remaining length of cord to the lowest ring on the left side of the shade for the left-hand cord. Thread the cords through the column of rings and through the screw eye in the mounting board at the top of the column. Thread all cords through the extreme left screw eye (Figure 9).

17 Place the cornice box on the mounting board. Install with 2" wood screws in the pilot holes. Pull the cords individually to take up slack. Trim the cord ends even. To raise the shade, gently pull the cords together, causing the fabric to gather. Secure the cords to the cleat with a figure-eight motion. To dress the gathers, raise the shade to its highest position. Secure the cords and arrange the gathers by hand. After several weeks, the pleats will develop "memory" and will no longer need to be dressed by hand. If the outside edges of the shade need additional weight for a more defined drop, open the hem and insert additional curtain weights. Release the cords to raise and lower the shade.

Patchwork takes on new meaning when you apply it to chair components. Attain the cottage-style charm of these slipcovers by combining as many as four fabrics on a chair. Coordinating fabrics from the same design line make it easy to successfully mix and match patterns.

cottage-style slipcovers

Give an easy chair the look of an old-fashioned flower garden with a combination of garden-inspired prints. To successfully mix several prints on one chair, vary color and scale, but make sure they have enough in common to blend into an eye-pleasing look. Divide the chair into logical units and keep the fabrics the same for each unit. Take your cue from the chair at left, where the main frame of the chair is covered in one print, the seat cushion in another, all the gusset or flat pieces in a third, and the welting in a fourth pattern. By blocking the patterns into large pieces, each fabric shows to its best advantage. In keeping with the garden look, choose florals for all but the welting, where a minicheck pattern works better.

Pin-fitting allows you to fit the cover properly before you sew and eliminates the need to refit each section as you add another. Use the seam and welting lines of the original cover as a guide to place the new construction and embellishment lines.

Each chair component is measured as a rectangle at the widest and highest points to determine the size of the fabric panel to use on that section. Add a seam allowance and tuck-in allowance to each piece (see the step-by-step instructions, beginning on the following page, for details). Allowances vary from 4 inches to 10 inches because some of the panels are tucked into the original upholstery to secure the slipcover.

materials

54"-wide decorator fabric for seat cushion top and bottom panels*

54"-wide decorator fabric for seat cushion gusset and arm front*

54"-wide decorator fabric for chair back panel, seat back panel, deck panel, inside arm panel, outside arm panel, and skirt*

54"-wide contrasting decorator fabric for welting*

$^6/_{32}$" filler cord*

Paper

Upholstery zipper as long as chair is high*

Upholstery zipper 9" longer than measured back edge of seat cushion*

sewing tools

Sewing machine and accessories

Needle and thread

Pins

Scissors

Vanishing fabric marker

Seam ripper

Iron and ironing board

Zipper foot

skill level: intermediate/advanced

time required: 4 to 5 days

*Purchase materials after taking measurements.

1 To determine the amount of welting for the chair, measure the approximate length of each seam into which you plan to insert welting: Measure the top edge of the chair back, the depth of each arm, around the front edges of each arm, and around the base of the chair at the top of the skirt. Also measure around the gusset of each seat cushion; double this figure.

2 Cut enough 1½"-wide bias strips from welting to equal the length calculated in Step 1 plus 36". Handle the bias strips carefully to avoid stretching. Sew the strips together at the narrow ends. Fold the bias strips, wrong sides together, around the filler cord, matching the long raw edges. Using the zipper foot and a long stitch length, baste close to the cord to encase it in the fabric. Set the welting aside.

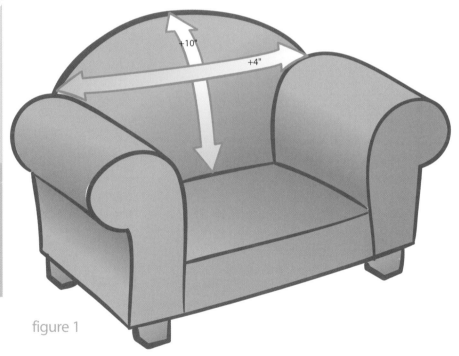

figure 1

3 Remove the seat cushion(s). Measure the back of the seat from side to side at the widest point and add 4". Measure the back of the seat from the top to the deck (the seat area that's normally covered by cushions) and add 10" (Figure 1). Note that on the original upholstery, the seam for the top of the seat back, may be over the top edge of the chair. Cut one seat back panel to this size from fabric .

4 Measure the deck of the chair from side to side at the widest point and add 10" (Figure 2). Measure from the back of the deck, over the edge of the deck, to the bottom of the chair front (or the top of the chair skirt) and add 10" (Figure 2). Cut one deck panel to this size from fabric.

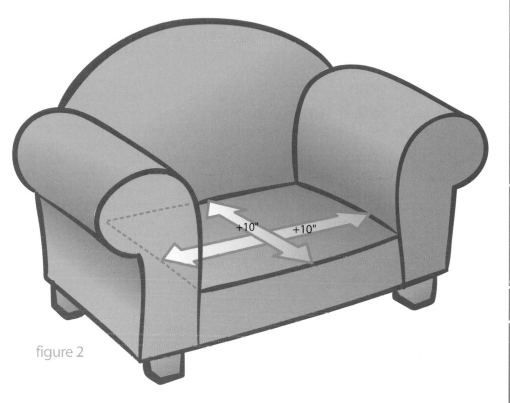

figure 2

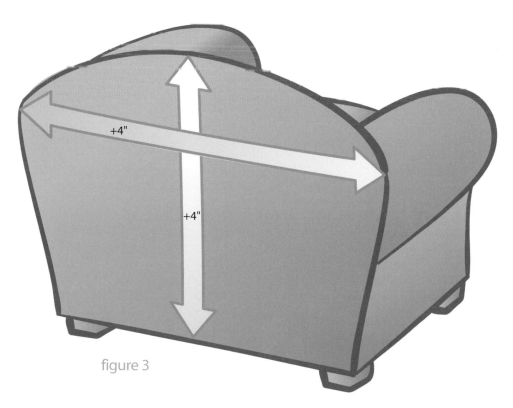

figure 3

5 Measure the back of the chair from side to side at the widest point and add 4". Measure from the top of the chair to the lower upholstered edge (or top of the chair skirt) and add 4" (Figure 3). Cut one chair back panel to this size from fabric.

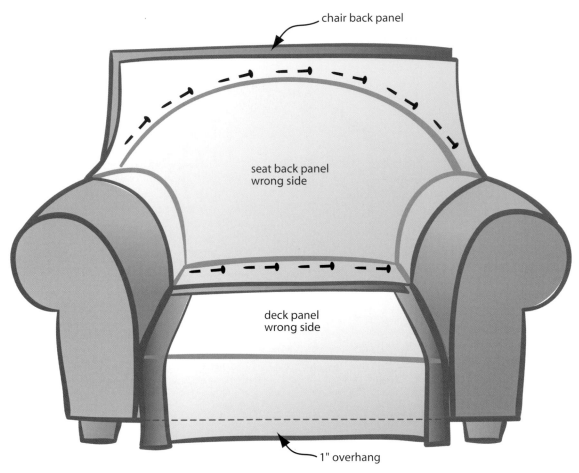

chair back panel

seat back panel
wrong side

deck panel
wrong side

1" overhang

figure 4

6 Place the panels on the chair with wrong sides out. Bring the raw edges of the seat and chair back panels together. If these edges are different lengths, center the panels on the top edge. Insert a line of pins following the top edge of the chair to make a temporary seam (Figure 4). Smooth the seat back panel over the seat back and onto the deck.

7 For the deck panel, leave a raw edge 1" below the upholstered edge (or top of the chair skirt), creating a 1" overhang. Center the panel on the deck, smoothing it in place. Bring the bottom edge of the seat back panel and the back edge of the deck panel together. Pin the panels together 1" from the short edge. Trim the seam allowance to 1" on each pinned seam.

8 | Remove the panels from the chair. Insert welting between the layers of fabric along the top edge, removing and replacing pins to add the welting. Using the zipper foot and a long stitch length, baste the pinned seam, catching the welting in the stitches. Baste the pinned seam at the back of the deck. Remove the pins. Replace the covers on the chair with wrong sides out. Lap the tuck-in allowance at the back of the deck on the top of the deck. Lap the allowances on the side edges.

9 | On the chair arms, draw an imaginary line from front to back along the top edge of the arm (Figure 5). Measure from this line to the deck and add 10". Measure from the chair back to the front edge of the arm and add 10" (Figure 5). Cut two arm panels to size from fabric. Make sure that prominent or directional patterns mirror each other across the seat of the chair.

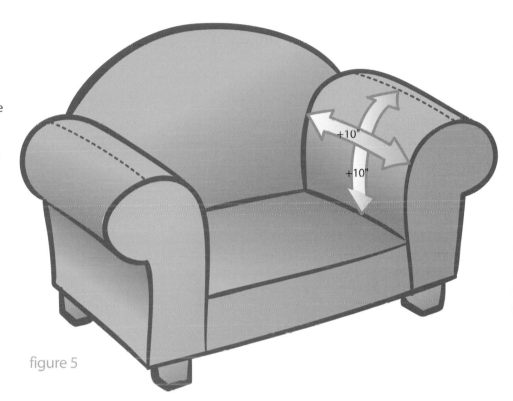

figure 5

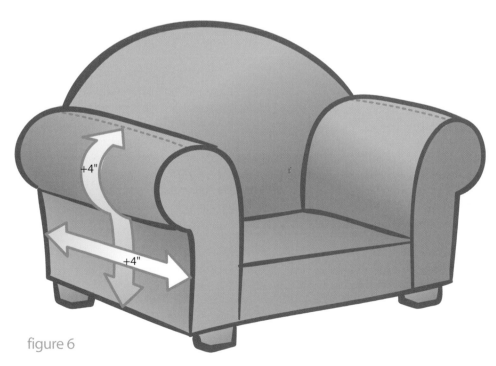

figure 6

10 | From the same imaginary line, measure down the outer side of the chair to the upholstered edge (or top of the chair skirt), following the chair contours, and add 4". Measure the side of the chair from front to back at the widest point and add 4" (Figure 6). Cut two side panels to these measurements from fabric. Make sure that prominent or directional patterns mirror each other so that the chair will look the same from either side. If possible, match patterns with the pieces cut in Step 9.

11 With right sides together and raw edges aligned, pin the tops of the arm and side panels together 1" from the edge. Insert welting between the fabric layers, removing and replacing pins to insert the welting. Baste the seam, catching the welting in the stitches. Remove the pins. Place the arm-side unit on the chair with wrong sides out and the seam lying along the imaginary line. Allow the panels to extend 1" over the front edge of the arm. Smooth the arm panels down to the deck. Fold the bottom edge of the arm panel onto the deck.

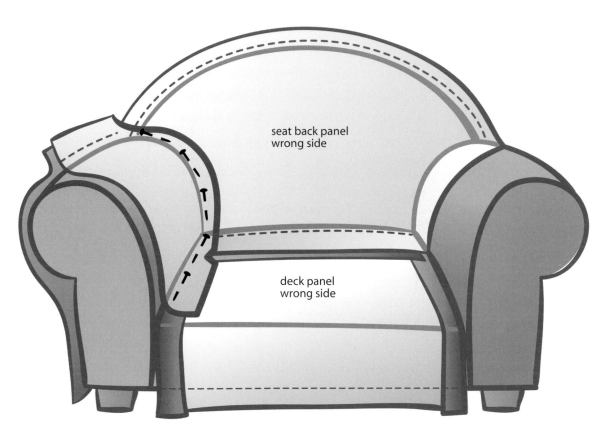

seat back panel
wrong side

deck panel
wrong side

figure 7

12 Bring the bottom edge of each arm panel and the side edges of the deck panel together (the inside arm panel may extend beyond the raw edge of the deck panel). Insert a line of pins parallel to the edge, 1" from the shorter edge, to make a temporary seam (Figure 7). Between this seam line and the inside corner of the chair, there will be a 2" to 3" tuck-in allowance. Trim the seam allowance to 1". Bring the back edge of the arm panel and the adjacent edge of the seat back panel together along the back edge of the arm. Beginning at the top of the seam, insert a line of pins to curve from the top of the arm to the deck. Place the pins so that the seam is close to the chair at the top of the arm and gradually looser as it reaches the deck. Trim the seam allowance to about 1".

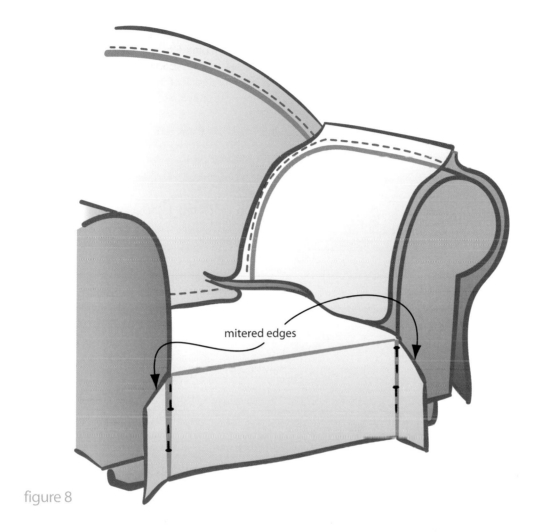

mitered edges

figure 8

13 Remove the panels from the chair. Use a long stitch length to baste the pinned seams on the bottom and back edges of each arm panel. Remove the pins. Place the panels on the chair. Tuck the seams around the deck into the original upholstery. On the front edge of the deck panel, fold each side to fit the section for the front panel, mitering the corners. Insert a line of pins as a temporary seam (Figure 8). Remove the panels. Baste the seam on the pinned line, then remove the pins.

14 Place the panels on the chair. Tuck the seams around the deck and at the back of the arms into the original upholstery. At each back corner, bring the edges of the chair back panel and each side panel together. Insert a line of pins parallel to the edge to make a temporary seam. Do not baste or sew these seams yet. Smooth the side panels to the front of the chair; check that the front edge extends at least 1" beyond the chair.

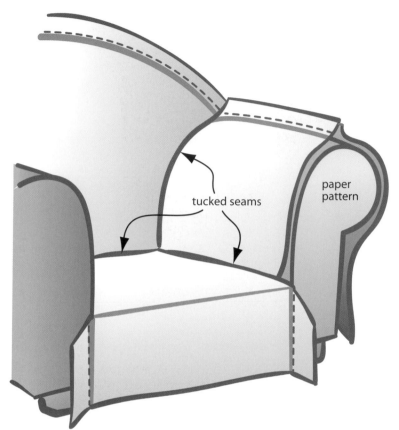

tucked seams

paper pattern

figure 9

15 Place a piece of paper on the arm front. Place the bottom edge of the paper even with the upholstered edge (or top of the skirt) on the original upholstery. Mark the front arm edge on the paper. Cut out the pattern. Compare the arm front pattern to the chair to ensure that the pattern is large enough (Figure 9).

16 Place the arm front pattern on the fabric. Add a 1" allowance around the pattern and cut out one arm front panel. Reverse the pattern and cut one more arm front panel for the opposite side.

17 Place each arm front on the chair, wrong side out. Bring the side, arm, and front panels to meet each arm front panel. Insert a line of pins about 1" from the raw edge of the arm front to make a temporary seam. Trim the seam allowance to 1". Clip the seam allowances of the side and arm panels to ease the fabric around the curves. Remove the pins from one corner on the back of the slipcover. Remove the panels from the chair.

18 Insert welting between the fabric layers along the edges of each arm front panel, removing and replacing pins to insert the welting. Using the zipper foot and a long stitch length, baste the pinned seam, catching the welting in the stitches and removing pins as you sew. Baste the pinned seam at one corner on the back of the slipcover; remove the pins. Turn the cover right side out.

19 Place the panels on the chair with right sides out. Tuck the seams around the deck and at the back of the arms into the original upholstery. At the open back corner, bring the edge of the chair back and side panels together. Insert a line of pins parallel to the corner to make a temporary seam. Check the fit of the cover: It should be slightly loose and true to the shape of the original upholstery. Adjust seams at any snug points. When satisfied with the fit, stitch each seam along the basting line with a regular stitch length. Leave one back corner open. Grade the seam allowances and clip the corners and curves. Press the seams. Turn the cover right side out. Lightly press the seams from the right side.

20 Place the cover on the chair, right sides out. Tuck the seams around the deck into the original upholstery. At the bottom edge, trim the excess fabric to make an even 1" allowance where the cover overlaps the upholstered edge (or the top of the skirt).

21 At the back corner, bring the side edge around the corner to the back. If necessary, trim the edge of the side panel to make an even strip on the back. Turn under the edge of the side panel one-half of the width. Turn under the raw edge of the chair back panel to meet the fold with the back corner of the chair. Pin and press. Trim the bottom edge of the cover 1" longer than the upholstered edge or the top of the existing skirt on the upholstered piece.

22 Measure the zipper against the chair back corner. Position the zipper tab 1" from the bottom edge of the panel. With the zipper closed, hand-stitch across the coils to shorten the zipper, if necessary, taking several stitches that will serve as a zipper stop. Leaving a 1" allowance, cut off the excess zipper length (Figure 10).

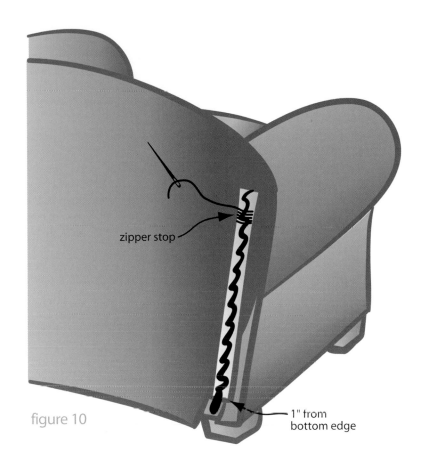

zipper stop

1" from bottom edge

figure 10

chair back panel

side panel

figure 11

23 Place the zipper tab down. Pin one tape under the folded edge of the side panel. Remove the cover from the chair. Using the zipper foot, stitch the zipper to the side panel. Place the folded edge of the chair back panel over the zipper and pin the free zipper tape to it. Using the zipper foot, stitch the panel to the tape (Figure 11).

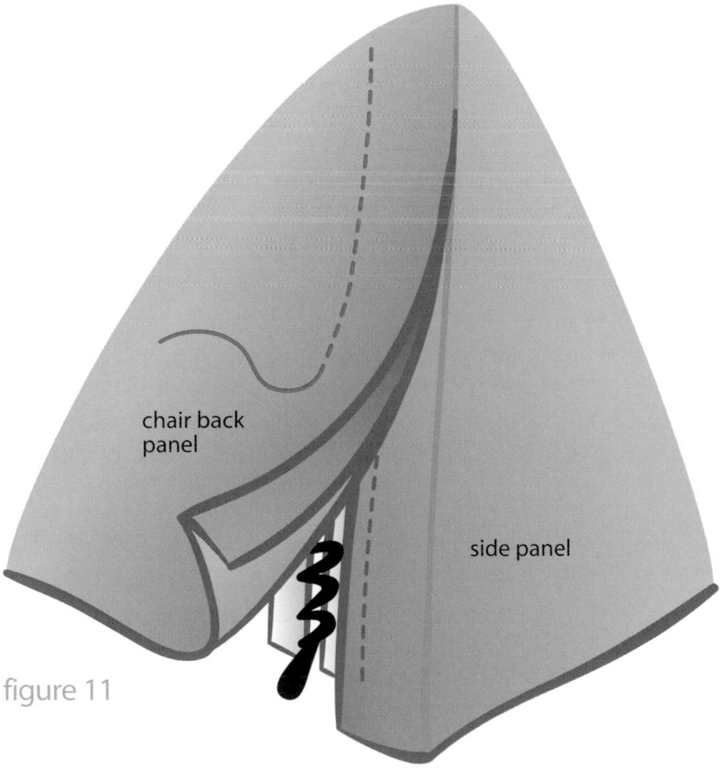

24 Pin welting on the right side of the bottom edge of the cover. Place the cord 1" from the raw edge and lay the seam allowance toward the raw edge. Turn the welting ends to the wrong side of the cover behind the zipper tapes. Using the zipper foot and a long stitch length, baste the welting to the cover.

25 Place the cover on the chair. Measure from the welting to the floor and add 3" for the cut width of the ruffle. Measure around the chair at the welting and multiply by 1½. From fabric, cut enough strips of this width to make the required length. With right sides together and raw edges aligned, stitch the strips together at the narrow ends, using a ½" seam allowance. On the hem edge, turn under 1" twice. Press. Edgestitch close to the folded edge. On each narrow end, turn under 1" twice. Edgestitch close to the folded edge.

26 Divide the remaining long edge of the ruffle into quarters, marking each quarter with pins. Divide the bottom edge of the slipcover into quarters. Set the sewing machine for a long stitch length and loosen the upper thread tension. Stitch the ruffle $1\frac{1}{4}$", 1", $\frac{3}{4}$", and $\frac{1}{2}$" from the raw edge, breaking the stitching at the quarter marks. Match the quarter marks on the ruffle to those on the slipcover. Pull up the bobbin thread of all four gathering lines to fit the ruffle to the slipcover edge. Adjust the gathers and pin the ruffle to the slipcover, with right sides together and raw edges aligned. Stitch the ruffle to the slipcover along the welting basting line, removing pins as you sew. Press the seam. To remove the visible line of gathering stitches below the welting, pull the bobbin thread and then the top thread. Place the slipcover on the chair and zip the cover closed. Tuck the seams around the deck and at the back of the arms into the original upholstery.

27 If the seat cushion is a regular shape, measure it from side to side and front to back and add 2" to each measurement. Centering any fabric motif on the panels, cut two pieces to these measurements from fabric for the top and bottom panels.

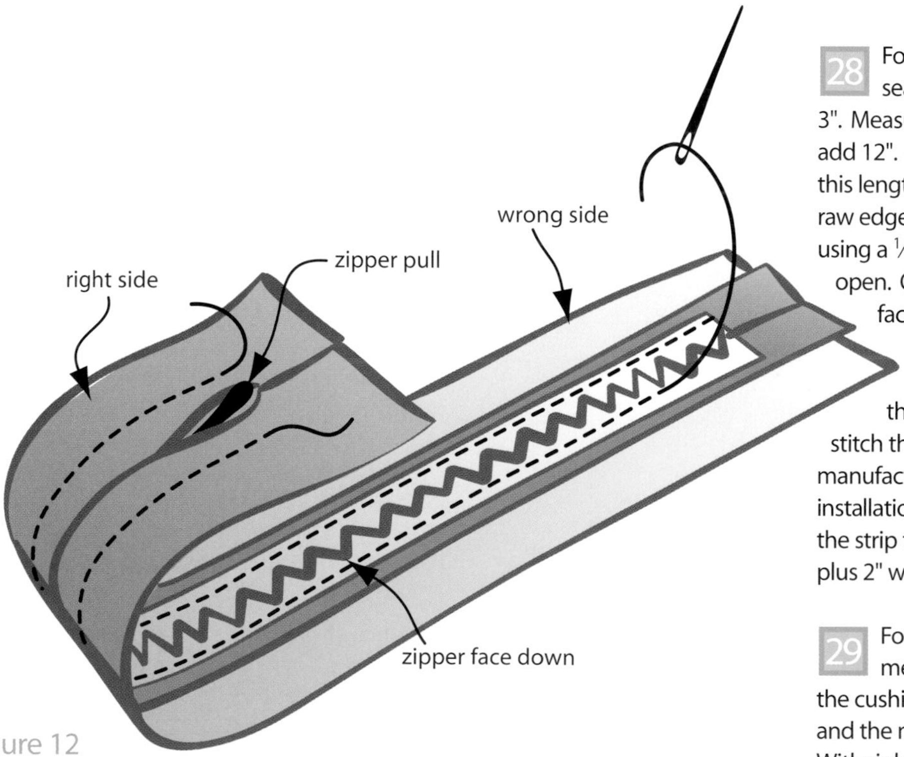

28 For the zippered gusset, measure the seat cushion gusset width and add 3". Measure the back edge of the cushion and add 12". Cut two 4"-wide strips from fabric to this length. With right sides together and long raw edges aligned, baste the strips together, using a $\frac{1}{2}$" seam allowance. Press the seam open. On the wrong side, center the zipper, face or tab side down, over the basted seam. Baste the zipper tapes to the fabric by hand (Figure 12). Turn to the right side. Using the zipper foot, stitch the zipper in place following the manufacturer's instructions for centered zipper installation. Remove the basting stitches. Trim the strip to the measured width of the gusset plus 2" with the zipper at the center.

29 For the remaining (front) gusset, measure the sides and front edges of the cushion. Cut a strip of fabric to this length and the measured width of the gusset plus 2". With right sides together and raw edges aligned, pin one end of the front gusset to the zipper-stop end of the zippered gusset. Use a 1" seam allowance to stitch the front gusset to the back gusset. Press the seam.

right side

zipper pull

wrong side

zipper face down

figure 12

30 Center the zippered back gusset on the back edge of the original cushion, folding the ends around the corners of the cushion. Wrap the front gusset around the cushion to the back gusset, leaving a little slack in the gusset for a smooth fit. How closely the gusset fits the original cushion will determine the fit of the finished cover. Leave some ease around the cushion. Where the gusset ends meet, make a 1½" tuck in the front gusset over the zipper-pull end of the zippered gusset. Pin the narrow ends of the gusset together. Using a 1" seam allowance, stitch the ends. Press the seam toward the front gusset (Figure 13).

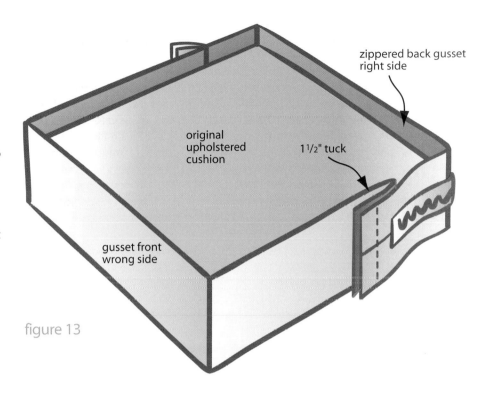

zippered back gusset right side

original upholstered cushion

1½" tuck

gusset front wrong side

figure 13

31 Place the gusset on the cushion with wrong sides out. Open the zipper and pin the edges of the open zipper together. Center the top panel, wrong side up, on the cushion. Bring the edges together with the gusset edges. Clip the gusset corner seam allowances. Insert a line of pins to make a temporary seam along the edges (Figure 14). Turn over the cushion and repeat to pin the bottom panel to the gusset. Check the fit; it should be snug. The gusset should be evenly pinned between the panels to keep it straight and smooth. When satisfied with the fit, trim the seam allowances to 1".

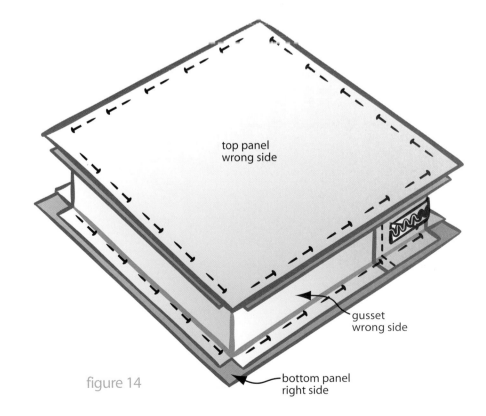

top panel wrong side

gusset wrong side

bottom panel right side

figure 14

32 Remove the pins from the zipper opening and remove the cushion. Insert welting between the fabric layers on each gusset edge, removing and replacing pins. Overlap the welting 2" and cut the ends (they will be finished in a later step). Using the zipper foot and a long stitch length, baste the pinned seam of the top panel and gusset, working with the top panel faceup and catching the welting in the stitches. Pivot the stitching at the corners. Clip the gusset and welting seam allowances at the corners. Baste the gusset to the bottom panel in the same manner, but with the gusset panel faceup.

33 Turn the cover right side out. Insert the cushion into the cover through the zippered opening. Check the fit of the cover, then remove the cushion. Turn the cover to the wrong side and adjust the seams, if necessary.

34 Where the welting ends meet, remove the basting stitches to loosen a 4" section of welting. Remove the stitches from the casing on each end of the welting. Cut the cord ends to meet. Refold one end of the casing over the cord; turn under the remaining casing end ½" to conceal the raw edges. Using the zipper foot and a long stitch length, baste the welting to the panel along the basting line.

35 Set the machine at a normal stitch length and work with the top panel faceup. Stitch the top panel to the gusset along the basting line, pivoting the stitching at the corners. Working with the gusset faceup, stitch the gusset to the bottom panel along the basting line, pivoting the stitching at the corners. Clip the corners and grade the seam allowances. Press the seam and turn the cover right side out. Insert the cushion into the cover. Close the zipper and place the cushion on the chair.

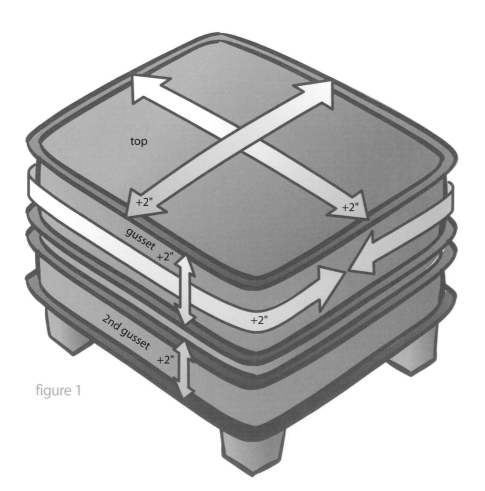

figure 1

OTTOMAN SLIPCOVER

1 Measure the top of the ottoman from side to side and front to back and add 2" to each measurement. Cut one top panel from fabric to this size. Measure the width of the gusset edge of the ottoman top and add 2". Loosely measure around the ottoman top and add 2" for the gusset length. Measure the ottoman platform from top to bottom and add 2" for the second gusset width. Loosely measure around the platform and add 2" for the second gusset length (Figure 1). Cut two gussets to size from fabric, matching patterns, if necessary.

OTTOMAN FABRIC REQUIREMENTS

54"-wide decorator fabric for top*
54"-wide decorator fabric for gussets*
54"-wide decorator fabric for skirt*
54"-wide contrasting fabric for welting*

*Purchase materials after taking measurements.

2 With right sides together and raw edges aligned, stitch the narrow gusset ends together, using a 1" seam allowance to make a loop. Check the fit of the gussets on the ottoman and adjust, if necessary. Press the seam. Stitch the second gusset in the same manner. Pin welting to the right side of each gusset along the bottom edge, placing the cord edge 1" from the raw edge, with seam allowances turned toward the raw edges. Clip the welting seam allowance at the corners. Overlap the welting 1" and cut the ends. Remove the stitching from the casing on both ends and cut the cord ends to meet. Refold one casing over the cord, turn under the remaining casing to conceal the raw ends, and wrap it around the cord. Using the zipper foot and a long stitch length, baste the welting to the gussets. Pivot the stitching at the corners. Baste welting to the right side of the top panel.

CALCULATING YARDAGE

When you take on a project, such as making a slipcover for an upholstered chair, you need a formula to calculate how much fabric you need for your particular chair.

■ Almost all fabric panels cut for slipcovers like the one shown on page 190 are cut so that fabric designs run in the same direction. Measure the width of the largest plane on the upholstered chair. Most often, the largest piece for a chair is either the chair back panel or the side panel. Measure the width of each to determine which of these planes is larger. If the width is less than 54", cut the panel as a single piece from one width of fabric; however, if the chair is wider, cut at least one additional segment to piece together a panel for that part of the chair.

■ Measure the width of each plane of the chair to determine the number of fabric widths or cuts for each panel. Make a chart of the planes on the chair, referring to them by the names given to the panels used to piece together the slipcover: For the chair frame—chair back, seat back, deck, arm (two each), side (two each); for the chair cushions—top panel, bottom panel, gusset front, and gusset back (multiples of these pieces if chairs have more than one loose cushion). In your chart, list each plane by panel name. List the width of the plane and the number of cuts or fabric widths needed to obtain that width. Also note the height or length of each plane in inches.

■ If you use solid fabric with no printed or woven design, multiply the number of fabric widths or cuts by the panel heights or lengths. Add the resulting figures to find the total length needed to make the slipcover. Purchase 10 to 15 percent more fabric to be sure you have enough.

■ If you choose fabric with a design or pattern, you will need the pattern repeat to finish your calculations. The repeat identifies the length of the fabric that contains the complete design (see page 117). If the fabric has a central motif, such as a floral bouquet, you will need enough repeats to center the motif on each panel.

■ If each of the panels measures less than the fabric repeat, multiply the number of cuts by the length of the repeat to find the required yardage. If a cut is larger than the repeat, rethink the height of the panel in terms of how many repeats are needed to make that panel. For example, rather than allowing for one 45"-long cut for the chair back panel, allow for 2½ repeats that are each 18" long.

■ Set up the panel cuts in terms of how many repeats each panel needs. Add the total number of repeats. Multiply the number of repeats by the length of one repeat to find the total yardage needed. Purchase one or two more repeats than you calculate to ensure that you have enough fabric. Look at the fabric to see where the last cut on the fabric is placed. Add partial repeats at the start of the fabric piece to the total to ensure the desired design placement.

3 With right sides together and raw edges aligned, pin the gusset top edge to the top panel over the welting. Clip the gusset seam allowance at the corners. Using the zipper foot and a long stitch length, baste along the previous basting. Remove the pins as you stitch and pivot stitching at the corners. Turn right side out and check the fit on the ottoman; adjust, if necessary. Stitch the top panel to the gusset along the basting.

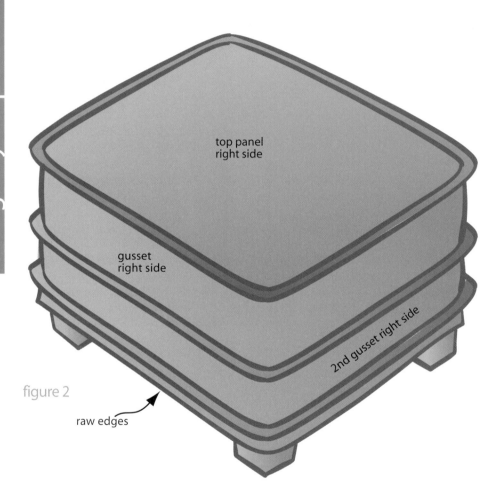

top panel
right side

gusset
right side

2nd gusset right side

figure 2

raw edges

4 With right sides together and raw edges aligned, pin the top edge of the second gusset to the first gusset over the welting. Using the zipper foot and a long stitch length, baste the gussets together. Turn right side out and check the fit of the unit on the ottoman (Figure 2); adjust, if necessary. Stitch the gussets together along the basting. Remove the pins.

5 Place the cover on the ottoman. Measure from the welting to the floor and add 3" for the cut width of the ruffle. Measure around the cover at the welting and multiply by 1½. Cut enough strips of this width from fabric to equal the required length. With right sides together and raw edges aligned, stitch the strips together at the narrow ends to make a loop, using a ½" seam allowance. On the hem edge, turn under 1" twice and press. Edgestitch close to the folded edge.

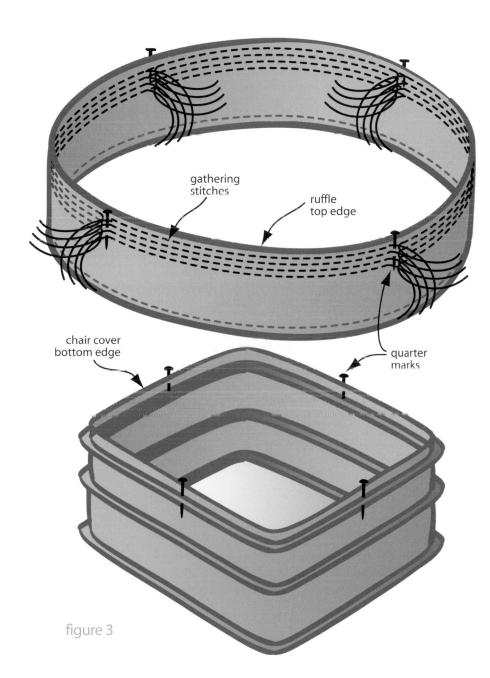

gathering
stitches

ruffle
top edge

chair cover
bottom edge

quarter
marks

figure 3

6 Divide the remaining long edge of the ruffle into quarters and mark each quarter with pins. Divide the lower edge of the ottoman cover into quarters. Set the machine for a long stitch length and loosen the upper thread tension. Stitch the ruffle $1\frac{1}{4}$", 1", $\frac{3}{4}$", and $\frac{1}{2}$" from the raw edge, breaking the stitching at the quarter marks (Figure 3).

7 Match the ruffle quarter marks to the slipcover quarter marks. Pull the bobbin thread of all four gathering lines to gather the ruffle to fit the edge of the slipcover. Adjust the gathers and pin the ruffle to the slipcover, with right sides together. Stitch along the basting line for the welting, removing pins as you sew. Press the seam. To remove the visible line of gathering stitches below the welting, pull the bobbin thread and then the top thread. Place the cover on the ottoman.

Brighten a sunroom with custom-made cushions for chair seats and backs to soften the appearance of wicker furniture. Envelope pillows, with a flap-front design, are interesting focal points against an array of basic pillows, making the furniture even more comfortable.

sensational sunroom

Bring a porch or sunroom to full bloom with floral-patterned cushions. Using one fabric for both back and seat cushions on each piece ties together different shapes and styles of furniture and blends them in a well-planned decorating scheme. Keeping with the style of the furniture and room, the look of the cushions is casual, with softly gathered corners and minimal detailing on each cushion. Standard-density upholstery foam adds to the ease of workmanship.

Accent the cushions with contrasting throw pillows in several related patterns. The fringe edging and rosette on the plaid envelope pillow shown at left impart a playful feeling that suits the casual porch setting. If the style of your room calls for simpler lines, replace the fringe in the seams of the pillow with welting in the same fabric as the cover. Or use contrasting piping for a clean edging that accents the pillow shape with color.

See page 48 for basic pillow instructions.

materials

3"-thick upholstery foam
for seat*
$\frac{1}{8}$"- to $\frac{1}{4}$"-loft bonded
polyester batting*
54"-wide decorator fabric*
Purchased welting*
Paper
1"-thick upholstery foam for
seat back*
Buttons with shanks (optional)

tools

Utility knife
Permanent marker
Vanishing fabric marker
Upholstery needle
Skewer (optional)

sewing tools

Sewing machine
Needle and thread
Pins
Iron and ironing board
Tape measure
Zipper foot

skill level: beginner
time required: 1 day
*Purchase materials after
taking measurements.

seat cushion

1   Measure the chair seat and cut one piece of 3"-thick foam to this size.
Place the foam on the chair to check the fit; there should be some room
for movement. Trim the foam, if necessary.

2   Wrap the foam with batting, pinning and trimming it to cover the foam
smoothly. Loosely hand-stitch the batting edges together. Remove
the pins.

3   Measure the foam
from side to side and
front to back and add 4" to
each measurement. Cut two
pieces to this measurement
from fabric for the top and
bottom panels. Set the
bottom panel aside. Center the
top panel, right side down, on
the batting-wrapped foam.
Smooth the fabric over the
sides of the foam. Using the
vanishing fabric marker, mark
the seam line along the center
edge of the foam (Figure 1). At
the corners, gather the fabric
with your fingers and mark the
seam lines.

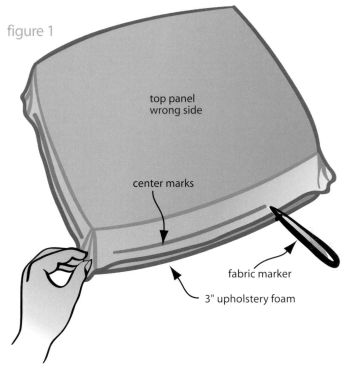

figure 1

top panel
wrong side

center marks

fabric marker

3" upholstery foam

4   Remove the panel from the foam. Measure $\frac{1}{2}$" from the
marked line and trim the excess fabric to make even seam
allowances. Mark curves around the corners. Trim the bottom panel
to match the top panel. Set the sewing machine for a long stitch
length and loosen the upper thread tension. On each panel, stitch
around the corners $\frac{3}{4}$", $\frac{1}{2}$", $\frac{3}{8}$", and $\frac{1}{4}$" from the raw edge (Figure 2).
At each corner, pull the bobbin thread of all four lines of stitching to
gather the corner to fit the panel neatly over the foam.

5   Pin the welting to the right side of the top panel,
beginning at the center of the back edge and aligning raw
edges. Overlap the welting 1"; cut. Remove the stitching from the
casing on both ends. Open the casing and cut the cord ends to
meet. Refold the casing over the cord, turning under one end to
conceal the raw edges of the casing. Using the zipper foot and a
long stitch length, baste the welting to the top panel. (One line of
gathering stitches will be visible in the top panel and will be pulled
out in a later step.) Press the seam toward the seat panel.

6   With right sides together, raw edges aligned, and using the
zipper foot, stitch the top and bottom panels together. Stitch
around the corners and leave an opening in one side for turning.
Press the seam. Turn the cover right side out. Remove the
gathering stitches at each corner by pulling the bobbin thread,
then the top thread.

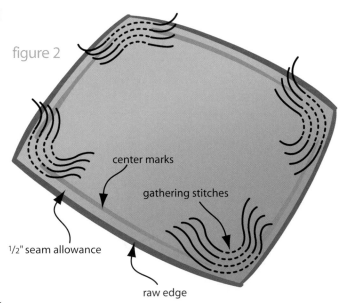

figure 2

center marks

gathering stitches

$\frac{1}{2}$" seam allowance

raw edge

7   Insert the foam through the opening.
Turn under the raw ends of the fabric
opening and hand-stitch the opening closed.

PATTERN PLACEMENT

For professional looking home decorating projects, consider pattern placement and repeat.

LARGE FLORAL MOTIFS
■ Center the largest bouquet or flower on each cushion (Figure 1, top).
■ On a bench or long cushion, place three large flowers along the span (Figure 1, bottom).

TOILE
■ Treat these scenic designs as florals, centering one portion of the design on each cushion (Figure 2).
■ To maximize the pattern, arrange motifs toward the cushion center, with fabric backgrounds along the cushion edges.

PLAIDS OR STRIPES
■ Center the repeat side-to-side on cushions. When cushions are used in a row, center the repeat on each cushion (Figure 3).
■ Match patterns on the front edge of the cushions to look as though the fabric wraps around the cushion (Figure 3). Because cushion sides will be obscured, they do not have to match from the top to the side.

welting

figure 1

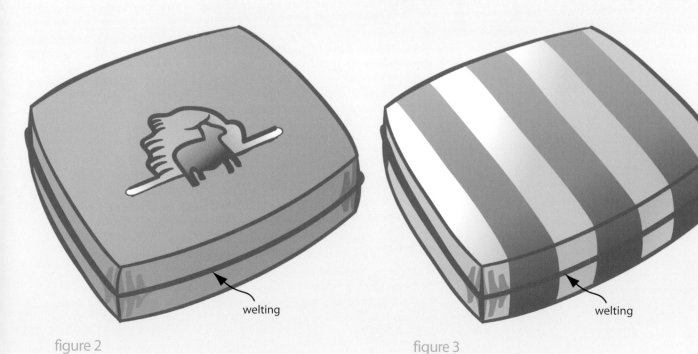

welting

figure 2

welting

figure 3

back cushion

1 Place a sheet of paper on the seat back and mark the edges. Cut out along the marked line to make a pattern. Crease the paper from top to bottom along the center. Place the paper on the chair back to check the fit and to determine button placement, if desired (Figure 1).

2 Using the pattern, cut the 1"-thick foam to size. If using buttons, transfer the button placement to the foam, using the permanent marker. Push a skewer straight through the foam at each mark to transfer the button placement to the back of the foam. Mark the button placement on the back. Use a utility knife to cut out a small cone shape, slightly larger than the button diameter, at each button mark. Wrap and smooth batting over the foam, pinning and trimming the batting to cover the foam smoothly. Hand-stitch the batting edges together. Remove the pins.

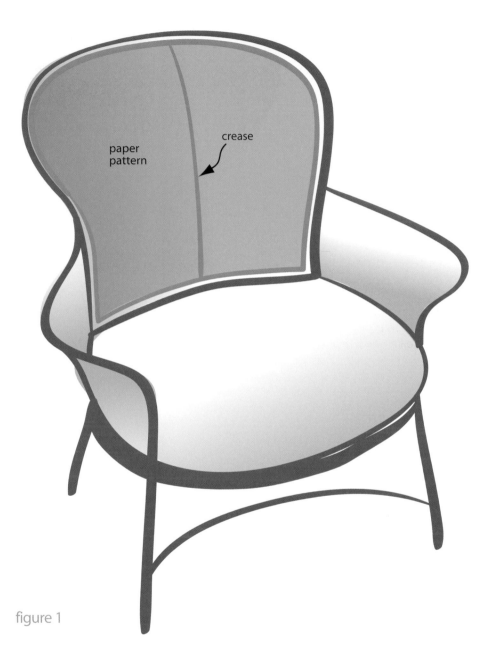

paper pattern

crease

figure 1

3 Place the pattern on the right side of the fabric, centering any design. Mark 1½" seam allowances beyond the pattern edges. Cut one front panel and one back panel along the marked lines. Center the front panel on the batting-wrapped foam, smoothing the fabric over the sides. Using the fabric marker, draw a line along the center of the foam side for the seam line. At the corners, gather the fabric with your fingers and mark for the seam line. If the top edge of the seat back is curved, gather the fabric along the curve to mark the seam line.

4 Remove the panel from the foam. Measure $\frac{1}{2}$" from the marked line toward the edge and trim the excess fabric for an even seam allowance. Trim the back panel to match the front panel. Set the sewing machine for a long stitch length, and loosen the upper thread tension. On the front and back panels, stitch around each corner and along the top curved edge $\frac{3}{4}$", $\frac{1}{2}$", $\frac{3}{8}$", and $\frac{1}{4}$" from the raw edge (Figure 2). Pull the bobbin threads of all four gathering stitches to gather the corners and curves, fitting the panel neatly over the foam.

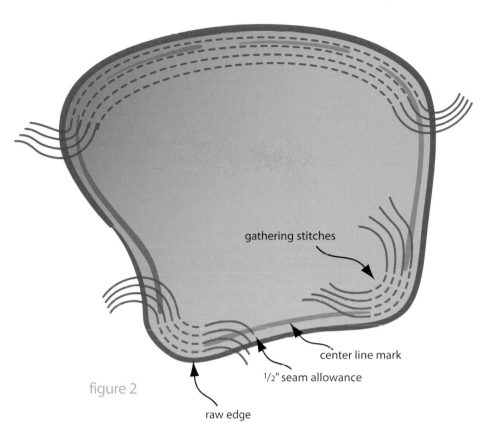

gathering stitches

center line mark

$\frac{1}{2}$" seam allowance

figure 2

raw edge

5 Pin the welting to the right side of the front panel, beginning at the center of the bottom edge and aligning raw edges. Overlap the welting ends 1" and cut. Remove the stitching from the casing on both ends. Unfold the fabric and cut the cord ends to meet. Refold one end of the casing over the cord. Turn under the casing $\frac{1}{2}$" on the opposite side and refold it to cover the cord. Using the zipper foot and a long stitch length, baste the welting to the front panel. (One line of gathering stitches will show on the front panel at each corner; these stitches will be pulled out in a later step.) Press the seam toward the panel.

6 With right sides together and raw edges aligned, stitch the front panel to the back panel along the welting stitches using the zipper foot. Stitch around the corners, leaving an opening in one side to turn and to insert the foam. Press the seam and turn the cushion cover right side out. To remove the visible gathering stitches, pull the bobbin thread, then the top thread.

7 Insert the foam for the seat back into the cushion cover. Turn under the raw ends of the opening and hand-stitch the opening closed.

8 To tuft the seat back with buttons, follow the manufacturer's instructions to cover a pair of buttons for each button position. Cut two 12" lengths of buttonhole thread. Treating two lengths as one, insert the thread through one button shank. Insert all four thread ends through the eye of an upholstery needle. Locate a button position by feeling through the cushion fabric. Insert the needle through the cushion to the backside and pull the thread to sink the button into the cushion. Pass the needle through the second button shank and pull the thread tightly. Knot the thread under the button. Repeat for the remaining button pairs. Place the cushion on the chair back.

envelope pillow

1 Cut a 24×32" rectangle from paper. Fold the paper in half, matching the long edges, and crease the fold. Open the fold and mark a point 4" from the corner on one long edge (Figure 1). Draw an angled line from this point to the fold. Refold the paper and cut both layers along the marked line, then reopen the fold.

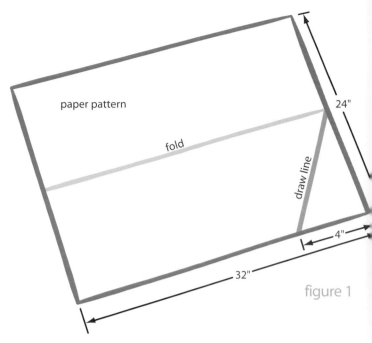

paper pattern

fold

draw line

24"

4"

32"

figure 1

2 Place the pattern on the right side of the fabric, positioning the pattern on the bias. Add a ½" seam allowance around the pattern and cut one back panel. Also cut a 25" square for the front panel, positioning it to take advantage of any fabric motif.

3 Place the pattern on the right side of the lining, positioning the fold line on the straight grain. Add a ½" seam allowance around the pattern and cut one back lining. Cut a 25" square for the front lining.

4 Lay the back panel right side up. Pin the braided edge of the fringe to the panel, aligning the edges (Figure 2). Gently round square corners to ease the fringe around the panel.

Where the fringe ends meet, overlap the ends ½". Apply liquid ravel preventer to the cut ends. Let dry. At the center of the overlap, turn the end of the fringe into the seam allowance. Using a long stitch length, baste the fringe to the panel.

5 Along one edge of the front panel, turn ½" to the wrong side (this will be the top edge). Press to crease. With right sides together and raw edges aligned, pin the front panel to the back panel on the side and bottom edges. Stitch the panels together following the previous basting line in the back panel (be sure to keep the fringe edge out of the seam). Clip the corners, press the seam, and turn to the right side. Press.

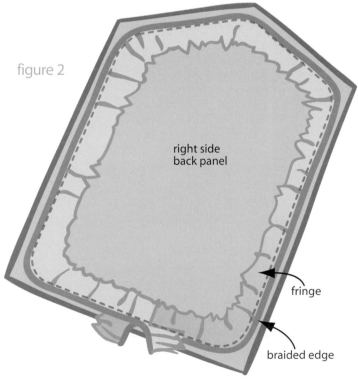

figure 2

right side
back panel

fringe

braided edge

6 On the top edge of the front lining panel, turn under ½". Press to crease. With right sides together and raw edges aligned, pin the front lining panel to the back lining panel on the bottom and side edges. Using a ½" seam allowance, stitch the lining panels together on three sides, pivoting the stitching at the corners. Clip the corners and press the seams open.

7 With right sides together and raw edges aligned, pin the lining to the back panel along the edges of the flap (Figure 3). Stitch the lining to the panel following the previous basting lines in the back panel. Start and stop stitching where the front panel has been attached. Clip the corners and press the seams. Turn the flap to the right side. Press the seam. Place the fringe on the edge of the flap and press flat.

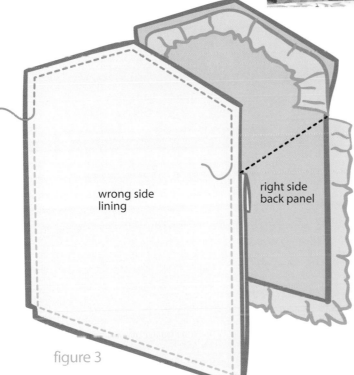

wrong side lining

right side back panel

figure 3

8 Tuck the lining inside the pillow cover. Align the folded edge on the front panel with the folded edge on the front lining. Edgestitch the panel and lining together along the edge. Using a needle and thread, hand-tack the side seams in the lining to the side seams in the outer cover. Insert the pillow form in the cover. Close the flap.

9 Apply liquid ravel preventer to the cut end of the fringe. To make a fringe rosette, coil fringe on a flat surface with the braid edge at the center of the circle; make the coil as tight as possible. Using a needle and thread, hand-tack the braid to close the coil. Make a second coil by inserting braid inside the first coil with the brush end of the fringe standing up (Figure 4). Tack the braid to itself as you work. At the center, cut the fringe. Apply ravel preventer. Let dry. Tuck the end into the center of the coil. Tack the end to the braid. Stitch the rosette to the right side of the flap by hand. The weight of the flap with the rosette will keep the pillow cover closed. If desired, invisibly stitch the tip of the flap to the front panel.

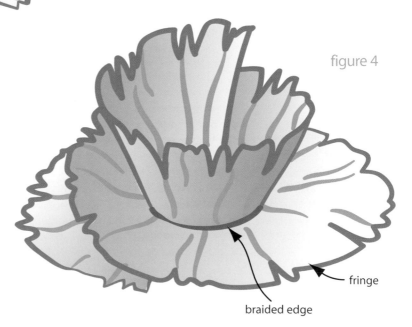

figure 4

braided edge

fringe

chairs: fabric selection and care

Choosing the best fabrics for slipcovers not only makes the finished items look better, but it also makes the construction process easier—and more pleasant.

Fashion fabrics may be pretty to look at, but few have what it takes to make long-wearing and successful slipcovers. Decorator and upholstery fabrics are designed to accommodate the shapes and styles of furniture. The techniques used in making slipcovers or upholstering chairs also factor into the manufacture of the fabric, so they will handle well when stretched, stitched, and gathered. A final consideration is how fabric will handle abrasion, cleaning, sunlight, and other facts of life for a fabric-covered chair.

When choosing a new fabric for a slipcover, analyze the original covering of the chair and try to determine why it was (or wasn't) successful. Also check out similar pieces of furniture in stores, homes, magazines, and books. Look at the pattern, texture, and weight and use that knowledge when buying fabric for a slipcover.

Weave

Fabrics stretched tightly over a cushion, seat, or the body of the chair take a great deal of wear, both during construction of the cover and when it is in use. Tightly woven fabrics are essential for this type of cover. A fabric with a tight weave should feel stable without seeming stiff. Pull the fabric horizontally, vertically, and diagonally as if you were stretching it over the chair; there should be very little give on the crosswise and lengthwise grains and minimal give on the bias. Slipcovers that are softly draped and will receive little wear do not need to be as stable or tightly woven.

Weight

Decorator fabric comes in three basic weights: upholstery, multipurpose, and lightweight. Upholstery weights are strongest, have better abrasion resistance, and are more

lightfast. They also tend to be heavier. This may mean that they will not gather as tightly or easily; it may be harder to form crisp folds for corners or pleats, and it may add bulk at seams. Drop-in seats, such as those that fit down into the frame of dining room chairs, may not fit into the chair if a heavy upholstery fabric is used to replace a lighter weight fabric. Velvet and tapestry are examples of upholstery-weight fabrics.

Multipurpose fabrics are lighter weight and have less abrasion resistance than upholstery-weight fabrics, but they are still adequate for most chair covers. They're easier to work with, especially when doing details such as pleats, gathers, or welting. Multipurpose fabrics should have a heavy feel and a tight weave but be more drapable and softer than upholstery fabrics. Chintz is an example of a multipurpose fabric.

Lightweight fabrics, such as organza, offer interesting alternatives in chair covers but should only be used in special circumstances. Slipcovers that will receive light or occasional wear and have a loose fit are good candidates for lightweight fabrics.

Pattern

Many people make their initial pattern decision based on what best coordinates with the room decor and their own personal preference; however, you should also consider scale, furniture shape, detail of the cover, repeat and matching of the pattern, and your sewing skills. Although plain fabrics may seem a safe choice, they are most likely to show sewing flaws; a pattern or texture can help hide minor mistakes.

Keeping the scale of the fabric pattern consistent with the scale of the chair makes the finished piece look coordinated and professional. A small chair doesn't always require a tiny print, but an oversize pattern may not fit the size of the chair. If possible, drape the fabric over a display or counter in the fabric store so it covers approximately the same amount of surface it would cover on the chair; then step back to see how bold the pattern looks from a distance.

Chairs with curves and shaping to the seat and back may be difficult to cover with bold patterns unless the pattern is a simple stripe. Plaids and other geometric designs may not work well with elaborate curves.

Covers with details such as ruching, pleats, gathers, mixed patterns, and welting work best with smaller prints. Large motifs get lost in all the detail, and the overall look becomes visually confusing.

A small repeat is more difficult to match than a large repeat. Narrow stripes or plaids, for example, involve matching along every seam, while large stripes or a large even plaid require minimal matching. A large central motif must be carefully positioned. Take a tissue paper tracing of the chair seat or back with you to the store and lay it over the fabric to see how the large motif will work on the size and shape of the chair.

Specialty Fabrics

Nontraditional fabrics, including chenille, hand-painted canvases, vintage fabrics, and quilts, offer an unusual style and an appealing look. When considering these fabrics, follow the same guidelines for weight and pattern as you would with traditional decorator fabrics. Most of these fabrics were not meant to be used for high-abrasion situations and may not wear well when sat upon. They are also not likely to have any sunlight- or stain-resistant properties, so reserve them for furniture that receives lighter wear. Chairs in a bedroom, entryway, little-used sitting room, formal living room, or guest room are places to utilize this fun look without having the fabric wear in a short time.

Finishes and Treatments

Stain-resistant finishes can be a part of the structure of the fabric, a chemical additive applied or integrated during the manufacture of the fiber or fabric, or a treatment applied at a later date. When purchasing fabric, ask about special finishes; a few are guaranteed.

Tightly woven polished fabrics, like glazed cotton, are naturally more stain-repellent than napped fabrics, such as velvets or corduroy, or highly absorbent ones, including canvas and denim. Even without an added finish, spills are more likely to bead up rather than soak in, allowing time to blot a spill.

Read the labels or brochure information on fabric finishes. Some have specific recommendations for cleaning, suggestions for cleaning agents, or a stain removal guide.

Spray-on stain repellents may be difficult to find. If you cannot find them in the laundry aisle, call fabric stores, furniture stores, and decorator fabric shops. To make sure the spray is compatible with the fabric's original finish and dye, test it on a scrap before applying it to the entire chair cover. Reapply the finish as recommended by the manufacturer.

Outdoor Concerns

New-generation synthetic outdoor fabrics offer resistance to the elements—sunlight, rain, soil, and heavy wear. Many new fabrics also are more comfortable and don't leave you sitting in a puddle of perspiration, like those of a few years ago. Although many decorator fabric stores carry these fabrics, also check with marine-supply stores and tent and awning manufacturers. Also inquire about special cushion material that breathes and dries well. Substitute plastic cording for cotton cording and, for large welting, use nylon rope from marine and hardware stores.

Care and Cleaning

Prevention is the best way to keep fabric clean and fresh. For slipcovers that are left in place, vacuum the furniture frequently using a soft upholstery attachment and a crevice tool. Check for loose buttons and threads before vacuuming. Make sure the vacuum attachment is clean and vacuum in one direction to avoid streaks.

Deep clean chairs every year or two depending on wear. Remove slipcovers when possible and have them professionally cleaned. If they cannot be removed, have them commercially cleaned or use a do-it-yourself foam or steamer. Test the cleaner on an inconspicuous spot before cleaning an entire piece.

For slipcovers that remove easily, freshen them by placing them in a clothes dryer on the air cycle. Place a tennis ball in the dryer with the slipcover to help loosen dust.

For pillows to use outdoors, choose sunproof, mildew-resistant fabrics intended for outdoor use.

bedding basics

Duvets (comforters)

Duvets have become a popular way to dress the bed because they provide snuggly warmth, as well as color and pattern—and the plump comforter makes any bed look irresistible and inviting. Keep the following in mind when buying a comforter.

■ Goose-down comforters are rated by fill power; 575 to 750 is best. Look for a cotton cover with a thread count of 250 to 350. The construction will depend on the manufacturer, but the most common types are box-stitched and channel-stitched. The construction should keep the down evenly distributed and prevent it from shifting to the edges of the comforter.

■ If you're allergic to down, consider cotton- or silk-filled comforters or hypoallergenic synthetic filler.

■ Comforters are generally 86 to 88 inches long and wide enough to hang 12 to 16 inches over each side of the bed. This is large enough to cover a standard-depth mattress, but if you have a pillow-top mattress (which can be 14 to 16 inches deep), the duvet will fall short on each side. In this case, consider dressing the bed with a coverlet and keeping the duvet folded at the foot of the bed.

■ Down-filled comforters may fluff up so much that they actually cover less of the mattress than the measurements on the package might indicate. You may need to choose one size larger to ensure that the comforter is long and wide enough to cover the mattress completely.

■ The duvet projects in this book allow for an 87-inch length and a standard mattress depth, so be sure to measure both your comforter and mattress and adjust measurements and yardage accordingly before buying fabric.

Common Comforter Sizes

Twin: 66-68x86-88 inches
Double: 81-84x86-88 inches
Queen: 86-88x96-100 inches
King: 102x86-88 inches
California King: 107-110x96-98 inches

Basic Mattress Sizes

Note that some manufacturers may add or subtract inches from the standard size.
Twin or Single: 39x75 inches
Twin Extra Long: 5 inches added to the length, which makes them more comfortable for adults.
Double (Full): 54x75 inches
Queen: 60x80 inches
Standard (Eastern) King: 76-78x80 inches
California King: 72x84 inches
Mattress depth: standard depth is 9 to 12 inches; pillow-top mattresses are 14 to 16 inches deep and sometimes even deeper. Before buying sheets, measure your mattress to make sure the fitted sheet is deep enough to accommodate its depth. Also, shop for the largest flat sheet in your size category; you need to be able to tuck in at least 8 to 12 inches at the end of the bed to hold the sheet securely in place.

Because mattress depths vary from manufacturer to manufacturer, measure yours to calculate yardage and to ensure the duvet or coverlet drop is deep enough to cover the mattress.

Common Pillow Sizes

Standard: 20x26 inches
Queen: 20x30 inches
European: 26x26 inches
King: 20x36-40 inches
Boudoir: 12x16 inches
Neckroll: 6x14 inches

Sheet Sizes:

Twin:
Fitted sheet 39x75 inches
Flat sheet 66x96 inches

Twin Extra Long:
Fitted sheet 39x80 inches
Flat sheet 66x102 inches

Double:
Fitted sheet 54x75 inches
Flat sheet 81x96 inches

Queen:
Fitted sheet 60x80 inches
Flat sheet 90x102 inches

King:
Fitted sheet 76-78x 80 inches
Flat sheet 108x102 inches

California King:
Fitted sheet 72x84 inches
Flat sheet 102x110 inches

Note: Some manufacturers offer slightly larger sheets for double, queen, and king-size mattresses to accommodate pillow-top mattresses.

Pillowcase Sizes

Twin, Twin Extra Long, Double: 20x26 inches
Queen: 20x30 inches
King and California King: 20x36-40 inches

U.S. units to metric equivalents

To convert from	Multiply by	To get
Inches	25.4	Millimeters (mm)
Inches	2.54	Centimeters (cm)
Feet	30.48	Centimeters (cm)
Feet	0.3048	Meters (m)

metric to U.S. equivalents

To convert from	Multiply by	To get
Millimeters	0.0394	Inches
Centimeters	0.3937	Inches
Centimeters	0.0328	Feet
Meters	3.2808	Feet

glossary

Align: to match pieces of fabric in a straight line; usually refers to meeting raw edges for sewing a seam or for matching pattern motifs.

All-over design: a pattern that covers the entire fabric and has no distinguishable central motif.

Apron: the part of a chair that extends vertically from the seat and forms a wide finished trim between the seat and legs; also refers to the part of a slipcover (usually a ruffle or pleated band) that extends in the same manner.

Baste: to hold pieces of fabric together temporarily with long, loose stitches, usually made by using the longest stitch length on your sewing machine; basting may be used as a guide for permanent stitches and removed after permanent stitching.

Batting: a bonded low-loft or high-loft material, commonly cotton or polyester, that adds softness and volume to an upholstered piece or seat; batting is made from natural and synthetic fibers.

Bias: the diagonal of the weave or a 45-degree line across the grain of a fabric from the selvage edge; fabric cut on the bias will stretch, allowing a smoother fit around curves.

Box pleat: one or a series of even-width pleats that are made by doubling a fabric strip back on itself. The width of the "box" (the front of the pleat) is created when two opposing folds meet on the underside.

Bullion fringe: fringe made of gold or silver threads.

Butt: to join two pieces or sections side by side to fit together perfectly without gaps.

Cargill: a type of long, silky fringe used to trim draperies.

Casing: a pocket or channel into which a rod or dowel is inserted; it may be formed by parallel lines of stitching through two layers of fabric or by folding a single layer fabric to the desired depth and stitching along the edge.

Chair back: the upright portion of a chair to lean against when sitting. The inside back is the part that faces the person when seated; the outside back refers to the upright portion at the back of a chair.

Chair seat: the portion of a chair to sit on. Many seats are a permanent part of the chair structure; a drop-in seat is separate from the rest of the chair and can be lifted out.

Clip: to make snips or tiny cuts into the seam allowance, up to but not through the stitching, so the seam will lie flat. On a concave curve, make triangular notches to allow for flattening the seam easily.

Cording: a ready-made upholstery trim with a ropelike surface; cording may be stitched decoratively to a surface or used as an edging. Cording can be used plain or covered with fabric for welting.

Cording with lip: cord that is covered with fabric and has a flat fabric extension (the lip) for sewing the cording into a seam line; also called cording with a flange or welting.

Cording with tassels: decorative cord in a set length with a tassel attached to each end.

Cornice: a wooden or metal box or band hung at the top of a window to hide the curtain mechanics; it may have a shaped crown or edge and may be covered with fabric or wallpaper for decorative effect.

Cotton padding: loose cotton fibers that are used to add softness and loft to a cushion or a piece of upholstered furniture.

Crosswise grain: the weft, or grain of the fabric going across the width of the fabric from selvage to selvage.

Cut: a length of fabric prepared for use in a sewing project. For example, to make a pair of curtain panels, you need two cuts of fabric for the pair.

Cut length: the measurement of a piece of fabric that includes allowances for hem, header, any gathers or pleats, and fabric repeat; the length to which you need to cut fabric before you begin sewing.

Cut width: the measurement of a piece of fabric that includes allowances for hems, gathers, or pleats; the width to which you need to cut the fabric before you begin sewing.

Deck: the structural framework of an upholstered chair that is below a drop-in seat; the seat platform below the seat cushion.

Directional pattern: a fabric design that has an obvious top or bottom; the direction needs to be considered when placing a pattern on the fabric. Also referred to as one-way design.

Dress pleats: the term refers to the technique of shaping and arranging pleats until you achieve the desired effect, then wrapping or otherwise binding them so the fabric develops a "memory" of the shape.

Ease: to fit a piece of fabric to one that is slightly shorter. The longer piece is gathered so slightly that the gathers do not show on the finished seam and the shorter piece is stretched slightly but not enough to distort the weave or pattern.

Edgestitch: to machine stitch close to the folded edge of the fabric with medium-length to short stitches.

Fabric marker: special pen, pencil, or chalk that is made for fabric; the marks can be easily brushed or washed away or fade out with time. Always test the marker on a scrap of the fabric to make sure it does not mark that type of fabric permanently, especially after pressing.

Facing: a piece of fabric or nonwoven material stitched to the raw edge of fabric and then turned to the wrong side; it produces a stiffer, more substantial edging than simply hemming a raw edge; it is often incorporated into a design to conceal raw edges.

Fat cord: oversize plain cotton cord that is used to make extra-large welting.

Filler cord: a mesh-wrapped fiber tube used to make welting or piping. Filler cord is available in a range of closely graduated sizes; the most common size for pillow trim is $6/32$ inch.

Fingerpress: using your fingers to press a crease or fold into fabric; the fold isn't as sharp or permanent as one made by pressing with an iron, but is sufficient to retain its shape.

Finish: to prevent raveling on the raw edges of a seam allowance or to create a neat edge by zigzag-stitching, cutting with pinking shears, binding with seam binding, or treating with liquid ravel preventer.

Flat-fell seam: used for lightweight fabrics to create a finished seam on both the right and wrong sides of the fabric; one seam allowance is trimmed narrower than the other; the wider one is folded and stitched over the trimmed allowance, encasing the allowance and its raw edge; a double row of stitching shows on the wrong side of the fabric; on the right side, a line of topstitching parallels a conventional-looking seam. See page 74 for instructions on making a flat-fell seam.

French seam: similar to flat-fell seams in that the seam allowances are enclosed, but the right side of the fabric looks like a conventional seam; the wrong side of the seam looks like a casing. No stitches are visible.

Gathering stitches: rows of medium-length stitches worked about 1/4-inch apart with thread tails to gather the stitches. Gathering stitches may be used as a guide for permanent stitches and removed after stitching permanently.

Gathers: fullness or ruffles created in a flat piece of fabric when the tails of gathering threads are pulled together.

Gimp: flat braid or round cording used to trim pillows, curtains, or upholstered pieces.

Grade: to trim the layers of fabric in a seam to different widths to eliminate bulk and create a smooth transition from the seam to the outer edge of the seam allowance.

Gusset: a piece of fabric inserted between two main components to ease the fit; a gusset often is sewn around the edge of a chair, joining the front and back pieces, or makes up the vertical edge of a seat to join the seat top and seat bottom.

Hand of the fabric: a subjective description of the way a fabric feels, its weight and finish, its degree of crispness or softness, and the amount of drape the fabric allows. The hand is often compared to a standard.

Heading: the top of a curtain panel or valance to which pleating tape, curtain hooks, tabs, ties, or drapery rings are attached.

Hem: a finished edge; an edge of the fabric that is folded over and stitched. Usually the hem is understood to be the bottom edge.

Hemstitch: worked by hand from the wrong side of the fabric, hemstitching secures a folded edge to the fabric by means of diagonal stitches. Draw the needle through the folded edge from underneath, pick up one or two threads of the flat fabric, then insert the needle in the folded edge and draw it through. Continue in this manner to secure the hem; the stitches should be nearly invisible from the right side of the finished piece.

High-density upholstery foam: firm polyurethane foam pads for use in cushions, bolsters, or pillows. Foam pads referred to as high density are resilient and resist crushing with heavy or prolonged use.

Hook-and-loop tape: a two-part fastening tape that has fuzzy material on one strip and plastic "teeth" on the other; strips are stitched or adhered to each side of an opening or to two surfaces that will be applied to each other.

Interfacing: nonwoven fabric, available in varying weights, that is used to stiffen fabric and strengthen seams. It is often used to keep bias-cut or loosely woven fabrics from stretching out of shape.

Interlining: a flannel-like fabric used between the lining and the wrong side of the decorator fabric.

In-the-ditch: a line of stitching worked on the seam line from the right side of the fabric so the stitching disappears into the seam; stitch in-the-ditch to secure facings behind seams.

Inverted pleat: a large pleat that has two folded edges meeting at the center of the pleat and the fullness of the pleat falling behind the folds; inverted pleats are often used at the corners of a chair to fit the skirt around the base of the chair.

Knife pleat: continuous narrow folds of fabric, 1 to 2 inches wide used to trim home decorating projects, such as dust ruffles; all folds run in the same direction.

Layout: the arrangement of fabric cuts or pieces on the original length of fabric; the plan by which pieces are arranged on the fabric to allow for matching patterns from curtain panel to panel or from piece to piece.

Leading edge: the edge of the curtain that falls toward the center of the window; the edge that will be pulled to draw the curtain closed.

Lengthwise grain: the fabric grain that runs parallel to the selvages.

Lining: a firmly woven, smooth-finish cotton used to back decorator fabric for a smooth finished appearance.

Liquid ravel preventer (seam sealant): a clear liquid adhesive applied to the cut edges of fabric or cording to prevent fraying.

Lockstitch: anchoring the beginning and ending machine stitches in place by making several stitches in the same place. Set the stitch length to zero so the needle does not move but goes up and down in the same spot. Lockstitching is less bulky than backstitching.

Loop shade tape: a ready-made strip of twill or polyester netting that has loops attached; it is intended for use in making shades and blinds. Loops may be hard plastic or soft fabric.

Monofilament thread: nylon thread that is transparent or smokey in color. When used in the top of the sewing machine, the stitches blend into the fabric.

Mounting board: a board installed inside the window frame to support a blind or shade, or attached to studs outside the window frame to support a cornice.

Notch: cutting small V-shapes from the seam allowances of a concave curve to allow the curve to lie smooth and flat.

One-way design: fabric that has a defined direction in pattern, texture, weave, or nap. To determine whether a fabric has one-way design, lay two panels side-by-side with one section in one direction and the other in the opposite direction; check whether the colors, patterns, and textures match and catch the light in the same way.

Oriented: pertaining to the direction a fabric design should appear on each piece of a project: the selvage edge notes "up" or "top" of the design.

Panel: the curtain itself, not including valance or swag; a pair of curtains consists of two panels.

Paper-backed fusible web: a heat-activated adhesive product that is used to bond fabric to fabric or fabric to other porous surfaces.

Passementerie: a French term for fancy trims such as fringe, braid, cording, and tassels that add texture and color to home decorating projects.

Pillow form: a ready-made cushion in one of a variety of standard shapes and sizes; the filling may be down, feather/down, or polyester fiberfill.

Pilot holes: starter holes for screws, made by drilling a short distance into the wood with a fine drill bit.

Pin-fit: to temporarily secure fabric pieces with straight pins or T pins; used in situations where basting stitches aren't practical, such as for fitting ruching to a padded headboard.

Pivot: with the sewing machine needle in the fabric, raise the presser foot, turn the fabric at a sharp angle, lower the presser foot, and continue stitching. Pivoting at corners and points is necessary to make a crisp point on the finished piece.

Plastic cord or tubing: weatherproof cord used to make welting for outdoor furniture; plastic cord or tubing is available at marine-supply stores and some hardware stores.

Platform cover: the piece of fabric on a dust ruffle that fits between the box springs and mattress.

Pleating tape: a ready-made band of twill or polyester netting into which a series of cords have been arranged. The band is fastened to the wrong side of a curtain panel or valance at the heading. The cords are drawn to create a preplanned pleated effect.

Pleats: a series of folds used to take up excess fabric and fit a longer piece to a smaller one, mainly for decorative purposes.

Pressing cloth: a lint-free piece of fabric used to protect an area that requires pressing with an iron. The cloth may be used damp or dry.

Prominent pattern: an obvious motif, such as a large floral bouquet set against a plain background.

Puddle: a decorator term describing draperies that are longer than the distance from curtain rod to floor, so the excess fabric can be folded under and arranged gracefully to suggest luxuriousness.

Repeat: the vertical length of a design or motif.

Return: the distance between the wall or window frame and the end of the curtain rod or the front of the curtain track.

Right side: the patterned, printed, or figured side of a piece of fabric; the side that is intended to show in the finished project.

Rod pocket: a channel formed by two rows of stitching at the top of a curtain panel or valance into which a curtain rod can be inserted.

Roman shade cord: See loop shade tape.

Ruche: to tightly gather or pleat a strip of fabric along the top and bottom edges; usually used on a gusset or trim piece.

Running stitch: a simple hand stitch worked from the right side of the fabric, made by taking two or three stitches on the needle at a time; stitches are worked in a straight line.

Seam: the line of stitching and the fabric from the stitching to the fabric edge where two pieces of fabric are joined.

Seam allowance: the fabric between the raw edge and the seam line; usually $1/2$ inch in home decorating projects.

Seam line: the line on which you stitch to join two pieces of fabric.

Selvage: the edge of a piece of woven fabric, finished by the manufacturer to prevent raveling; the selvages are cut off before you begin sewing. Selvages provide information as to the manufacturer, the colors in the fabric, and the direction of the design or pattern repeat.

Spray fabric protector: a specially designed spray that helps fabrics repel dirt, stains, water, and sun damage. Spray fabric protectors should be reapplied as the fabric wears, is exposed to the elements, or is laundered.

Stitch-in-the-ditch: a line of stitching worked on the seam from the right side of the fabric so the stitching disappears into the seam; stitch-in-the-ditch to secure facings behind seams.

Stitch width: needle setting on a sewing machine that sets the width of each stitch in a line of stitching to a specified measurement.

Straight grain: the grain that runs the length of the fabric, parallel to the selvages.

Tack: to secure with a few small hand stitches.

Tassel fringe: a decorative trim that consists of a gimp or braid portion combined with a fringe comprised of tassels.

Tension: the balance between the bobbin and needle threads on a sewing machine; correct tension ensures a perfect stitch.

Topstitch: a line of stitching worked from the right side of the fabric to reinforce a seam and/or to make a decorative effect.

Tuck: a small fold or pleat in a fabric or trim.

Tufting needle: long needle for sewing a button to a pillow front from front to back.

Turn under: to turn the edge of a piece of fabric to the wrong side, usually by a prescribed amount, such as $1/2$ inch.

Understitch: to turn the facing and seam allowance straight out, extending from the fabric piece, and to stitch parallel to the seam ($1/8$ inch), catching the facing and the seam allowances in the stitching.

Unit: a term that may be used to designate a joining of two or more fabric pieces or sections.

Upholstery foam: (see high-density upholstery foam).

Valance: a fabric treatment hung at the top of curtains to hide the curtain fixture.

Vanishing fabric marker: a fine- to medium-point water-soluble marker that generally marks the fabric with a blue line; the line disappears when dampened with water. Remove marks completely before pressing; heat will set them permanently.

Welting: fabric-covered filler cord used to trim edges or seams.

Whipstitch: to sew in small circles, catching the fabric as if to tack. Insert the needle through the fabric and bring it out, around the edge, and back through the fabric in the same manner; the effect is similar to the way the wire coils in a spiral binder.

Wrong side: the back of the fabric, not intended to be seen in the finished project.

Zipper foot: a sewing machine attachment designed for installing zippers; the design of the foot allows the needle to stitch close to bulky items such as zippers and cording.

Zipper stop: the barlike piece at the end of the zipper teeth that prevents the zipper head from going too far, allowing the two segments of the zipper to separate completely.

credits

Waverly products shown in this book were available as of publication date. Please note that items may be discontinued without notice. If a fabric you like is no longer available, call consumer information at 800/423-5881.

Page 10: Designer, stylist: Catherine Kramer; photographer: Hopkins Associates. Walls: Waverly paints WP136 Snow White, colorwashed with WD303 Lichen. Roman shade: Limerick/White 647091; pillows, swag, and banding on shade: 664423; sofa: 664370; chair seats: Limerick/Ruby 647106; chair seat skirts and fabric picture mats: Check It Out/Cherry 664404; area rug: Limerick/Nile 647119, Limerick/Khaki 647096; solid pillows: Old World Linen/Daffodil 645606, Navy 645622.

Page 22: Designer: Rhea Crenshaw, Rhea Crenshaw Interiors, Memphis, TN; photographer: Emily Minton; stylist: Julie Azar; workroom: Unique Decor, Memphis, Tennessee. Draperies, side chair seats, pillow trim: Hanover/Colonial 661080; sofa: Ranger/Maize 630002; armchair: Arcadia/Boxwood 601549.

Page 32: Styling: Heather Lobdell; photographer: Jeff McNamara; accessories: Waverly Home.

Page 36: Draperies: Spring Morning/Primrose 664790 trimmed in Seasons Texture/Spring 647480; chair and ottoman: May Flowers/Primrose 664860; pillow on chair: Seasons Texture/Spring 647480; sofa and pillows: Pretty Plaid/Primrose 664780; pillows on sofa: Spring Morning/Primrose 664790, Seasons Texture/Spring 647480.

Page 42: Window: Simple Stripe/Sage 664425 and Country Fair/Sage 647433; sofa, chair, pillows: Last Summer/Sage 664351; pillows: Field of Flowers 647423, Summer Stripe 664361.

Page 46: Designer: Rhea Crenshaw, Rhea Crenshaw Interiors, Memphis, TN; photographer: Emily Minton; styling: Julie Azar; workroom: Unique Decor, Memphis, TN. Center pillow: Garden Lane 663393; right pillow: Lunette 600965.

Page 54: Curtains: Simple Stripe/Cobalt 664422; table skirt: Cherry Blossom/Cobalt 664381; table topper and slipcovers: Check It Out/Cherry 664404; wallpaper: Cherry Blossom/Cobalt 573931, Cherry Plaid/Cobalt 573951; border: Cherry Plaid Border/Cobalt 573941.

Page 64: Designer, stylist: Catherine Kramer; photographer: Hopkins Associates. Walls: Waverly paints: WT110 Buttercream, WP237 Azure Blue, WD238 Delft; overdoor valance: Parfait/Sky 663981; chair pads, napkins by Waverly.

Page 70: Wallpaper: Demitasse Companion/Lake 572211, Demi Check/Porcelain 572220, Demitasse Border/Lake 572201; chairs: Demitasse/Lake 663541; tablecloth: Perfection/French Blue 647207; table topper: Perfection/Buttercream 647198; trim: Wickerwork/Royal 660872.

Page 76: Left: wallpaper: Aqua; Blossomtime 573350; borders: Blossomtime Border 573360, Doina 573413; windows, chair skirts: Blossomtime/Aqua 663780; valance, chair pads: Heritage/Chambray 647070; chair skirt trim and ties: Heritage/BarnRed 647066; center: wallpaper: Berry Toss/Bright 574251, Bountiful Check/Lemonlime 572178; border: Parfait Border/Lemonlime 574220; window: Party Plaid/Marigold 647301; placemats: Fruit Salad/Lemonlime 663930; napkins, slipcovers: Parfait/Lemonlime 663980; right: wallpaper: Botanica/Victorian 571470; border: Botanica Border/Victorian 571510; chairs, pillows, table runner: Parlour Plaid/Poppy 600723.

Page 82: Designer: Rhea Crenshaw, Rhea Crenshaw Interiors, Memphis, TN; photographer: Emily Minton; stylist: Julie Azar; workroom: Unique Decor, Memphis, TN. Wallpaper: Pantry Plaid/Blush 570961; valance, window seat cushion: Charade Vintage/Crimson 662550; shade and pillows: Country Fair/ Citron 662687.

Page 102: Designer: Sally Draughon, Previews Interior Design, Macon, GA; photographer: Emily Minton. Draperies: Brilliant/ Lemon 602123; table runner: Greenbriar Damask/Persimmon 631546; chair seats: Chaplin/Straw 601105, Chaplin/ Tomato 601102.

Page 112: Designer: Deborah Hastings; photographer: Emily Monton; dust ruffle, valance: Picnic/Aqua 663790; shams: Spring Fling/Aqua 663800, piping Harmoney/Peony 655934, ruffle and dressing table chair: Vacation/Aqua 663810; bed curtains, cafe curtains: Blossomtime/Aqua 663780; table skirt: Spring Fling/Aqua 663800 with miller/White 614830 overlay; wicker chair set cushion: Glosheen/Nugget 645509, piping Harmony/ Peony 655934.

Page 126: Designer, stylist: Catherine Kramer; photographer: Hopkins Associates; duvet: Checkmate/Sunwashed 664215; dust ruffle and folding screen panel: Glosheen/Bluebell 645531; screen panels: Glosheen; pillows: Garden Trellis/Vanilla 664171.

Page 138: Ottoman, scarf trim: Stockholm Stripe 647260; chair, pillows: Inga 664032; Nicholas Plaid 664022; coverlet, pillows: Baltic Brocade 664052; pillows, scarf: Hans 664062, Eugenia 664002; canopy: Greta 664072, Gustavian Stripe 664012; shades: Fredrick 663992, Oyster; sheers: Caprice/ Cream 631302.

Page 158: Designer, stylist Elizabeth Dooner; photographer: Emily Minton; walls: Waverly paint WA156/Olive; coverlet: Chandler from The Luxury Collection; Euroshams, duvet, drapery, neck roll pillow: Windsor Washed Velvet/Toffee 631561; pillows, bed skirt: Mountaineer/Brick 631614; green pillows: Windsor Washed Velvet/Taffy, Copper Olive 631572; leopard pillow: Rondeau/Natural 660090; chair and ottoman: Bouclette/Wheat 603130.

Page 168: Color: Sky; table skirt: Parfait 663981; border: Block Party 664204; seat cushion: Checkmate 664214.

Page 172: Designer: Michael Buchanan; styling: Cynthia Doggett; photographer: Tria Giovan. Pillows: Check It Out 664403, Floral Festival 663971, Picnic 663792.

Page 176: Wallpaper: Giardino (Champagne) 5501730; pillows: Giardino (Champagne) 666641; bench: Pisa (Champagne) 666531.

Page 182: Designer: Rhea Crenshaw, Rhea Crenshaw Interiors, Memphis, TN; photographer: Emily Minton; stylist: Julie Azar. Wallpaper: Camilla/Sage 572892; window shade: Castlebury/Stone 663711.

Page 206: Designer: Rhea Crenshaw, Rhea Crenshaw Interiors, Memphis, TN; stylist: Julie Azar; photographer: Emily Minton. Folding screen, seat cushions: Westbourne/Loden 663670; scalloped table topper, pillows: Highgrove/Loden 647247; table skirt, round pillow: Prescott/Apple 663682; plaid envelope pillow, iron chair cushion: Cabin Plaid/Laurel 602422.

index

index

index